A POKE IN THE EYE

(*with a* SHARP STICK)

A POKE

IN THE

EYE

(*with a* SHARP STICK)

EDITED AND INTRODUCED
BY GRAHAM McCANN

CANONGATE
Edinburgh · London

First published in Great Britain in 2012 by Canongate Books Ltd,
14 High Street, Edinburgh EH1 1TE

www.canongate.tv

1

British Library Cataloguing-in-Publication Data
A catalogue record for this book is available on
request from the British Library

ISBN 978 0 85786 734 6

Designed and typeset by Cluny Sheeler, Edinburgh

Printed and bound in Great Britain by Butler, Tanner & Dennis

CONTENTS

A POKE IN THE EYE
‹with a sharp stick›

HER MAJESTY'S THEATRE, HAYMARKET, S.W.I. Ist, 2nd, 3rd April 1976 II.30 pm.

JOHN BIRD

ELEANOR BRON

TIM BROOKE-TAYLOR

GRAHAM CHAPMAN

N CLEESE

C/ L CLEVELAND

PETER COOK

JOHN FORTUNE

GRAEME GARDEN

TERRY GILLIAM

BARRY HUMPHRIES

ERIC IDLE

NEIL INNES

DES JONES

ALAN BENNETT

TERRY JONES

JONATHAN LYNN

JOE MELIA

JONATHAN MILLER

BILL ODDIE

MICHAEL PALIN

FOR IMMEDIATE RELEASE

AMNESTY INTERNATIONAL ANNOUNCES:

For the first time ever, all the performers listed on this page are appearing together in one show. We are delighted that these performances will be in aid of Amnesty International.

As I am sure you will realise, such a cast represents the history of revue from the early sixties until today. 'Beyond the Fringe', 'Cambridge Circus', 'Making Faces', 'Monty Python's Flying Circus', 'The Goodies', 'Not Only - But Also', 'I'm Sorry, I'll read that again', 'Hello Cheeky', 'Rutland TV' and 'Fawlty Towers' are just a few of the innumerable shows represented by the performers.

Some of the sketches will be old favourites and some will be new. Some will see performers together again after many years. It will be a memorable evening !

Amnesty International works for the release of non-violent prisoners of conscience all over the world and campaigns for the abolition of torture. The profits from these shows will mean a fantastic boost for work that has never been more vital.

17th February 1976

In Aid Of:

Further information from Peter Luff or David Simpson 01-242 187
01-328 199

Amnesty International, British Section, 55 Theobald's Road, W.C

amnesty internationa

THE ASSAULT OF LAUGHTER
A FOREWORD FROM AMNESTY INTERNATIONAL

As a human rights organisation, we hadn't yet celebrated our fifteenth birthday when 'A Poke in the Eye (With a Sharp Stick)', the first of the three shows that began the sequence of Secret Policeman's Balls, was staged over three nights at Her Majesty's Theatre in London in April 1976.

The idea of fundraising for Amnesty by putting on anarchic evenings of comedy sketches – a cross between a *Beyond the Fringe*-style revue and a night of stand-up – was hatched the previous year by Amnesty International's then assistant director Peter Luff and John Cleese, star of the comedy hit of the decade, *Monty Python's Flying Circus*, and of that year's new TV sensation, *Fawlty Towers*. Luff had asked Cleese, an Amnesty supporter, if he had any fundraising ideas, and Cleese suggested he'd arrange a comedy benefit gig featuring 'a few pals'. They turned out to be the cream of UK comedy talent, including most of the *Python* team, Peter Cook, Alan Bennett and Jonathan Miller from *Beyond the Fringe*, Eleanor Bron and Dame Edna Everage (aka Barry Humphries). It all came about with a kind of happy serendipity – and it happened at a crucial time in Amnesty's history.

The Amnesty story began in November 1960 with the personal outrage of an English lawyer called Peter Benenson. He told of reading a newspaper article about two Portuguese students who, in a Lisbon bar one evening, raised a toast 'to freedom'. Students often do things they regret in pubs, but toasting freedom isn't usually one of them. Under Antonio Salazar's regime, however, they were reported to the authorities and sentenced to seven years in prison. The regime's absurd response to this so-called crime moved Benenson to write an article in the *Observer* newspaper called 'The Forgotten Prisoners'. Published in May 1961, it urged readers to write letters on behalf of 'prisoners of conscience' – those imprisoned simply for peacefully expressing their political, moral or religious beliefs – throughout the world. Benenson's appeal sparked an international grassroots campaign to protect human rights, and Amnesty International was born.

The new organisation quickly built a reputation for meticulous research, political neutrality and impartiality, and this gave Amnesty a moral authority that meant we were listened to – even by those who would rather not hear what we had to say. By 1976, thousands of prisoners had been released, in whole or in part because of pressure from Amnesty. Our annual report, a detailed country-by-country summary of the human rights situation around the world, was recognised by governments and organisations such as the United Nations. And we broadened our agenda to include campaigns on specific issues such as torture and the death penalty in recognition of the fact that human rights abuses against individuals would continue to proliferate until such practices were outlawed everywhere. As our public profile grew, so too did international recognition. In 1977, the organisation was awarded the Nobel Peace Prize for our work against torture and for having 'contributed to securing the ground for freedom, for justice, and thereby also peace in the world'.

Throughout our fifty-year history, Amnesty has grown, developed and changed in response to global challenges, consistently promoting *all* the rights enshrined in the Universal Declaration of Human Rights while campaigning on specific abuses. From our early focus on prisoners of conscience and political prisoners in the Cold War era, we have increasingly exposed other forms of cruelty and oppression (for instance, at one point researchers concluded that there were 'no political prisoners in Guatemala, only political killings'). 'Disappearances', control of the arms trade, poverty, discrimination of all kinds and corporate responsibility have all become part of our human-rights campaign agenda, as have abuses connected with the rise of armed conflicts – mass killings, widespread displacement of people, the use of child soldiers and the unchallenged impunity of mass abusers. We also find constructive ways of working with other organisations and grassroots movements; for example, Amnesty's campaign to end violence against women produced effective joint actions with local women's groups all over the world. Individual casework remains the backbone of our work, reminding us always that the concept of human rights is not abstract – it is about real people.

The Secret Policeman's Balls have been part of this journey. In the first fifteen years, Amnesty's principles, purpose and practices were clear and well developed. By the time of the first show, we had approximately 70,000 individual members in sixty-five countries, with some 1,600 active Amnesty campaigning groups in thirty-three countries. The organisation was highly respected by governments, campaigners and everyone concerned with protecting human rights. But to become even more effective and to put human rights at the forefront of the worldwide conversation, Amnesty needed to reach out to the millions of potential supporters who were *not* already committed human rights activists. The UK comedy fundraisers proved a surprisingly good vehicle.

Is there a contradiction between the deadly serious work that we are engaged in, and the laughter generated by the Secret Policeman's Ball? Many of the prisoners of conscience we try to defend spend years in prison, sometimes in horrific conditions. Many are tortured or otherwise abused. Some are murdered or simply 'disappear'. There's nothing remotely funny about what happens to these people. Yet the Secret Policeman's Balls are all about laughter – the more of it the better! The *Private Eye* editor and *Have I Got News For You* star Ian Hislop once described feeling that 'humour and Amnesty are unlikely bedfellows' after announcing the winners at an Amnesty Media awards ceremony.

How, he wondered, is it possible to laugh about things such as torture and the death penalty? 'I went on stage following a catalogue of extremely distressing reports of human rights abuses. It didn't seem the ideal time to make such a joke, but I felt obliged because one of the winning entries had contained such a good joke that it would have been unfair not to pass it on. It was about a secret policeman who was ordered to catch a lion in the desert. This seemed an impossible task until the policeman revealed his secret. He would catch a rabbit and force it to confess it was a lion.' The audience loved the joke. He said, 'This is black humour, gallows humour, even, but it does indicate that even in the worst of circumstances people want to laugh and that laughter has the power to make them feel better.'

But the relationship between comedy and satire and Amnesty's purpose in defending freedom of expression goes beyond making people feel better when the world looks bleak. Laughter and freedom of expression are intimately linked. More than a hundred years ago, the American writer Mark Twain said, 'Against the assault of laughter, nothing can stand.' It is a powerful, non-violent weapon against those forces that would deny freedom. Dictators hate laughter, especially when it is directed at them.

Freedom of expression – or rather, the lack of it – lies at the heart of many of the human rights violations that Amnesty deals with. We believe that everyone in the world has the right to speak and write freely, without fear of persecution, provided thay are not violating someone else's rights. One can measure freedom within a society by the attitude its government has towards free speech, particularly that of high-profile voices such as dissidents, political and religious figures, artists, musicians, writers and comedians. Regardless of what we might think about any particular government in Britain or the United States, a comedian can walk on stage and insult a leader without fear of imprisonment and torture. But millions of people around the world aren't so lucky, which is why Amnesty defends the right to freedom of speech, and fights for the release of thousands of political prisoners around the world.

When oppressive regimes clamp down on their citizens, freedom of speech is normally the first thing to go. But what does a dictator and his army of thousands have to fear from a peaceful lone voice? Quite a lot, actually. Authoritarian leaders live in fear of dissent. And they know that an idea, spoken by a single voice, can spread virally and inspire a whole nation to stand up for change. The Burmese comedians the Moustache Brothers, aka U Pa Pa Lay and U Law Zaw, spent seven years in a labour camp with shackles on their legs, for singing a funny song about the country's ruling generals. They say, 'Jokes share the suffering. That's what government is afraid of. Jokes are like wildfire. They want to hide deep problems under the covers. But jokes spread the word.'

The world has changed dramatically in the fifty years since Peter Benenson's newspaper article, but many of the problems we face remain the same. Bloggers in Egypt are detained. Access to the internet is blocked in Iran. Students in Azerbaijan are arrested for posting comments on Facebook – just like, back in 1960, those Portuguese students got in trouble for raising a glass in defiance of a dictator. In the internet age, Amnesty's role is as important as ever. In many parts of the world, social media and the internet increasingly attract the attention of the security apparatus of oppressive regimes, because of the speed with which they transmit ideas and stimulate debate. The freedom to impart and receive information is an integral element of freedom of expression.

We now have three million supporters, branches in fifty-two countries, and ambitious plans for expansion in the 'global south'. Does pressure from Amnesty really make a difference? Does all the laughter – and all the donations – at the Secret Policeman's Balls actually help to change the world? As an organisation, we never claim sole credit when a prisoner is released, when death sentences are commuted or when a government changes its laws and practices. However, former prisoners, torture victims and others who have suffered human rights abuses often say very clearly that international pressure secured their freedom and saved their lives. Femi Kuti, the musician and son of Nigerian jazz star and dissident Fela Kuti, has no doubt that his father's release from prison was connected to his father having been adopted as a prisoner of conscience by Amnesty International. 'I am one of the thousands of people whose lives have been directly affected by Amnesty's work,' he says.

Every year, Amnesty receives messages of thanks and solidarity that inspire us to keep working for human rights. They show that, together, we can make a difference. And they show generals, torturers and secret policemen everywhere that, at the end of the day, the joke's on them.

Amnesty International
October 2012

Join Amnesty.
Protect the Human.
www.amnesty.org.uk/join

'It is vital that we use our liberty to promote the liberty of others.'

Aung San Suu Kyi

A POKE IN THE EYE

with a **(SHARP STICK)**

HER MAJESTY'S THEATRE
APRIL 1976

1, 2, 3 April
11.30pm
**Her Majesty's
Theatre**

write QUICKLY to
Amnesty Box Office
Her Majesty's
Theatre
Haymarket SW1
(enclose s.a.e.)

Call in person or
'phone 01-839 2110
from
23 February 1976

Prices
**£150
(for not coming)
£100 per box**
£50.07, £10, £5,
£3, £2

Cheques & postal orders
made out to
AMNESTY
INTERNATIONAL

with
John Bird
Eleanor Bron
Tim Brooke-Taylor
Graham Chapman
John Cleese
Carol Cleveland
Peter Cook
John Fortune
Graeme Garden
Terry Gilliam
Barry Humphries
Eric Idle
Alan Bennett
Neil Innes

Des Jones
Terry Jones
Jonathan Lynn
Joe Melia
Jonathan Miller
Bill Oddie
and
Michael Palin

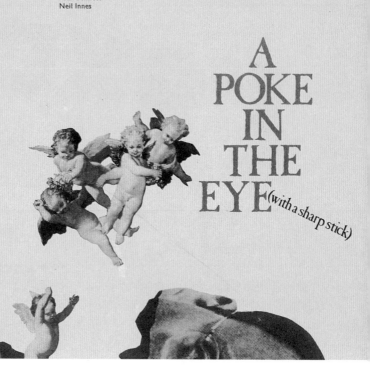

A
POKE
IN
THE
EYE (with a sharp stick)

BEGINNINGS
AN INTRODUCTION

It started with a cheque. Signed 'J. Cleese', it arrived in the post at Amnesty International's London headquarters early in 1976 and ended up on the desk of its Assistant Director, Peter Luff. The timing could not have been better.

'We were getting steadily poorer,' Luff recalls. 'Most of our fundraising came from authors such as John Fowles, Samuel Beckett or Margaret Drabble giving us their manuscripts to auction.' The sight of that cheque from John Cleese, late of *Monty Python's Flying Circus* and now more popular than ever thanks to *Fawlty Towers*, sparked a bright idea for a bold new approach: a high profile comedy event, featuring Cleese and 'a few friends' – the most illustrious of his fellow performers – staged in support of Amnesty on the occasion of its fifteenth anniversary.

The novelty of such a possible collaboration was obvious. British comedians had no track record of working hand-in-hand with charities (the most notable fundraising event in recent memory had been mounted to help *Private Eye* pay off its legal fees) nor – since the satire boom of the early 1960s – had there been any significant comic intervention into politics, aside from *Private Eye*. George Orwell might have claimed that 'every joke is a tiny revolution', but most of the nation's joke-tellers preferred to err on the side of conservatism. Amnesty International, however, was about to challenge the cosy world of charity fundraising. With the help of John Cleese and friends, they were about to invent something completely different.

Even during the economic and political turmoil of Cold War Britain, few comedians in the mid-1970s seemed inclined to get involved in the great debates of the day. John Cleese was about to prove an exception to the rule. As he later explained, he had joined Amnesty International after he 'suddenly realised how nice it was to live in a country where people didn't come to your front door at 2 a.m., and take you away and hand you over to people who've been specially trained to hurt you as much as possible'.

When Peter Luff called him, therefore, Cleese was happy to help. 'It seemed like the most obvious thing in the world,' Cleese recalled about the stage show. 'Because that's the one thing, I guess, that I knew how to organise.' Indeed, Luff found that Cleese was eager to snap into action: 'He said, "If I'm going to do this, we've got to do it for two or three nights – there's no point in doing it just for one night. You find the theatre, I'll give you the telephone numbers of the people, and if you can get them we'll go ahead." And except for a couple of them, who were away or couldn't manage it, they all said yes.'

London theatres proved harder to secure. They were fully booked with on-going productions. Undaunted, Amnesty simply decided to start the shows after the audience had left from that night's production. Her Majesty's Theatre was the chosen venue, and on 1, 2 and 3 April (Thursday, Friday and Saturday nights) in 1976 a new comedy genre was born.

Among the friends and colleagues whom Cleese recruited were his fellow Pythons (minus Eric Idle, who was otherwise engaged), The Goodies and the former members of the *Beyond the Fringe* quartet (minus Dudley Moore, who was working in America), as well as the likes of Eleanor Bron, John Fortune, John Bird, Neil Innes and Barry Humphries. In piecing together such a cast, Cleese was effectively uniting two generations of great British (and Australian) comic talent to revive their best routines.

In a way, the artists who were unable to appear were as important to establishing the future format of the shows as the artists who were able to make it. Python members played Dudley Moore's roles in *Beyond the Fringe* sketches and Peter Cook became an honorary Python. Audiences loved seeing these unique collaborations and this became an enduring element of future Balls.

Cleese chose, as a working title for the show, *An Evening Without David Frost*, as it seemed that the man whom Peter Cook had dubbed

'The Bubonic Plagiarist' was the missing link to everyone else in the cast. Thinking better of it, he then decided to name the event *A Poke in the Eye (With A Sharp Stick)*.

With artists and venue booked, everyone met for lunch at Bertorelli's restaurant in Bayswater to discuss how the project should proceed. Luff recalls: 'Alan Bennett suggested that alphabetical billing on the posters and programmes would help, until John Fortune responded wryly that it would certainly help Alan.' Consensus was quickly achieved when it came to deciding on the contents of the show: everyone's 'greatest hits' – which would not only be relatively easy to rehearse but would also serve as a celebration of a quarter of a century of the country's most distinctive and distinguished comedy material.

Cleese and Amnesty agreed the atmosphere should be relaxed and informal. The shows were starting close to midnight, the already warmed up audience of comedy fans would be coming from pubs and other shows – and the unprecedented assembly of artists should have fun onstage with their peers and enjoy the backstage camaraderie. Tickets for the shows, advertised exclusively in *Private Eye*, sold out within four days. Intrigued, the filmmaker Roger Graef persuaded Amnesty to grant him access to make a *cinema verité*-style documentary of the event.

Rehearsals soon dispelled any fears of clashes between competing egos among the comedy greats. 'I must admit,' Jonathan Miller (who directed) remembers, 'there was a moment in that chilly theatre on that first, cold Sunday morning when I felt the idea had no justification and it might well be a disaster. But people were greeting each other, getting together again, and it was very companionable.' John Cleese would agree, noting how eager everyone seemed to be to promote a positive atmosphere: 'I think the fear of being *thought* competitive is greater than the desire to *be* competitive.' The only minor tensions occurred when the always-inventive Miller suggested ways to 'improve' the other performers' routines, such as Cleese's memorably bad-tempered clash between the Pope and Michelangelo. (Cleese's co-star Jonathan Lynn recalls that Miller 'suggested I play my part a little camp – because Michelangelo was gay. And I remember I saw John shaking his head solemnly behind him.')

When the first night finally arrived the cast were taken aback at the welcome they received. 'John Cleese walked out onto the stage with a parrot cage and the theatre erupted,' Peter Luff recalls. 'We had no idea people would laugh so much.' Buoyed by the warmth of the reaction, each performer began to relax, improvise and extend their routines: 'You didn't really need a director,' Alan Bennett observed dryly. 'You wanted a snatch squad, really, to go on and get them off, because everybody did twice as much as they said they were going to do.' The planned two-and-a-half-hour running time was thus stretched out to four, but there were no complaints from the audience, who knew they were witnessing a very special moment in comedy history.

Buoyed by the success of the event, Amnesty staged another one the following year, and a new tradition was duly established. Some thirty-two years on from Orwell's famous remark, British comedy was at last ready and willing to spark some tiny revolutions.

THE DEAD PARROT SKETCH

JOHN CLEESE & MICHAEL PALIN

A customer, carrying a bird cage, enters a pet shop.

CLEESE: I wish to register a complaint.

(The owner doesn't respond.)

PALIN: Sorry, we're closed for lunch.

CLEESE: Never mind that, my lad. I wish to complain about this parrot what I purchased not half an hour ago from this very boutique.

PALIN: Oh yes, the, uh, the Norwegian Blue . . . What's, uh . . . What's wrong with it?

CLEESE: I'll tell you what's wrong with it, my lad. It's dead, that's what's wrong with it!

PALIN: No, no, 'e's, uh . . . he's resting.

CLEESE: Look, matey, I know a dead parrot when I see one, and I'm looking at one right now . . .

PALIN: No, no, he's not *dead*, squire, he's, he's *restin'*! Remarkable bird, the Norwegian Blue, innit, eh? Beautiful *plumage*!

CLEESE: The plumage don't enter into it. 'E's *stone dead*.

PALIN: No, no, no, no, no, *no*! 'E's *resting*!

CLEESE: All right then, if he's restin', I'll wake him up! (*Shouting at the cage.*) 'Ello, Mister Polly Parrot! I've got a nice fresh cuttlefish for you if you wake up . . .

(*Owner hits the cage.*)

PALIN: *There* – he moved!

CLEESE: No, he didn't – that was *you* hitting the cage!

PALIN: I never!!

CLEESE: Yes, you did!

PALIN: I didn't do anything!

CLEESE: (*Yelling and hitting the cage repeatedly.*) 'ELLO, *POLLY*!!!!! Wakey wakey!!!! (*Removes parrot from cage and bangs it on counter.*) Testing! Testing! (*Bangs parrot a couple more times on counter.*) This is your nine o'clock alarm call! (*Thumps its head on the counter yet again, then throws it up in the air and watches it plummet to the floor.*)

CLEESE: Now that's what I call a dead parrot.

PALIN: No, 'e's stunned!

CLEESE: *STUNNED*?!?

PALIN: Yeah! You stunned him, just as he was wakin' up! Norwegian Blues stun easily!

CLEESE: Now listen, matey, I've definitely had enough of this. That parrot is definitely deceased, and when I purchased it not 'alf an hour ago, you assured me that its total lack of movement was due to it being tired and shagged out following a prolonged squawk.

PALIN: Well, he's . . . he's, ah . . . probably pining for the fjords.

CLEESE: *PININ' for the FJORDS*?!?!?!? (*Palin corpses.*) *PININ' for the FJORDS*?!?!?!? What kind of talk is that? (*Palin still struggles to regain his composure.*) This is nothing to laugh at! Look, why did he fall flat on his back the moment I got 'im home?

PALIN: The Norwegian Blue prefers kippin' on its back! Remarkable bird, ain't it, squire? Beautiful *plumage*!

CLEESE: Look, I took the liberty of examining that parrot when I got it home, and I discovered the only reason that it had been sitting on its perch in the first place was that it had been *NAILED* there.

PALIN: Well, of course it was *nailed* there! If I hadn't nailed that bird there, it would have muscled up to those bars, bent 'em apart with its beak, and VOOM!

CLEESE: *'VOOM'*?!? Mate, this bird wouldn't 'voom' if you put four million volts through it! 'E's bleedin' *demised*!

PALIN: No, no! 'E's *pining*!

CLEESE: 'E's *NOT* pining! 'E's *passed on*! This parrot is no more! He has ceased to be! It's a stiff! 'E's snuffed it! Bereft of life, he rests in peace! 'E's in-du-bit-ab-ly extinct! THIS IS AN *EX*-PARROT!!

PALIN: (*Pausing to reflect on this information.*) Well, I'd better replace it, then.

(*He goes off in search of a replacement but soon returns empty-handed.*)

CLEESE: What's the news?

PALIN: Sorry, squire, I've had a look out the back, and uh, we're right out of parrots.

CLEESE: (*Testily.*) I see, I see, I get the picture.

PALIN: I got a slug.

CLEESE: (*Cautiously.*) Does it talk?

PALIN: Yeah.

CLEESE: Right, I'll have that one then!

'No, no, he's not dead, squire, he's restin'!'

Michael Palin

T.E. LAWRENCE
ALAN BENNETT

The spotlight picks out Alan Bennett, hands tucked into tweed pockets, staring into space with the distracted air of an Oxbridge academic.

T.E. Lawrence – the man, and the myth. Which is man, and which is myth? Is this fact, or is it lies? What is truth, and what is fable? Where is Ruth? And where is Mabel?

To some of these questions I hope to be able to provide the answer.

No one who knew T.E. Lawrence, as I did – scarcely at all – could fail but to be deeply impressed by him. It was in pursuit of this legend that I first sought him out, in June of 1933, at his cottage at Cloud's Hill in Dorset. It was a simple cottage, but I thought I detected Lawrence's hand in the rough whitewashed wall, the stout paved doorstep, and the rough oak door, upon which I knocked, lightly. It was opened by a small, rather unprepossessing figure – slight of frame, fair-haired – with the ruddy, gleaming face of a schoolboy . . .

. . . It *was* a schoolboy. I had come to the wrong house.

'Horrance,' the Arabs called him, for they are unable to pronounce their Ls . . . as distinct from the Chinese, who can pronounce little else . . . It's interesting – though fruitless – to speculate, but had fate taken him to China, he would have been known as 'Lollance'. That is by the way . . .

'Shaw', or 'Ross' as Lawrence now called himself, returned from the East in 1919. Shyness had always been a disease with him, and it was shyness and a longing for anonymity that made him disguise himself. Clad in the magnificent white silk robes of an Arab prince, within his belt the short curved gold sword of the Ashrab descendants of the Prophet, he hoped to pass unnoticed through London. Alas, he was mistaken.

'Who am I?' he would cry, despairingly. 'You are Lawrence of Arabia!' passers-by would stop him and say, '. . . and I claim my five pounds.'

HAPPY, DARLING
ELEANOR BRON & JOHN FORTUNE

A young couple are sitting down, the man with his arms wrapped around the woman's shoulders like a thick winter scarf.

FORTUNE: Happy, darling?

BRON: *Mmmm.*

FORTUNE: What are you thinking?

BRON: Oh, nothing. I was just thinking of something you once said. About there being three phases which always crop up when an affair's coming to an end. The first was: 'Happy, darling?' The second was: 'What are you thinking?' Ha, I can't remember what the third one was.

FORTUNE: Ha, silly, darling. (*Hugs her tighter.*) I love you.

BRON: Oh yes, *that's* it!

SPUNK
DAME EDNA EVERAGE

Dame Edna's elderly pianist crosses the stage and sits at the piano. Dame Edna then makes her entrance, carrying a large bunch of gladioli, to rapturous applause and wolf whistles. She bows and blows kisses.

Oh, you're gorgeous! (*Laughs.*). I'm going to, if I may, on this delightfully festive occasion, sing you a little ditty dedicated to a country I've always had a lot of time for – Mother England. Dedicated to the courage and fortitude of you poor, wretched, little people.

Now, I know a lot of people say rude things about you. They *do*! Just because you have the lowest standard of living in the world. And I don't think that's *fair*! I think that's mean and horrid and I think they're *awful*. Because I know that England will rise again. It *will*! It *will*! Say to the level of Sicily, or Ethiopia. It *will*! You see – I feel a song coming on . . .

(*Sings.*)

> The English have a quality,
> I'd like to sing about,
> It's not the sort of quality,
> Bestowed on wog or kraut.
>
> When things are on the sticky side . . .
> You never throw a tizz,
> A special something sees you through,
> I'll tell you what it is . . .

Spunk! Spunk! Spunk!
You're so full of British spunk.
You're never in a panic,
And you're never in a funk.

So in a time of crisis,
There's nothing quite so nice as,
Singing spunk, spunk, spunk, spunk,
Spunk, spunk, spunk!

The Black Hole of Calcutta,
Was a very nasty place.
The curry was disgusting,
And the toilet a disgrace.

The grubby Indian menu
Gave you very little choice,
So the hungry British patrons
All cried out, as with one voice – you've guessed it –

Spunk! Spunk! Spunk!
We're so full of British spunk,
Though our club rooms are all rambling
And ours members sadly drunk.

So in a time of crisis,
There's nothing quite so nice as
Singing spunk, spunk, spunk, spunk,
spunk, spunk, spunk!

(*Her pianist breaks briefly into the theme from* The Dambusters.)

A chappie who saw the Second World War,
Has somewhere wisely written,
'If it wasn't for a handful of ex-public schoolboys,
Who bravely manned the Spitfires,
We'd never have won the battle of Britain.'

But up spoke Winston Churchill,
Above the battle's din,
'You poor little Poms,
Will be safe from the bombs
If you sing with Vera Lynn . . .'

Spunk! Spunk! Spunk!
You're so full of Bri-i-i-tish spunk,
Though the place is full of Arabs,
And sterling has had a bunk.

But in this time of crisis,
There's nothing quite so nice as
Singing Spunk! Spunk! Spunk!
You're so full of Bri-i-i-tish – (*Cymbal crash.*) – Spunk!

(*She flings the gladioli into the audience and exits.*)

'I know that England will rise again. It will! It will!'

Dame Edna

MINER
PETER COOK

The scene reveals E.L. Wisty, sitting alone on a park bench, talking to the audience.

Yes, I would've liked to have been a judge, but I never 'ad the Latin . . . I never 'ad sufficient Latin to get through the rigorous judging exams. They're very rigorous, the judging exams, they're noted for their rigour. People come staggering out saying, 'Oh my God, what a rigorous exam!'

So I become a miner instead. A coalminer. They're not so rigorous, the mining exams. They only ask you one question. They say, 'Who are you?' And I got seventy-five per cent on that. So I was allowed to join the mining community.

The only trouble with the mining community is that the conversation tends to be a bit on the boring side. If you want to hear a boring conversation, just pop down my mine. Stuff like: 'Hello, I've just found a lump of coal.'

'Have you really?'

'Oh, yes, no doubt about it. This black substance is coal, all right'.

'Jolly good, the very thing we're looking for.'

I've tried to inject a little intellectual substance to conversation down the mine. I said to a fellow miner the other day, I said, 'Have you heard of Marcel Proust?' He said, 'No. He must work down another mine.'

So I explained to him that Marcel Proust was a very famous writer. He used to dip biscuits in his cup of tea and suck on the biscuits, and all his memories would come flooding back. And he wrote them down into a wonderful novel.

But I've done a bit of writing myself. I've written a book called *My Experiences Down the Mine*. It's very largely based on my experiences. Down the mine.

It's a story of this man who comes down the mine one day, and he sees a lump of coal. And he grabs hold of it and throws it on a trolley, which disappears down a long dark tunnel and he never sees it again.

It's a very short story. But it is extremely boring.

I took it along to a publisher, and he confirmed my opinion. He said it was without doubt *the* most boring story he had ever read in all his life. And he's not a man who's given to superlatives. He said, 'The trouble with your story is that it lacks everything. You name it, it lacks it. And above all, it lacks the elements of sex and violence so vital in these troubled times.'

So I've rewritten it a bit. I've given it a new title. I've called it *Sex and Violence Down the Mines*. And chapter one begins with these three nude ladies: Beryl, Stella and Margaret. And they are completely nude. And they're wandering around the desert. Violently.

Nude and violent, they wander around the desert. Every day they get more violent. Every day they get more nude. Till eventually the leader of the nude, violent ladies, Beryl Whittington, sees a disused mine shaft. 'Come on, girls!' she shouts, a wicked glint in her eye. 'Let's all rush down that mine shaft and do disgusting things to each other!'

So, as one man, the three nude, violent ladies rush down the mine shaft and start doing disgusting things to each other. They start hurling lumps of coal at each other. Nudely and violently. They hurl the lumps of coal until they're all black and blue from bruises, and covered in coal dust. And they sink exhausted in a coma to the floor.

Now comes the wry twist. A miner, whose character is very loosely based on myself, happens upon the three nude, violent, comatose ladies. But as they're all black and blue from bruises, and covered in coal dust, he mistakes them for lumps of coal. And he grabs hold of them and throws them on a trolley, which disappears down a long dark tunnel and he never sees them again.

Whoooooops! Did you notice for no apparent reason I suddenly went *Whoooooops*! It's an impediment I got from being down the mine. Because one day I was wandering along in the dark and I stumbled across the body of a dead pit pony. *Whoooooops*! I went with surprise. And ever since then I've been going *Whoooooops*! unexpectedly.

And that's another reason why I couldn't be a judge.

It would destroy the dignity of the court, you see. I mean, I might have been up there one day, sentencing away, all majestic and dignified and in my robes, saying to some criminal: 'You have been found to be a heinous criminal, and it is my solemn duty to sentence you to *Whoooooops*!'

And the trouble is, you see, under English law, that would have to stand.

But the trouble with being a miner, is that as soon as you're too old and tired and ill and sick and stupid to do your job properly, you 'ave to go. Well, the very opposite applies with the judges.

So on the whole, I'd rather have been a judge than a miner.

COURT ROOM SKETCH

TERRY JONES: Judge
PETER COOK: Michael Norman Smith
JOHN CLEESE: Counsel for the Defence
MICHAEL PALIN: Counsel for the Prosecution
GRAHAM CHAPMAN: PC Pan Am

The scene is a crowded court room. The judge bangs his gavel impatiently and the court falls into an expectant silence.

JUDGE: Michael Norman Smith, you stand here charged with the murder of Arthur Edward Hopcraft, Brian Graham Whittaker, the Reverend John Claude Motson, Father Kevin Joyce O'Malley, Monseigneur Jean-Paul Reynard, Padre Robert Henry Noonan, Rabbis Edwin and Carey Makepiece Goodgold, Pope Mario Marcotti, Divisional Fire Officer Karl-Heinz Biarritz, Archbishop Stavros Nikolas Abquinnel, His Most Holy and Invisible Oneness Wan-Kai Song, Bombardier Arthur Buddah and Nicholas Parsons . . . on or about the morning of the third Sunday in January. Mr Smith, have you anything to say before this court considers your case?

SMITH: Er . . . yeah . . . I did them.

(Groans of disappointment are heard in court.)

SMITH: I did, you know, the murders, but, as you're all so looking forward to this, I thought I'd plead 'Not Guilty'.

(*Sounds of relief and excitement are heard.*)

JUDGE: I'll bear that in mind when I'm sentencing you.

SMITH: Thank you, Michael!

JUDGE: Don't call me Michael in court!

SMITH: Sorry.

JUDGE: Counsel for the Prosecution . . . Just a minute – where is the Counsel for the Defence?

COUNSEL FOR THE PROSECUTION: Ah, he is not here yet, m'lud, he's asked me to start without him.

JUDGE: Oh, very well, carry on.

COUNSEL FOR THE PROSECUTION: M'lud, this terrifying and heinous case –

(*The Counsel for the Defence arrives, carrying a plastic bag.*)

COUNSEL FOR THE DEFENCE: Sorry I'm late, I couldn't find a kosher car park. Don't bother to recap, I'll pick it up as we go along. (*Moves towards witness box.*) Now, you are Michael Norman Smith? Alias 'Michael Norman Smith'?

SMITH: That's right, sir.

COUNSEL FOR THE DEFENCE: I suggest that you murdered these people.

SMITH: Yes, sir, I did.

COUNSEL FOR THE DEFENCE: I put it to you that you murdered these people.

SMITH: Yes, sir, I did.

COUNSEL FOR THE DEFENCE: I submit that you murdered these people.

SMITH: I did murder these people.

COUNSEL FOR THE DEFENCE: *DID YOU OR DID YOU NOT MURDER THESE PEOPLE?*

SMITH: Yes, I murdered –

COUNSEL FOR THE DEFENCE: YES OR NO?

SMITH: Yes, I murdered these people!

COUNSEL FOR THE DEFENCE: *ANSWER THE QUESTION!!!!*

SMITH: *I murdered these people!*

COUNSEL FOR THE DEFENCE: (*Triumphantly.*) *Ah! Ha ha! Ha ha ha HA!! We've wheedled it out of you at last!! AH HA HA HA!*

JUDGE: Er, Mr Bartlett, um, you do realise you're meant to be the Counsel for the *Defence*?

(*The Counsel for the Defence suddenly stops grinning, rubs his brow and then grimaces.*)

COUNSEL FOR THE DEFENCE: Sorry! Sorry, *sorry*, everyone! Shit! What a goof!

JUDGE: Mr Bartlett, would you like to proceed for the *Defence*?

COUNSEL FOR THE DEFENCE: Certainly, m'lud, I'd like to call the first Defence witness. Call the late Arthur Aldridge!

(*Two policemen carry a coffin into court.*)

JUDGE: The 'late' Arthur Aldridge? How do you hope to question the deceased?

COUNSEL FOR THE DEFENCE: I beg your pardon, m'lud?

JUDGE: Well, er, the witness *is*, er, dead?

COUNSEL FOR THE DEFENCE: Yes, m'lud. Well, *virtually*, m'lud. Now, Mr Aldridge –

JUDGE: He's not *completely* dead?

COUNSEL FOR THE DEFENCE: No. He's not completely dead, m'lud, no. But he's not at all well. Mr Aldridge –

JUDGE: Well, if he's not completely dead, what's he doing in the coffin?

COUNSEL FOR THE DEFENCE: Er, it's merely a precaution, m'lud. Now, if I may be allowed to continue? (*Approaches the coffin.*) Mr Aldridge, you were, you *are*, a stockbroker of 10 Suvurna Close, Wimbledon?

(*A loud knock comes from inside the coffin.*)

JUDGE: What was that knock?

COUNSEL FOR THE DEFENCE: It means 'Yes', m'lud – one knock for 'Yes', two knocks for 'No'. (*Addressing the coffin again.*) Mr Aldridge, would it be fair to say that you are not at all well?

(*A loud knock comes from inside the coffin.*)

COUNSEL FOR THE DEFENCE: In fact, would you be prepared to say that you are, as it were, in a manner of speaking, what is commonly known as 'dead'?

(*There is silence. Everyone stares intently at the coffin, ears pricked. The Counsel for the Defence looks puzzled.*)

COUNSEL FOR THE DEFENCE: I think he *is* dead, m'lud.

JUDGE: Where *is* all this leading?

COUNSEL FOR THE DEFENCE: That will become apparent in one moment, m'lud. (*Trying to appear in control of the situation, he looks at the coffin again and raises his voice.*) Mr Aldridge? Are you thinking, or are you just dead?

(*Once again, there is silence. The Counsel for the Defence lifts up the lid of the coffin far enough to peek inside. He stares for a moment, then drops the lid back down and moves away.*)

COUNSEL FOR THE DEFENCE: (*Calmly.*) No further questions, m'lud!

(*He sits down. The judge is exasperated.*)

JUDGE: Mr Bartlett, you can't just come in and dump dead bodies in this court! (*Looks around and gestures to a policeman.*) Get rid of that thing! (*Turns back.*) Counsel for the Prosecution!

COUNSEL FOR THE PROSECUTION: Thank you very much, m'lud. I'd like to call my first witness. Call Police Constable Pan Am!

(*A police constable races into court, truncheon raised, and heads straight to the witness box, where he has to be physically restrained from hitting Mr Smith about the head and neck.*)

JUDGE: Stop that, Constable! There'll be plenty of time for that later on!

COUNSEL FOR THE PROSECUTION: You are Police Constable Pan Am?

PC: (*Shouting excitedly.*) No! I shall deny that to the last breath in my body! (*Stops and thinks.*) Ooh, sorry: Yus!

COUNSEL FOR THE PROSECUTION: Do you recognise the defendant?

PC: No, I've never seen him before in my life – I swear it! (*Sees Counsel gesturing to him furtively.*) Oh, yus, he's the one! You're right – I'd recognise 'im anywhere!

COUNSEL FOR THE PROSECUTION: Would you tell the court in your own words, PC Pan Am, what happened?

PC: Oh, yus! (*Starts reading from notebook.*) I was proceeding in a northerly direction up Al Italia Street when I saw the deceased from an upstairs window baring her bosom to the general public. She then took off her – no, wait a minute, that's the wrong story! (*Turns page.*) Oh, yus: there were these three nuns on a train, and the ticket inspector – (*Looks at Counsel, who is shaking his head.*) No? Oh. Anyway, I clearly saw the deceased –

COUNSEL FOR THE PROSECUTION: The defendant!

PC: The defendant. Doing whatever he's accused of, red-handed! There's no doubt about that! (*Consults notebook again.*) When kicked – er, when *cautioned* – he said: 'It's a fair cop. I did it, all right. No doubt about that!' Then, bound as he was to the chair, he assaulted me and three other constables while bouncing round the cell. The end!

JUDGE: Excellent evidence, Constable! (*The PC is applauded as he steps down.*) Counsel for the Prosecution?

COUNSEL FOR THE PROSECUTION: I take you back to Germany, 1944.

JUDGE: *Why* must we go back to Germany, 1944?

COUNSEL FOR THE PROSECUTION: Because, m'lud, I shall seek to prove that on one occasion, alone, half dead and without weapons of any kind, he nevertheless managed to bite to death the entire staff of the First SS Panzer Division stationed in Basingstoke.

JUDGE: Basingstoke in Hampshire?

COUNSEL FOR THE PROSECUTION: No, no, no, sir. (*Continues with his speech.*) The complete negation of the basic codes of civilisation –

JUDGE: Basingstoke *where*?

COUNSEL FOR THE PROSECUTION: (*Dismissively.*) Basingstoke in Westphalia, sir.

JUDGE: Oh, I see. Carry on!

COUNSEL FOR THE PROSECUTION: This utter disregard for the sanctity of human life by this monster –

JUDGE: Er, I didn't know there *was* a Basingstoke in Westphalia.

COUNSEL FOR THE PROSECUTION: (*Rattled.*) It's on the *map*, sir.

JUDGE: What map?

COUNSEL FOR THE PROSECUTION: The map of Westphalia as used by the Army, sir.

JUDGE: Well, *I've* certainly never heard of a Basingstoke in Westphalia.

COUNSEL FOR THE PROSECUTION: (*Eager to move things on.*) It's a municipal borough, sir, thirty miles north of Southampton, principal manufacturers of leather –

JUDGE: Is there a *Southampton* in Westphalia?

COUNSEL FOR THE PROSECUTION: Yes, sir.

JUDGE: Who compiled this map?

COUNSEL FOR THE PROSECUTION: Cole Porter, sir.

JUDGE: *Cole Porter*??? Who wrote *Kiss Me Kate*?

COUNSEL FOR THE PROSECUTION: No, that's not him, sir. This is the one who wrote 'Anything Goes'.

JUDGE: That's the same one! (*Starts singing.*) 'In olden days a glimpse of stocking was looked on as something shocking, now heaven knows, anything goes!'

COUNSEL FOR THE PROSECUTION: Oh, no, this one's different, sir.

JUDGE: How does it go?

COUNSEL FOR THE PROSECUTION: (*Sounding shifty.*) Sir, I . . . I'd rather –

JUDGE: Come on, how does it *go*? How does *your* 'Anything Goes', go?

COUNSEL FOR THE PROSECUTION: (*Pauses, clears his throat, breathes in, then starts singing.*)

Anything goes in.
Anything goes out!
Fish, bananas, old pyjamas.
Mutton! Beef! and Trout!

JUDGE: No, that's not it.

SMITH: I want to go home.

JUDGE: What do you want to say?

SMITH: I'll have to admit the fact that I am an habitual mass murderer, preferring to murder en masse than any other method of murdering. But I'll have to say in my defence that I come from a society which is in itself –

(*Irritated noises from court.*)

JUDGE: Oh, shut up!

SMITH: . . . if it wasn't for the Vietnam War –

JUDGE: If you don't shut up, I'll shoot you!

SMITH: Just as I thought, you see! There's an example of the –

(*The judge pulls out a gun and shoots him.*)

COUNSEL FOR THE DEFENCE: (*Suddenly gets up.*) M'lud, I really must protest about you shooting my client!

JUDGE: I'm in charge of this court! Stand up! (*Everyone stands up.*) Sit down! (*Everyone sits down.*) Go 'MOO!' (*They go 'Moo!'.*) Titter! (*They all titter.*) Now . . . on with the pixie hats! (*He puts his on. The rest follow suit.*) And order in the skating vicar! (*The skating vicar appears.*)

JUDGE: Come on!

(*The judge gets up and starts singing, soon accompanied by the others in court.*)

> Anything goes in!
> Anything goes out!
> Fish, bananas, old pyjamas.
> Mutton! Beef! and Trout!
>
> Anything goes in!
> Anything goes out!
> Fish, bananas, old pyjamas . . .

'I clearly saw the deceased – the defendant! – doing whatever he's accused of, red-handed!'

Graham Chapman

PROTEST SONG
NEIL INNES

Innes appears as a very bad Bob Dylan-wannabe folk rock singer, wearing a red baseball cap, sunglasses, a blue-and-white striped shirt, blue-and-white spotted trousers that hang high above his ankles and a pair of silver platform boots. He speaks in what he thinks is a 'cool' American-accented drawl.

This next song is a protest song. (*Random, out of tune guitar strumming.*) Ladies and gentlemen, I've suffered for my music, and now it's your turn.

(*Awful harmonica playing.*)

> All the prophets of doom
> Can always find room
> In a world full of worry and fear
> Tip cigarettes
> And chemistry sets
> And Rudolph, the Red-Nosed Reindeer.
> So I'm goin' back
> To my little ol' shack
> And drink me a bottle of wine
> That was *mis en bouteille*
> Before my birthday
> And have me a fuckin' good time!
>
> Rain on a tin roof, sounds like a drum
> We're marchin' for freedom today – yay!
> Turn on your headlights and sound your horn
> If people get in the way.

(*More awful harmonica playing.*)

Let me turn you on
To the chromium swan
On the nose of a long limousine
Even hire it for the day
It is somethin' to say
But what the hell does it mean?
I may be accused
Of bein' confused
But I'm average weight for my height
My phil-o-so-phy
Like colour TV
Is all there in black and white.

Rain on a tin roof sounds like a drum
We're marchin' for freedom today – yay!
Turn on your headlights and sound your horn
If people get in the way.

———————————————

THE LAST SUPPER

JOHN CLEESE & JONATHAN LYNN

The scene is a room in the Vatican. The Pope (John Cleese) is looking with some displeasure at a painting of the Last Supper.

FOOTMAN 1: Michelangelo to see the Pope.

FOOTMAN 2: Michelangelo to see the Pope . . . Michelangelo Buonarroti to see the Pope.

(*Michelangelo enters.*)

MICHELANGELO: Evening, Your Grace.

POPE: Evening, Michelangelo. I want to have a word with you about this Last Supper of yours.

MICHELANGELO: Oh, yes?

POPE: I'm not happy with it.

MICHELANGELO: Oh, I know, you don't like the kangaroo.

POPE: *What* kangaroo?

MICHELANGELO: I'll paint it out, no problem.

POPE: I never saw a kangaroo!

MICHELANGELO: Well, it's right at the back . . . but I'll alter, no sweat . . . I'll make it into a disciple.

POPE: That's the problem . . .

MICHELANGELO: What is?

POPE: The disciples.

MICHELANGELO: Are they too *Jewish*? I made Judas the *most* Jewish . . .

POPE: No, no . . . it's just that there are TWENTY-EIGHT of them.

MICHELANGELO: Well – another one would hardly notice, then. So . . . I'll make the kangaroo into a disciple and—

POPE: No.

MICHELANGELO: All right, all right, we'll lose the kangaroo altogether, I don't mind . . . I was never completely happy with it.

POPE: That's not the point . . . there are TWENTY-EIGHT DISCIPLES!

MICHELANGELO: Too many?

POPE: *OF COURSE IT'S TOO MANY!*

MICHELANGELO: Well, in a way . . . but I wanted to give the impression of a *huge* get-together. You know, a *real* Last Supper – not just any old supper but a proper, final *treat* – a real mother of a blowout.

POPE: There were ONLY TWELVE DISCIPLES at the Last Supper.

MICHELANGELO: Well, suppose some of the others happened to drop by?

POPE: There were only twelve disciples *altogether*!

MICHELANGELO: Well . . . maybe they'd invited some friends . . .

POPE: There were only the twelve disciples and Our Lord at the Last Supper. The Bible clearly says so.

MICHELANGELO: No friends?

POPE: No friends.

MICHELANGELO: Waiters?!

POPE: No!

MICHELANGELO: Cabaret?!

POPE: *No*!!

MICHELANGELO: I like them. They fill out the canvas. I suppose we could lose three or four of them, you know, make –

POPE: *THERE WERE ONLY TWELVE DISCIPLES.*

MICHELANGELO: I've got it – I've got it! We'll call it the Penultimate Supper!

POPE: What?

MICHELANGELO: I mean, if there was a *last* one there must have been one *before* that, right?

POPE: Yes . . .

MICHELANGELO: Well, right, so this is the Penultimate Supper. The Bible doesn't say how many people were *there*, does it?

POPE: No, but . . .

MICHELANGELO: Well, there you are, then!

POPE: Look! The Last Supper was a significant event in the life of Our Lord. The Penultimate Supper was not, even if they had a conjurer and a steel band! Now, I commissioned a Last Supper from you, and a Last Supper I want . . . with TWELVE disciples, and ONE Christ!

MICHELANGELO: *ONE*??!!!

POPE: Yes, one. Now will you please tell me why in God's name you have painted this with *three* Christs in it?

MICHELANGELO: (*Shouting.*) IT *WORKS*, MATE!

POPE: It does *NOT* work!

MICHELANGELO: It *does*! It looks great! The fat one balances the two skinny ones!

POPE: There was only ONE Saviour!

MICHELANGELO: Well, I *know* that, *everyone* knows that . . . but what about a bit of artistic license?

POPE: ONE Redeemer!

MICHELANGELO: I'll tell you what *you* want, mate – you want a bloody *photographer*, not a creative artist with some *imagination* . . .

POPE: (*Shouting.*) I'll tell you what I want . . . I want a Last Supper, with *one* Christ, *twelve* disciples, *no* kangaroos by Thursday lunch – or you don't get paid!

MICHELANGELO: *You bloody fascist!*

POPE: Look – I'm the bloody *Pope*, mate! I may not know much about art – *but I know what I like*!

TELEGRAM

ALAN BENNETT

Bennett is sitting in a comfortable chair and is talking on the telephone.

Hello . . .? Hello, I want to send a telegram, please, if I may. Ah, yes, I am the subscriber, and *my* name is Desmond. (*Listens.*) Yours is Glynis? No, you misunderstand me. My *surname* is Desmond. (*Listens.*) Yours is Budd? Yes, we seem to be drifting into a kind of redundant intimacy . . . Ah, I only want to send a telegram. Yes. (*Fiddling with his nose as he speaks.*) My address is 23 Gloucester Crescent, NW1, telephone number 4858319. (*He pulls out a hair from his nose.*) And the telegram is going to a Miss Tessa Prosser, that's Tes-sa Pros-ser, 16 – one six – Chalcott Square, SW14.

   (*Pauses.*) Right. Here we go . . . (*Listens.*) No, 'Right, here we go' is not the telegram. No. Here goes: (*Starts speaking louder and clearer, pronouncing each word with consummate care.*) 'Bless your little' (*Listens.*) Yes, 'Bless your little . . . BOTTY BOOES.' (*Listens.*) '*BOTTY BOOES.*' Well, I've never been called upon to spell it. Ah, I suppose it's B-O-double T–Y, B-double O-E-S, though I think that probably the last E is not statutory. (*Listens.*) Yes, well, it's a diminutive of 'bottom', really, isn't it? (*Listens.*) No, Miss Prosser *doesn't* have a diminutive bottom – that's partly the joke, you see, ha ha. (*Listens and then winces and looks quizzically at the receiver.*) Yes, so that's: 'BLESS YOUR LITTLE BOTTY BOOES.' Then I want to sign it: 'DESMOND DONKEY-DRAWERS.' (*Listens.*) Well, ah, it's . . . it's a nickname, it's a term of affection Miss Prosser is wont to use at moments of heightened excitement. (*Listens.*) Yes.

   So that's the corpus of the message: 'BLESS YOUR LITTLE BOTTY BOOES. DESMOND DONKEY-DRAWERS.' Then I want to end it, if I may: 'NORWICH.' (*Listens.*) Norwich, yes.

Well, it's an idiomatic way of saying: 'Knickers Off Ready When I Come Home'. You see it's the initial letters of each word. (*Listens.*) Yes, I *know* 'knickers' is spelt with a k! I *was* at Oxford – it was one of the first things they taught us. And in an ideal world it would be 'KORWICH' but I don't think it carries the same idiomatic force.

(*Listens.*) 'BURMA'? No, I *hadn't* come across that. What's that? (*Listens.*) 'Be Upstairs Ready My Angel'? Well, yes, I like that, ah, but I don't think it will do in this case for strictly topographical reasons, because, er, Miss Prosser lives in a basement flat. And if she *was* upstairs 'ready', she *would* in fact be in the flat of the window dresser from Bourne & Hollingsworth. And I don't *think* she would want that. And I *certainly* don't think *he* would.

(*Listens.*) What? 'NORWICH' obscene? Oh, no, certainly not. What about the Bishop of Norwich? When he signs his letters 'Cyril Norwich', does he *mean* 'Cyril Norwich' or 'Cyril Knickers Off Ready When I Come Home'? One doesn't know. Goodbye, goodbye.

NOT AN ASP
PETER COOK & JOHN FORTUNE

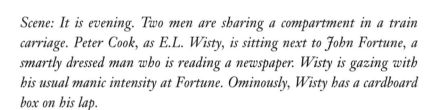

Scene: It is evening. Two men are sharing a compartment in a train carriage. Peter Cook, as E.L. Wisty, is sitting next to John Fortune, a smartly dressed man who is reading a newspaper. Wisty is gazing with his usual manic intensity at Fortune. Ominously, Wisty has a cardboard box on his lap.

COOK: I've got a viper in this box, you know.

FORTUNE: (*Ignoring him.*) Really. Good gracious me.

COOK: Oh, yes. It's not an *asp*. Looks rather like an asp, but isn't one. It's a viper.

(*Fortune sighs and continues reading.*)

COOK: Some people can't tell the difference between a viper and an asp. More fool them, I say. *Har har har har.*

FORTUNE: Yes.

COOK: Cleopatra had an asp. It bit her in the bra . . . *I'd* rather have a viper, myself.

FORTUNE: (*Still not looking up.*) Well, that's all right then, isn't it?

COOK: Not that they're cheaper to run! Oh, no. If anything, the viper is more voracious than the asp. My viper eats like a horse.

FORTUNE: Like a horse, eh?

COOK: Oh, yes, yes. Yes, I'd like a horse. Yes. I've always yearned for a horse. I'd, er, I'd love to have a horse. Mind you, you'd never cram a horse into a little box like this, you see. It's too small for a horse . . .

FORTUNE: (*Vaguely.*) Yes, it would be difficult, I can see that.

COOK: (*Indignant.*) It wouldn't be *difficult*, it would be bloody *impossible*!

(*Fortune continues to stare at his newspaper.*)

COOK: Cram a horse into a little box like this? You *try* it! No, thank you very much! You can't go cramming horses into a little box like this, thank you very much!

FORTUNE: (*Testily.*) Yes. I realise that.

(*Cook taps his box.*)

COOK: I haven't got a fish in here. There's no fish in *my* box, you see. It's only *cardboard*, this box, you see. So if you had a fish in here, you'd get the water seeping through onto your knees, you see. So it's ideal for a viper, but no good for a fish. They haven't invented waterproof cardboard yet. Or if they have, they haven't told me. Or if they've told me, I've forgotten. One way or another.

(*Fortune tries to lose himself in his paper.*)

COOK: Some people think I've got a toad in here . . .

FORTUNE: Really?

COOK: A toad, in *here*? If they knew *me*, they'd know I wouldn't have a *toad* in here. I can't *abide* toads. Vipers devour toads, you know. They *devour* them – they come up slinkily behind the crouching toad, and suddenly –

(*Fortune starts to corpse, prompting Cook to suppress a snigger. The audience laughs.*)

COOK: There's nothing to smile about here! And suddenly – *Bleeaaah*! – the toad goes all the way down the viper's belly. You can see it, starting off large in its throat, and then it gets smaller and smaller and smaller, until it is ejected. Like a small, black biro . . .

(*Fortune looks sickened.*)

COOK: Serpents hear through their *jaws*, you know. It's the bone structure that does it. Oh, yes, there's no doubt about it. It's the bone structure.

FORTUNE: (*Sounding as indifferent as he can be.*) Yes, I suppose it would be.

COOK: A *bee*? A *BEE*?? I haven't got a *bee* in here, thank you very much! You'd hear it *buzzing*, if there was a bee in here! (*He holds the box up close to Fortune's head.*) 'Ere, you have a *listen* to my viper – you won't hear any buzzing!

FORTUNE: (*Recoiling.*) No!

COOK: (*Still holding the box close to Fortune's head.*) Can you hear any buzzing?

FORTUNE: (*Squirming.*) No, thanks, I believe you!

COOK: No fangs? No *FANGS*?? You won't find fangs on a *bee*, thank you very much! That's one thing you *won't* find on a bee is *fangs*! Serpents bite – bees sting. That's how you tell the difference between the bee and the serpent.

FORTUNE: (*Curtly.*) I see. Now look: I'm *trying* to read my paper – will you *please* be quiet?

COOK: 'Bee quiet?' Bees aren't *quiet*! Bees make this terrible *BUZZING* noise: '*All bzzz-bzzz-bzzz goes the bumble bee, tweedly-diddly-dee goes the bird*!' No. (*Points at box.*) No noise from here!

FORTUNE: PLEASE! I wish you would SHUT up!

COOK: Oh, it's *shut up*, all right. You wouldn't catch me setting a viper loose in a railway carriage, thank you very much! Not my viper loose in a railway carriage, no, thank you *very* much! It's completely shut up!

(*Fortune snaps, folding up his newspaper, getting up and heading for the door.*)

COOK: 'Ere, where are you going?

FORTUNE: (*Turning back and glowering.*) I am going into the next compartment.

COOK: I don't see why. I'm not going to let my viper loose.

FORTUNE: It's not that. If you don't mind my saying so, it's just that I find your conversation a bore!

COOK: I beg your pardon?

FORTUNE: I said a bore: B-O-R-E. A *BORE*. Goodnight!

(*He departs.*)

COOK: (*Bemused*) I haven't got a *boar* in 'ere! What could possess him to think I've got a *BOAR* in 'ere? It's a viper, all right. It's not an asp!

 'They haven't invented waterproof cardboard yet. Or if they have, they haven't told me. Or if they've told me, I've forgotten. One way or another.'

PORTRAIT FROM MEMORY

JONATHAN MILLER

ANNOUNCER: Ladies and gentlemen, I am delighted to announce that Bertrand Russell has kindly returned from the dead to be with us tonight for a few brief reminiscences of his early days at Cambridge. Thank you . . .

(Miller shuffles on as the elderly philosopher.)

One of the advantages of living in Great Court, Trinity, I seem to recall, was the fact that one could pop across at any time of the day or night and trap the then young G.E. Moore into a logical falsehood by means of a cunning semantic subterfuge.

I recall one occasion with particular vividness. I had popped across and had knocked upon his door. 'Come in,' he said. I decided to wait a while in order to test the validity of his proposition. 'Come in,' he said once again. 'Very well,' I replied, 'if that is in fact *truly* what you wish.'

I opened the door accordingly and went in, and there was Moore seated by the fire with a basket upon his knees.

'Moore,' I said, 'do you have any apples in that basket?'

'No,' he replied, and smiled seraphically, as was his wont.

I decided to try a different logical tack. 'Moore,' I said, 'do you then have *some* apples in that basket?'

'No,' he replied, leaving me in a logical cleft stick from which I had but one way out.

'Moore,' I said, 'do you then have *apples* in that basket?'

'Yes,' he replied.

And from that day forth, we remained the very closest of friends.

APPEAL
ELEANOR BRON

The spotlight is on Bron. She is wearing a formal evening dress and is reading nervously and hesitantly from a piece of paper.

I do think . . . that we cannot . . . let an occasion of this nature . . . go by . . . without stopping . . . for a moment . . . just to say a few words about . . . what a worthwhile and enjoyable, erm, occasion . . . it is. Erm, we all of us take things for granted too easily – I know I do . . . um . . . and I do think that unless somebody stands up, er, and just bothers to put it into words . . . we might all just sit here, um, without realising quite what a worthwhile and enjoyable time . . . we were all having.

Oh, and, er, I must just say here, before I forget, would people please not put unwanted sandwiches, and, erm, other matter, into the heating vents? I know . . . I know how easy it is for little fingers to do, um, and perhaps for fingers that are not quite so little . . . but, um, getting out, getting out small pieces of decayed fish paste, erm, with knitting needles, and, er, surgical forceps – as we had to do last year – does waste a great deal of the, er, very limited time available to the committee.

Um, I should just like to say a word of thanks to the many people involved in making tonight such a success . . . (*Laughs stiffly.*) I'm sure that having their names mentioned was the last thing they had in mind in the first place . . . and, er, they'll probably never forgive me . . . er, but, er . . . I hope they'll forgive me if there are any names I forget to mention.

And of course, no occasion of this nature could be allowed to pass without mention of Mrs Hussey and her loyal support on the teapot.

(*Modest applause.*)

Um – how we should ever have got through committee meetings without Mrs Hussey and her tea and biscuits I don't know! (*Sadly.*) I think some of us only come to committee meetings for the refreshments.

And I must also mention the noble work performed by so many others too numerous to mention . . . (*Studies piece of paper intently.*) – Mrs Shortstreet, Mrs Flowerdew, Mrs Wales, Mr Chert, Mr Hapforth senior, Mrs Winterbourne, Miss Tumelly, Mr Pettigrew. And, last, but not least, I should like to thank all of you, for coming here tonight, and working so hard to enjoy the entertainment . . . that all these good people have worked so hard to provide. It is particularly gratifying to see so many young faces here tonight. We often think that young people today are only out for a good time. Well, that certainly can't be said of *these* young people.

It's also very gratifying to see all these other people who are not quite so young . . . Er, I know how tempting it is, believe me, just to sit in front of a good fire and watch your favourite television programme . . . (*To herself.*) . . . and there are one or two rather good programmes on tonight. I know how tempting it is to think, oh, let someone *else* go out this time and get themselves entertained! I . . . I must say it is remarkable how – how an occasion of this nature does seem to bring out the best in people, it's just like . . . in the war, or at a great . . . rail crash . . . everybody cheerfully rallies round and, and makes the best of it.

I would just like to say, in all sincerity, that it is . . . people like you . . . that make an occasion of this nature . . . the sort of occasion it is.

SO THAT'S THE WAY YOU LIKE IT

PETER COOK, JONATHAN MILLER, ALAN BENNETT & TERRY JONES

Peter Cook enters wearing his own clothes but a bizarre Shakespearean hat. He fixes the audience with a steely gaze.

COOK: Sustain thee now! A time when petty lust and overweening tyranny offend the ruck of state. Thus fly we now, as oft with Phoebus did fair Asterope, unto proud Flanders shores, where the warlike Warwick – like unto the kite that sat on Hector's head – is bound for England, and for *WAAAAAAR!*

(Miller, Bennett and Jones enter in Shakespearean dress.)

MILLER: And so we bid you welcome to our court, fair captain Albany, and you, our sweetest Essex – take this my hand, and you, fair Essex this, and with this bond we'll cry anon, and shout 'Jack Cock o'London' to the foe!

COOK: Jack Cock o'London!

JONES: Jack Cock o'London!

MILLER: Approach your ears, and kindly bend your conscience to my piece; our ruddy scouts to me this hefty news have brought. The naughty English, expecting now some pregnance in our plan, have with some haughty purpose bent Aeolis unto the service of their sail. So even now while we to the wanton lute do strut, is brutish Bolingbroke bent fair upon some fickle circumstance!

BENNETT/COOK/JONES: Some fickle circumstance?!

MILLER:

> Get thee to Gloucester, Essex. Do thee to Wessex, Exeter.
> Fair Albany to Somerset must eke his route.
> And Scroop, do you to Westmoreland, where shall bold York
> Enrouted now for Lancaster, with forces of our Uncle Rutland,
> Enjoin his standard with sweet Norfolk's host.
> Fair Sussex, get thee to Warwicksbourne,
> And there, with frowning purpose, tell our plan
> To Bedford's tilted ear, that he shall press
> With most insensate speed
> And join his warlike effort to bold Dorset's side.
> I, most royally, shall now to bed,
> To sleep off all the nonsense I've just said.

(*They all leave the stage.*)

(*Bennett and Jones return. Jones is dressed as a jester with a lute, Bennett as a courtier.*)

JONES: (*Sings.*) Oh, death his face my shroud hath hid . . .

(*Plucks lute string – plink!*)

JONES: (*Sings.*) And Lethe drowned my poor love's grave . . .

(*Plucks lute string – plink!*)

JONES: (*Sings.*) Oh, let us flee to Pluto's Realm . . .

(*Plucks lute string – plink!*)

JONES: (*Sings.*) And in his arms I shall grow old.

(*Plucks lute string – bing!*)

BENNETT: Wise words in mouths of fools do oft themselves belie . . . Good fool, shall Essex prosper?

JONES: Aye, prosper . . .

BENNETT: Marry, then, methinks we'll prosper. And saying prosper, do we say, to cut the knot which crafty nature hath within our bowels lock-ed up. But soft, and who comes here?

(*Enter Cook in a state of agitation.*)

COOK: Oh, good my lord! Unstop your ear and yet prepare to yield the optic tear to my experience. Such news I bring as can only crack ope the casket of your heart. Not six miles hence there grows an oak, whose knotty thews engendered in the bosky wood doth raise itself most impudent towards the solstice sun . . . So saying, did there die. And dying, so did say!

(*Exit Cook.*)

BENNETT: God! This was most gravely underta'en! And underta'en Essex gravely answered it. Why then, we'll muster, and to the field of battle go, and unto them our English sinews show!

(*Exit Bennett and Jones. Re-enter Miller and Cook, both carrying swords. Rather too much atmospheric smoke begins to creep in with them.*)

MILLER: Why, then, was this encounter nobly entertained? And so by steel shall this, our contest, now, be buckled up. Come, sir—

(*Miller fans some of the smoke away.*)

MILLER: Let's to't!

COOK: Let's to't! Good steel, thou shalt thyself in himself, thyself, embowel.

MILLER: Come, sir!

(*They fight.*)

MILLER: Ah ha, a hit, a hit, a hit! (*Laughs manically.*)

COOK: No, sir, no hit, a miss!

MILLER: Thou art fop i' the mouth.

COOK: Art more fop i'the brain than fop i'the mouth!

MILLER: Well, sir, again!

(*They resume fighting, and Cook lays a fatal blow on Miller.*)

MILLER: Oh, God! (*He staggers.*) Fair cousin, thou hast done me wrong!

(*Miller staggers about, expiring very noisily.*)

MILLER: Now is steel 'twixt gut and bladder interposed!

(*Miller finally collapses and dies.*)

COOK: Oh, saucy Worcester! Dost thou lie so still?

(*Bennett and Jones return.*)

BENNETT: Now hath mortality her tithe collected, and sovereign Albany to the worms his corpse committed. Yet weep we not; this fustian life is short; let's on to Pontefract to sanctify our court . . .

'I, most royally, shall now to bed,
To sleep off all the nonsense I've just said.'

Jonathan Miller

THE LUMBERJACK SONG

MICHAEL PALIN & THE CAST

Michael Palin, dressed as a lumberjack, walks on jauntily with Carol Cleveland on his arm. Behind them is a chorus of Mounties, played by Jonathan Lynn, John Bird, Terry Jones, Terry Gilliam, Tim Brooke-Taylor, Graham Chapman, Bill Oddie, John Cleese and Eleanor Bron.

PALIN: (*Spoken.*) The smell of fresh cut timber! The crash of mighty trees! With my best girl by my side, we sing – *sing* – *SING*!

PALIN: (*Sings.*)

> I'm a lumberjack and I'm okay,
> I sleep all night and I work all day.

CHORUS:

> He's a lumberjack and he's okay,
> He sleeps all night and he works all day.

PALIN:

> I cut down trees, I eat my lunch,
> I go to the lavatory.
> On Wednesdays I go shopping
> And have buttered scones for tea.

CHORUS:

> He cuts down trees, he eats his lunch,
> He goes to the lavatory.
> On Wednesdays he goes shopping
> And has buttered scones for tea.

PALIN/CHORUS:

> He's a lumberjack and he's okay,
> He sleeps all night and he works all day.

PALIN:

> I cut down trees, I skip and jump,
> I like to press wild flowers.
> I put on women's clothing,
> And hang around in bars.

CHORUS:

> He cuts down trees, he skips and jumps,
> He likes to press wild flowers.
> He puts on women's clothing,
> And hangs around . . . in . . . *bars?*

(*The chorus is confused but picks up the song.*)

PALIN/CHORUS:

> He's a lumberjack and he's okay,
> He sleeps all night and he works all day.

PALIN:

    I cut down trees, I wear high heels,
    Suspenders and a bra.
    I wish I'd been a girlie,
    Just like my dear papa!

CHORUS:

    He cuts down trees, he wears high heels?
    Suspenders . . . and a *bra*?

(*Alarmed, the chorus breaks up noisily but then, when the music resumes, hastily reassembles to finish the song.*)

PALIN/CHORUS:

    . . . He's a lumberjack and he's okay,
    He sleeps all night and he works all day.
    He's a lumberjack and he's *okaaaaay*!

(*Lights down.*)

THE MERMAID FROLICS

HIGHLIGHTS OF THE <u>AMNESTY</u> INTERNATIONAL GALA!

JOHN
CLEESE & BOOTH CONNIE
WACKY TWOSOME

PETER
USTINOV
WELL KNOWN CELEBRITY

JULIE
COVINGTON
HIT PARADE SONGSTRESS

JOHN
'MR. GUITAR'
WILLIAMS

PETER
COOK
T/V's KING OF SATIRE

JONATHAN
MILLER
DOCTOR IN THE HOUSE

TERRY
JONES
MONTY PYTHON MIRTHMAN

THE
BOWLES BROTHERS BAND
LATEST RAVE COMBO

PETE
ATKIN
MUSICAL MAESTRO

AS SEEN ON TV
60 MINS OF SONGS & SMILES!

★

THE
MERMAID
FROLICS

★

**MERMAID THEATRE
8 MAY 1977**

THE MERMAID FROLICS, 1977

Relatively few comic performers (due to logistics or other commitments) were available for the second Amnesty event (which, as it was held at Sir Bernard Miles' Mermaid Theatre, was originally called *An Evening Without Sir Bernard Miles*), so Terry Jones, its director, was obliged to broaden the show's appeal by recruiting some musicians to complement the comedy.

Those comedians who did appear worked hard to maintain the same high standards of flair, rigour and literacy set by the previous year's participants. Peter Cook returned to perform another E.L Wisty routine; John Cleese (taking the place of the absent Alan Bennett) and Jonathan Miller revived another *Beyond the Fringe* sketch (this time the wonderfully accurate satire of Oxbridge academic pretension entitled 'Words . . . and Things'); and Cleese was joined by his estranged wife and *Fawlty Towers* co-writer Connie Booth to reprise a sketch ('Bookshop') he and Graham Chapman had written in the 1960s for the TV series *At Last the 1948 Show*. New material included several predictably wry and witty anecdotes by Peter Ustinov and a darkly comic song by Terry Jones called 'Forgive Me'.

There would have been more of Peter Cook had it not been for Dudley Moore's unexpected no-show (an absence Cook acknowledged in one routine by sniping at such 'sinners' as 'Diminished British people who go to Hollywood thinking they're stars and don't turn up for fucking *charity* shows they're supposed to be performing at!'). Terry Jones was co-opted to take Dudley's role in a couple of routines – including what became a quasi-blasphemous version of the 'Bishop of the World' sketch, in which Peter, in somewhat 'enhanced' condition, sailed way past the comedic limits of what was then acceptable to a Sunday night theatre audience or on TV.

QUEEN MARY
PETER USTINOV

For such a distinguished audience and for such a necessary cause, one shouldn't experiment too much, so I'll just tell you one or two things which are already formed and have made complete entities, in my mind, one of them told me by my mother, who was a painter and a scene designer, and who did the designs for the *Sleeping Beauty* in 1938, when President Lebrun paid his state visit to London, in order to ensure the solidarity which . . . got as far as Dunkirk.

At the gala, my mother was told that, together with Constant Lambert, and Dame Ninette De Valois, she was to be presented to Queen Mary, who came, of course, not alone, but accompanied by several ladies, including one – I don't know now which one it was, but I think it was the Grand Duchess of Teck-Pless-Nassau-Gotha-Coburg and Mecklenburg-Schwerin – who lived in Hampton Court and had a tiara, which was brought out for these occasions, and followed everywhere *viz a very strooong* German accent.

And my mother was told that you don't look *at* the Queen Mother – she was the queen then – you look straight forward, and you wait. So, my mother stood and Queen Mary came in with her toque, and went to Constant Lambert, who was at the end of the line, and my mother heard . . . (*Ustinov makes indistinct female royal speech, then obsequious male speech. Then more indistinct female royal speech, then the male voice again.*)

Then there was a pause, and Queen Mary moved one nearer. And my mother still looked straight ahead. And she heard . . . (*Does slightly louder but still incomprehensible Queen Mary voice.*)

And Dame Ninette said . . . (*Does incomprehensible woman's voice, then performs the whole incomprehensible conversation between the two.*)

Then there was a pause, and Queen Mary landed in front of my mother, and said . . .

(*He mimes Queen Mary struggling, and eventually failing, to think of something to say.*)

– and left.

So the Grand Duchess following her – now caught between a need to run after Queen Mary, and to repair this omission – had just time to say to my mother, 'What a *pity* about ze *revolution*!'

WORDS . . . AND THINGS

JONATHAN MILLER & JOHN CLEESE

The scene is a Senior Common Room somewhere in Oxford or Cambridge. Cleese is slumped almost horizontally in an old leather armchair, his chin resting on his chest. Miller, sprawled on the nearby stairs, addresses Cleese in a donnishly self-important adenoidal voice.

MILLER: Wittgenstein says, doesn't he, Wittgenstein *says*, doesn't he, in *The Blue and Brown Books*, mmm? The, erm, the statement 'Fetch me that slab', you see, the statement 'Fetch me that slab', implies, implies there *IS* a slab . . . you see, there is a slab, there is a slab . . . such that, were I to fetch it, the statement 'Fetch me that slab' would be disjunctively denied by the opposite state . . .

CLEESE: (*Thoughtfully, as if much is at stake.*) Ye-es . . .

MILLER: (*Getting to his feet and striding oddly around the room.*)

Well, you see, it seems to me, seems to *me*, seems to *ME*, that Wittgenstein has made really a rather *primitive* category mistake here, I would say . . . rather a primitive *category mistake*, in the sense that the unfetched slab, you see, the unfetched slab, the unfetched slab . . . can claim to *exist*, you see . . . really no more than the unseen tree in the quad.

(*Cleese, his fingers pressed against either side of temples, furrows his brow and thinks very hard indeed.*)

CLEESE: Hmm . . . Oh, no, no, no . . . no, no. I think *you're* making rather a primitive category mistake here.

(*Worried, his index finger pressed down tightly on his bottom lip, Miller stops dead and stares.*)

MILLER: *Really?*

(*Cleese nods gravely. Then, eyes darting from side to side, he suddenly looks alarmed.*)

CLEESE: No, *you're* not – it's *me*! Oh, I'm *terribly* sorry!

(*Buoyed by this, Miller walks around in an even more eccentric fashion while Cleese curls up in his chair like a tortured Kafkaesque insect.*)

CLEESE: I'm sorry, I'm sorry!

MILLER: You see—

(*Cleese recovers some composure and sits up, gently gnawing on his fist.*)

CLEESE: Yes, *yes* . . .

MILLER: Now tell me, tell me – are you using 'Yes' here . . . in the affirmative sense?

(*Cleese ponders this for a moment.*)

CLEESE: No . . . No, you see, I *like* the paper. *Like* it, because it has to bear on something I'm considering myself (*He gets to his feet.*) at the moment, namely, what part, what, erm, *role* –

MILLER: Role –

CLEESE: (*Suddenly speaking very quickly.*) . . . we – as philosophers – have to play in this, this, this, confusing and heterogeneous, confusing and confused, jumble of political and social and economic relations we call society . . .

MILLER: Yes, quite, yes, yes, yes, yes . . .

CLEESE: . . . And other people have jobs to do, don't they? I mean, what, what, what, what jobs do people do . . . these days? *Hmm?*

MILLER: Um . . .

(*They both puzzle over this for a while. Miller turns to the wall, reaches up and rests his fingers on a shelf as he looks down at the ground, and Cleese stands scratching his head.*)

MILLER: They chop down trees?

CLEESE: They chop down trees! They drive buses . . .

MILLER: Yes, yes . . .

CLEESE: . . . they play *games!*

MILLER: Ah . . . ha . . . ha . . .

(*Grinning, they point at each other knowingly.*)

CLEESE: (*Smugly.*) Now we *also* play games, but as philosophers . . . we play language games? Games, erm . . . *at* language?

MILLER: Yes, yes, yes, yes, I'm with you, yes . . .

CLEESE: Now, when you and I go onto the cricket pitch, we do so secure in the knowledge that a game of cricket is in the offing.

(*Almost boyishly, a grinning Miller mimes bowling an off-break.*)

CLEESE: But when we play *language* games –

MILLER: Yes, yes, yes . . .

CLEESE: . . . we do so rather in order to find out *what game it is that we are playing.*

(They both seem delighted with this notion and caper around the room in a sort of ecstasy of pomposity.)

CLEESE: In other words—

MILLER: Yes?

CLEESE: *. . . why do philosophy at all?*

MILLER: Yes, yes . . .

CLEESE: Why?

MILLER: Yes, yes . . .

CLEESE: Why?

MILLER: Yes, yes . . .

(Cleese sits back down again and rubs his brow. Miller continues to stride around the room.)

CLEESE: Hmm? *Why?*

MILLER: Yes, yes. No. No, *no*. In *that* case, in that case, you see, I think the burden is fair and square on your shoulders, Bleaney, you see, to explain to me the exact role that philosophy has in everyday life. I mean, do you think you can do that?

(*Cleese gets off his chair and kneels down, his face resting on the floor and his hands folded tightly over the back of his head. He then leaps up to his feet.*)

CLEESE: Yes! I think I can do this! Now, erm, this morning, I walked into a shop, and . . . a shop assistant was having an argument with a customer. The shop assistant said, 'Yes', you see, and the customer said, 'What do you mean, *yes*?' . . . and the shop assistant said, 'I mean . . . yes.'

MILLER: Yes, yes. This is very exciting!

(*Both men run about excitedly, hunched over, with their hands stuffed deep in their pockets.*)

CLEESE: Now here we have a splendid example, a *splendid* example, of two, two – very ordinary – people, asking each other what are innocent, and yet metaphysical, questions. Um, um, 'What do you mean, "yes"', 'I mean "yes"', and so forth, and so forth, where I – as a philosopher – could, erm, could help them.

MILLER: Yes. *Did* you?

CLEESE: Well, no. They were in rather a hurry . . .

E.L. WISTY: FROM BEYOND THE VEIL

PETER COOK

E.L. Wisty, bathed in a cold white light, is sitting on a chair, a blank expression on his face, and looking straight out at the audience.

Good evening. It's one minute before opening time up here. It's always one minute before opening time. They're forming a queue. They usually do, the newcomers, form a queue. For weeks they form a queue. Well, it's not really weeks, because although our watches go round there's only one time, which is: one minute before opening time.

We've been looking down at what's going to happen tonight. We've seen it several times.

We're very sorry about Mr Prendergast and the number 9 bus. I know he's out there listening. And I know he thinks that by knowing about it in advance he can avoid it. But it's no good, Mr Prendergast. You could sit in the theatre all night. It would still get you. Personally I think it would be more sensible to pop out and be run down in the street. At least there's some *logic* to that. But if you want a bus to come careering into the theatre, that's up to you. That's what freedom of choice is all about.

But let's not be too morbid. Let's think of the happy stories the newspapers never print. Let's think of all the millions of people who will *not* be run down by buses tonight. When did you last read a story in a newspaper: 'Millions of people get through the day reasonably successfully without being run down by a bus'? They don't print that kind of story.

(The light flickers.)

I'm beginning to fade slightly now. But if any of you out there below would like to get in touch, just speak to me if you want news of your loved ones, or bad news about those you hate. Speak and I shall answer ye. Do I hear voices coming to me . . . ?

(*Someone in the audience: 'What about inflation?'*)

Inflation here . . . is worse than what you have down there. We are running at 118 per cent. And that's one minute before closing time.

(*Another audience member: 'What about the bourgeois problem?'*)

We've eaten that.

(*Someone else in the audience: 'What about my budgerigar?'*)

Your deceased budgerigar? Or the one you have hidden about you?

(*'The dead one.'*)

Your dead budgie feels much the same as he did when alive. Terrible.

(*Another audience member: 'What about the Liberals?'*)

(*The light flickers again.*)

Fading gradually now – like the Liberals.

If I am never here again, don't worry, I'm still here. At one minute before closing time . . .

'Let's think of all the millions of people who will *not* be run down by buses tonight.'

FORGIVE ME

TERRY JONES

Forgive me, for loving you the way I do, dear
Forgive me, please do not say that we are through, dear
I know my manners aren't polite, and I insulted you last night
But please forgive me, the way you always do, dear.

Forgive me, for being such a crashing bore last night
Forgive me, for doing all that on the floor last night
I'm really glad that you complained
Please do not think I'm not ashamed
But just forgive me, and love me like before last night.

Forgive me, for being sick inside the car and then
Forgive me, for going just that bit too far and when
You slapped my face and I saw red
To my disgrace, I hit your head
And as I said, now that you're dead

Forgive me, for being late to your cremation
Forgive me, I left the flowers at the station
And now I'm here, I tried to shed
A single tear, and yet instead
I have this feeling of incredible elation.

SIR JOHN GIELGUD
PETER USTINOV

How do these things start? What are the comic moments that occur in life which people with an addiction to comedy notice? Other people hear them but don't always notice them.

It reminds me of a moment in St Louis, Missouri, where I was on the road with a play and got home to the hotel afterwards and switched on the television, and on the local channel I was very surprised to find Sir John Gielgud being interviewed by a local intellectual. And he had just played the *Ages of Man* in half a ball park – I think there was a game going on in the other half – and the American interlocutor said: (*Puts on a very earnest-sounding American accent.*) 'Well, er, I think we just have time for one final, er, question, um, Sir . . . Sir Gielgod. I'd like to ask you this: did you in your long and, er, well, not only *long* but also very *wonderful* career . . . did you have, oh, well, we *all* have, a person – a man, or, well, uh, ha ha, a woman – that you point at and say, "Yes, this person is the one responsible, you know, and that I look at now with, er, considerable gratitude . . . "?' By then John had understood what he was being asked, and he said, in the middle of Missouri: (*Impersonates Gielgud.*) 'Yes, I think there *was* someone. I remember with great gratitude, at the Royal Academy, Claude Raines. I don't know *what* happened to him – I think he *failed* and went to America.'

PIETER DE HOOGH
PETER USTINOV

Another anecdote told me – I wasn't there – by a friend who knew, very well, a Dutch professor who had lived a very orderly, quiet and hard-working life, a man of rather placid temperament who had devoted his whole mature existence to classifying all of the paintings by Pieter de Hoogh, and putting them into a magnificent colour edition, which is on the market. And at the age of sixty-two he felt that he had done his bit and was invited at that moment to a large English country house owned by a duke. And to his horror – one can imagine the horror – saw on the wall three Pieter de Hooghs that nobody had ever heard of or seen.

So he got very excited and said to my friend: (*Puts on the Professor's Dutch accent.*) 'But these are Pieter de Hooghs!'

(*Puts on a very crusty, absent-minded-sounding English accent.*) 'Er, I don't know *what* they are, er, ha ha . . .'

(*Professor:*) 'But . . . but . . . can I *ask* about them?'

(*Friend:*) 'Yes, ah, I should ask the duke.'

(*Professor:*) 'How does one call the duke?'

(*Friend:*) 'You call him "His Grace".'

(*Professor:*) 'His Grace?'

(*Friend:*) 'Yes, His Grace is, ah, ordinary, ah, with the duke . . .'

So he found the duke and said: 'Ah, His Grace! (*Pointing excitedly at the pictures.*) His Grace, these are Pieter de Hooghs!'

(*The Duke, sounding even more posh and absent-minded:*) 'They're *what?*'

(*Professor:*) 'These pictures are from Pieter de Hoogh!'

(*Duke:*) 'Eh? Oh, I don't know *what* they, ah, ha ha . . . (*Points at one of them.*) I know *that* one because it's painted on wood, you understand.'

(*Professor:*) 'Yes, I know! Very often they were painted on wood!'

(*Duke:*) 'Yes, that one, because when I was younger I, ah, used to throw a *ball* against it, the *bounce* was a very *true* one . . . (*Looks at another painting.*) I don't know *that* fellow at all . . . nor, nor the other one . . . I think they were in the other *wing* and, ah, must have come over here after the *fire* . . . I never went there . . . um . . . Do you want to *know* about them?'

(*Professor:*) 'YES! Yes, I would very much *appreciate* it, His Grace!'

(*Duke:*) 'Oh, well then, I'll, er, I'll get the Black Book.' (*He rings the service bell.*) And the butler appears at the end of the gallery. (*Duke:*) 'Oh, Bellamy: Black Book, please.' (*The butler mumbles and departs, and the Duke continues.*) 'Yes, ah, when the Black Book comes, you see, you'll find that on the *frames* are little tiddlywinks, or they may be paper, I can't remember, with a *number* on them. You tell me the *number* – your eyesight is certainly better than mine – and I'll, er, look up it up in the Black Book, you see, and I'll tell you all about it, ha ha!'

The book arrived and the Dutchman said: 'Sixty-four, sixty-five and sixty-seven.'

(*Duke:*) 'Oh . . . wonder what happened to sixty-six? Oh, well . . . er, what did you say they were?'

(*Professor:*) 'Pieter de Hooghs!'

(*The Duke consults the Black Book:*) '. . . *Oh*, ha ha, full marks! What *is* that? German? *German* painter?'

(*Professor:*) 'No, Dutch!'

(*Duke:*) 'I beg your pardon?'

(*Professor:*) 'Dutch!'

(*Duke, gesturing to his ear:*) 'I'm sorry, ah, hmmm?'

(*Professor:*) 'The Netherlands!'

(*Duke, still puzzled:*) 'Er, ha, um, I'm very sorry, ah . . . ?'

(*Professor:*) 'Holland! Er, the LOW COUNTRIES!'

(*Duke:*) 'Oh, the *Low Countries*! Oh, *really*?'

He's about to shut the book when the Dutchman said, 'Oh, before you shut the book, could tell me where you *acquired* them?'

(*Duke, puzzled again:*) 'Eh?'

(*Professor:*) 'Where you ACQUIRED them?'

(*Duke:*) 'Oh, where we *acquired* them. Ah, just a sec . . . (*He consults the book again, and then reports in the most disarmingly casual of tones.*) Yes, ah, we acquired them, ah, from the painter.'

BOOKSHOP
JOHN CLEESE & CONNIE BOOTH

A woman enters a small bookshop. A man stands behind the counter, writing a note. She rings a bell to attract his attention.

BOOTH: Good morning!

CLEESE: Good morning.

BOOTH: Can you help me? Do you have *Thirty Days in the Samarkand Desert with the Duchess of Kent* by A.E.J. Eliott, O.B.E.?

CLEESE: (*Puzzled.*) Well . . . I don't know the book, madam . . .

BOOTH: Oh, never mind. How about *101 Ways to Start a Fight*?

CLEESE: Er . . . by . . . ?

BOOTH: An Irish gentleman whose name eludes for the moment.

CLEESE: Er, no, well, we haven't got it in stock.

BOOTH: Not to worry, not to worry. Can you help me with *David Copperfield*?

(*Delighted to hear a familiar title, Cleese turns immediately and starts scouring the shelves.*)

CLEESE: Ah, yes, Dickens!

BOOTH: No.

CLEESE: (*Looking back at the customer.*) I beg your pardon?

BOOTH: No, Edmund Wells.

CLEESE: I . . . think you'll find Charles Dickens wrote *David Copperfield*, madam.

BOOTH: No, no, *David Copperfield* was written by Charles Dickens with two Ps. This is *David Coperfield* with one P by Edmund Wells.

CLEESE: *David Coperfield* with one P?

BOOTH: Yes, I should have said.

CLEESE: Yes, well, in that case we don't have it.

(*Rattled, Cleese returns to writing his note, so Booth has to address the top of his head.*)

BOOTH: Funny, 'cause you got a lot of books here.

CLEESE: (*Brusquely.*) Yes. But we don't have *David Coperfield* with one P by Edmund Wells.

BOOTH: You're quite sure?

CLEESE: Quite!

BOOTH: It's not worth just looking?

CLEESE: Definitely not.

BOOTH: How about *Great Expectations?*

(*Cleese looks up.*)

CLEESE: Yes . . . well, we have that.

(*He starts to move towards the shelves.*)

BOOTH: That's *G-R-A-T-E Expectations.* Also by Edmund Wells.

(*Disappointed, he turns back to the counter.*)

CLEESE: Yes, well, um, in that case, we don't have it. We don't have anything by Edmund Wells, actually: he's *not* very *popular.*

(*He returns once more to writing his note.*)

BOOTH: Not *Knickerless Knickleby?* That's K-N-I-C-K-E-R-L-E-S-S.

CLEESE: Nope.

BOOTH: A *Christmas Karol* with a K?

CLEESE: No.

BOOTH: How about *A Sale of Two Titties*?

(*Cleese merely looks up, gives her a withering stare and shakes his head.*)

BOOTH: Sorry to have troubled you.

CLEESE: (*Muttering.*) Not at all.

(*She starts to head for the door, but then pauses, turns back and rings the bell again.*)

BOOTH: I wonder if you might have a copy of *Rarnaby Budge*?

CLEESE: No, as I said: we are right *out* of Edmund Wells!

BOOTH: No, not Edmund Wells. Charles Dikkens.

CLEESE: Charles Dickens?

BOOTH: Yes.

CLEESE: You mean *Barnaby Rudge*.

BOOTH: No, *Rarnaby Budge* by Charles Dikkens. That's Dikkens with two Ks, the well-known Dutch author.

CLEESE: (*Sighing and then snarling.*) No, well, we don't have *Rarnaby Budge* by Charles Dikkens with two Ks, the well-known Dutch author, and perhaps to save time I should add that we don't have *Karnaby Fudge* by Darles Chickens, or *Farmer of Sludge* by Marles Pickens, or even *Stickwick Stapers* by Farles Wickens with four Ms and a silent *Q*!!! Why don't you try W.H. Smith's?

BOOTH: I did. They sent me here!

CLEESE: (*Indignantly.*) DID they!

BOOTH: I wonder if you might have *The Amazing Adventures of Captain Gladys Stoutpamphlet and Her Intrepid Spaniel Stig Amongst the Giant Pygmies of Beckles* . . . volume eight?

CLEESE: (*Sarcastically.*) No, we don't have it. Funny – we've got a lot of *books* here! Well, I mustn't keep you standing around here –

BOOTH: I wonder if you –

CLEESE: No, no, no, we haven't!

BOOTH: No, but I –

CLEESE: *NO!* We haven't! (*Gestures at his watch and moves to the front of the counter in a bid to shepherd her out of the shop.*) We're closing for lunch, I'm sorry!

BOOTH: I *saw* it over there!

CLEESE: What?

BOOTH: Er, *Olsen's Standard Book of British Birds!*

CLEESE: (*Confused.*) *Olsen's Standard Book of British Birds?*

BOOTH: Yes.

CLEESE: (*Suspiciously.*) O-L-S-E-N?

BOOTH: Yes!

CLEESE: B-I-R-D?

BOOTH: Yes!

(*Cleese stares at her quizzically for a moment, then heads back to the shelves.*)

CLEESE: Yes, well, we do have that as a matter of fact.

(*He reaches up and has his hand on the spine when the customer speaks again.*)

BOOTH: The expurgated version.

(*He freezes. He then takes the book down and avoids making eye contact with her.*)

CLEESE: I'm sorry, I didn't quite catch that.

BOOTH: The expurgated version.

(*Cleese cracks, spinning round with a look of fury in his eyes.*)

CLEESE: The *EXPURGATED* version of *Olsen's Standard Book of British Birds*?!?!?!

BOOTH: The one without the gannet.

CLEESE: 'The one without the gannet'?! They've *ALL* got the gannet!! It's a *Standard* British bird, the gannet, it's in *all* the books!!!

BOOTH: Well, I don't like them. They wet their nests.

(*Raging, Cleese opens the book, searches for the entry and rips out the page.*)

CLEESE: It's gone – any other birds you don't like?

BOOTH: I don't like the robin.

CLEESE: Right, the robin, the robin, the robin . . . here we are! (*He tears out another page.*) Anything else?

BOOTH: The nuthatch.

CLEESE: The nuthatch, the nuthatch, right . . . (*He tears out another page.*) There you are! No gannets, no robins, no nuthatches!

(*He slams the expurgated volume down on to the counter.*)

CLEESE: There's your book!

BOOTH: I can't buy that – it's torn!

(*She looks over at the shelves.*)

BOOTH: I wonder if you have, um . . .

CLEESE: Go on – ask me for another – we've got *lots* of books here, this is a bookshop!

BOOTH: How about *Biggles Combs His Hair*?

(*Cleese seems now not so much angry as exhausted. His hands are in his pockets and he almost looks resigned to his fate.*)

CLEESE: No, no, we don't have that one. Funny.

BOOTH: *The Gospel According to Charlie Drake?*

(*He glances half-heartedly at the shelves, pretending to search.*)

CLEESE: No . . . no . . . no, try me again.

BOOTH: Oh, I know! *Ethel the Aardvark Goes Quantity Surveying!*

CLEESE: No, no, no . . . (*Suddenly, his eyes pop open wide, he thinks for a moment and suddenly seems excited.*) Wh-Wh-*What* did you say?

BOOTH: *Ethel the Aardvark Goes Quantity Surveying!*

CLEESE: *Ethel the Aard . . . WE'VE GOT IT!!!* (*He suddenly swings round and rushes towards the shelves, looks up, down and sideways and then grabs a book and races triumphantly back to the counter.*)

CLEESE: There we are! *Ethel the Aardvark Goes Quantity Surveying!* There's your book! Now: *BUY IT!*

BOOTH: (*Suddenly panicking.*) I- I- I don't have enough money. I- I- I don't have *any* money.

CLEESE: I'll take a cheque!

BOOTH: I don't have a cheque book.

CLEESE: I've got a blank one!

BOOTH: I don't have a bank account!

(*Cleese is silent for a while, tensed up and twitching. He thinks.*)

CLEESE: Right: *I'll* buy it *for* you!

(*He opens the till and takes out some money.*)

CLEESE: Here you are, here's your change and some money for a taxi home! (*He picks up the book and runs round to the front of the counter straight at his startled customer.*) Here's your book, here's your book!

(*Booth backs away until she is trapped by the door, then gives out a cry of distress. Cleese leaps up and down with frustration.*)

CLEESE: What?? WHAT??? *WHAT???* ***WHAT IS IT NOW???***

BOOTH: *I CAN'T **READ**!*

(*Cleese stares in disbelief.*)

CLEESE: You can't read? (*He thinks for a moment.*) Right! SIT!

(*He drags her to a chair, sits down and pulls her onto his lap. Then he opens the book and starts reading.*)

CLEESE: 'Ethel the Aardvark was hopping down the river valley one lovely morning, trottety-trottety-trottety, when she met a nice little quantity surveyor . . .'

THE SECRET POLICEMAN'S BALL

HER MAJESTY'S THEATRE
27-30 JUNE 1979

Amnesty International
PROUDLY PRESENT

THE SECRET POLICEMAN'S BALL

CAST IN ORDER OF APPEARANCE

JOHN CLEESE
PETER COOK
BILLY CONNOLLY
MICHAEL PALIN
TERRY JONES
ELEANOR BRON
JOHN FORTUNE
ROWAN ATKINSON

THE SECRET POLICEMAN'S BALL

First Half

1. JOHN CLEESE & PETER COOK
'Interesting Facts' (4.44)

2. BILLY CONNOLLY
'The Country & Western Supersong' (7.35)

3. MICHAEL PALIN & TERRY JONES
'How Do You Do It?' (2.56)

4. ROWAN ATKINSON
'School Master' (7.09)

5. PETER COOK & ELEANOR BRON
'Pregnancy Test' (1.14)

6. JOHN CLEESE & TERRY JONES
(with guest celebrities: Mike Brearley,
Clive Jenkins, Anna Ford and Melvyn Bragg)
'The Name's The Game' (7.20)

7. MICHAEL PALIN & ROWAN ATKINSON
'Stake Your Claim' (1.17)

Second Half

1. PETER COOK
'Entirely A Matter For You' (9.54)

2. JOHN CLEESE & MICHAEL PALIN
(with Bouzouki: Richard Harvey
Greek Dancers: Dr. Rob Buckman
and Dr. Chris Beetles)
'Cheese Shop' (6.41)

3. ELEANOR BRON & JOHN FORTUNE
'Please' (1.01)

**4. JOHN CLEESE, MICHAEL PALIN,
TERRY JONES & ROWAN ATKINSON**
'Four Yorkshiremen' (4.20)

5. BILLY CONNOLLY
'Two Little Boys In Blue' (5.53)

6. PETER COOK & THE ENTIRE CAST
'The End Of The World' (5.05)

Produced by Martin Lewis. Edited by John Lloyd. Stage Show *slightly* Directed by John Cleese.
Executive Producers Martin Lewis and Peter Walker. A 21st Century Leisure Ltd. Production for Amnesty International.
Recorded at "The Secret Policeman's Ball" The 1979 Amnesty International Comedy Gala,
at Her Majesty's Theatre, London on 27th, 28th, 29th and 30th June 1979.

Recorded by the Island Mobile. Engineered by Howard Kilgour. Assisted by Andy Lyden.
Mixed and edited at the Berwick Street Recording Studio. Engineered by John Middleton. Editing Assistance by Lisa Braun.
Mastered by George Peckham.
Billy Connolly appears by courtesy of Polydor Ltd. Doctors Buckman and Beetles feel appear by kind permission of EMI Records.
Artist's Impression of a Secret Policeman by Colin Wheeler. Layman's Impression of a sleeve design by Martin Lewis.

Amnesty International would like to offer its very real thanks to all of the above,
especially the performers (who gave at their services entirely free of charge),
and also to the following (without whom the ball would not have rolled):
The Ken Campbell Roadshow, Terry Gilliam, Neil Innes, Clive James, Das Jones,
Tom Robertson, Pete Townshend, John Williams, John Altman, Ray Bland, Robert Cavendish,
Suzanne Church, John Cohen, Ruth Cowan, Michael Friend, Roger Greet, Joan Pakenham-Walsh,
Tom Schwalm, Judy Wuring and Paul Cox, Simon Fowler and John Halsall of LFI.

ISLAND

Manufactured and distributed by EMI Records Limited.

PROFITS FROM THIS ALBUM GO TO
Amnesty International

CHANGING THE GUARD
AN INTRODUCTION

Amnesty's collaboration with comedy was resumed two years later, in 1979, one month after Margaret Thatcher's Conservatives became the new Government. The new shows arrived bearing a brand new name – *The Secret Policeman's Ball* – and an increasingly diverse range of participants. When John Cleese got the team together at his Holland Park home, the quest for a name, among other things, was on the agenda. Sparked by Cleese's musing on 'An Evening Without the Secret Police', Martin Lewis (co-producer with Amnesty's Peter Walker) struck gold with *The Secret Policeman's Ball*. Completing the new look and feel was an instantly iconic image – the secret policeman in his gabardine raincoat – created by political cartoonist Colin Wheeler as a show logo. The *SPB* brand had thus been established.

It was a turning point for Amnesty's comedy enterprise. The shows had already been successful – strikingly so – in winning new members for Amnesty and raising awareness and support among previously detached audiences. From a fairly static 1976 level of 3,000, Amnesty membership in the UK was rising rapidly (reaching 23,000 by 1979, a growth of more than 700%). Equally clear, however, was the realisation that the shows offered a prime opportunity to reach out to far bigger audiences. Interest was growing, comedy fans were primed and expectations were high.

The challenge now was to make the shows bigger and more marketable to audiences well beyond the theatre on the night. Building on the old blend of the familiar and the unexpected, it was time to push the boundaries. In Thatcher-era politics, gritty 'alternative' comedy and music were on the rise. Could the Amnesty shows become a bit more rock and roll than Oxbridge smoker? The first shows, albeit containing some of the most memorable live *Fringe* and *Python* performances ever, had the cosy familiarity of a

Cambridge revue. Was it time, in Lenny Henry's words, to bring some funk to the Amnesty barbed wire?

The *SPB* team (with Peter Walker replacing Roger Luff for Amnesty and joining Cleese, Roger Graef and Martin Lewis) thought so, and started looking beyond the classic generation of Cook and Cleese to supplement the cast with talent representative of a younger and broader section of Britain's comedy community, beginning with the up and coming 24-year-old Oxford graduate Rowan Atkinson and the Glaswegian stand-up comic and former dockworker, Billy Connolly. It was Cleese who suggested the smart and versatile Atkinson, having seen him recently in revue at London's Hampstead Theatre. For Atkinson, taking his place in the Four Yorkshiremen sketch 'was living a fantasy, being on stage with *Monty Python*, doing a sketch with *Monty Python*'. In fact, Atkinson went on to steal the show, particularly when he stood in for Dudley Moore in the 'End of the World' sketch. Featuring new talent alongside the big names thus became a speciality of future shows.

Music was also to play a more important role from 1979 onwards. There had been a few comedic songs and light musical interludes in the first two shows; now Amnesty was adding top contemporary musicians to play a supporting role alongside the comedians. They enlisted the services of The Who's driving force Pete Townshend, not only to play his first high profile solo acoustic set but also to perform a duet with the classical guitarist John Williams, and the new-wave singer-songwriter Tom Robinson, who recently had a hit with 'Glad to be Gay'. The 1979 show, as a consequence, established the *SPB* stage as a platform for memorable and unique musical performances and collaborations for many years to come.

The success of these musical acts apparently had the unintended consequence of temporarily alienating Amnesty's original comedy patron, John Cleese. Already stressed by the need to control a show in which everyone seemed intent on over-running, there were added problems for Cleese as the backstage area morphed from something akin to a relaxed senior common room to a high-profile rock gig,

abuzz with groupies, roadies and publicists. Cleese would later confirm this, complaining about all the 'pop people' who swanned about 'like Elizabeth Taylor and Richard Burton' and 'packed the wings with hundreds of total strangers'.

The subsequent success of the show itself, however, and of the new combination of music and comedy, allowed Amnesty to increasingly exploit the commercial appeal of the shows. They staged publicity stunts, packaged Roger Graef's film for TV and released two separate record albums (one devoted to comedy and the other music) as money-spinning souvenirs. Peter Cook's performance as the Thorpe judge summing up in 'Entirely a Matter for You' was so successful that it was released as a special 12" EP entitled *Here Comes the Judge*. ITV had already negotiated a deal to televise the *SPB* as a Christmas special, but amazingly decided to drop Peter Cook's judicial summing up – the notoriously conservative programme buyer Leslie Halliwell declaring, 'It is quite obvious who this sketch is about. It is not suitable for television.'

By 1981 the format was truly established, the *Secret Policeman's Ball* tag was retained and Amnesty International had become accustomed to being able to call on support from the top comedy and music stars of the day. 1981's *The Secret Policeman's Other Ball* took the same template and added more musicians and edgier comedy, aiming to attract a broader audience with a bold range of talents and tastes – all to be filmed by the young and unconventional director Julian Temple.

John Cleese began tackling the need for more women in the shows by recruiting Victoria Wood and Pamela Stephenson, and Amnesty's desire to introduce new talent led them to recruit the brilliantly aggressive stand-up comic Alexei Sayle. Fellow comedian Lenny Henry, a later recruit, remarked, 'To have Alexei doing "What's on in Stoke Newington" in there was pretty anarchic. It's very unapologetic. It was sensational . . .' Sayle himself wryly commented that because the previous show 'had really made the career of Rowan Atkinson, I thought [the *SPB*] would do the same for me . . . it didn't really work out like that.' It was becoming clear, however, just how highly the Balls were regarded professionally – as Jennifer Saunders later pointed out, 'It was quite a big thing in those days to be asked to do an Amnesty gig, because everyone was so jealous when Alexei became the first person off the circuit to do it.'

The music line-up in 1981 featured chart-toppers and stadium-fillers of the day, including Sting, Phil Collins, Eric Clapton, Jeff Beck, Donovan and Bob Geldof – for whom, according to Sting, the event was the inspiration that led to Live Aid. Revered rock stars Eric Clapton and Jeff Beck joined the young Sting and others for the musical finale, Bob Dylan's 'I Shall Be Released'. Phil Collins described how Sting 'kind of led . . . he was a pushy little bloke really'. Sting later confirmed that he is indeed 'kinda bossy when it comes to music. So I found myself bossing Eric around and bossing Jeff Beck – these two icons. And I'm thinking, "I can't believe I'm doing this. I'm telling them what I think they should do!"'

The *Secret Policeman's Ball* had become an instantly recognisable brand, and a profitable, as well as popular, series of events. Amnesty now had its own ongoing social, cultural – and commercial – phenomenon.

The very first routine – 'Interesting Facts', featuring Peter Cook and John Cleese – set the pattern for the entire night. Down on the running order as lasting a maximum of three minutes, it actually, thanks to all of Cook's ad libs and Cleese's corpsing, stretched out to nine minutes. So here was *The Secret Policeman's Ball* – bigger and more ambitious than the previous two Amnesty events, but, in its own way, just as charmingly chaotic.

The 'bright young thing' of the show was Rowan Atkinson, then still largely unknown, who mesmerised the audience with his 'Schoolmaster' routine. He then took part in the 'End of the World' sketch and, deputising for Dudley Moore, came up with a strange croaky voice that, years later, would help inspire the character of Mr Bean. He also took part in the first performance in an Amnesty event of the classic sketch that became synonymous with the *Secret Policeman's Ball* – 'The Four Yorkshiremen', this time with John Cleese, Michael Palin, Terry Jones and Rowan Atkinson. Although many think this sketch originated on *Monty Python's Flying Circus*, it actually comes from Python precursor *At Last The 1948 Show*, and the original Four Yorkshiremen were Tim Brooke-Taylor, John Cleese, Graham Chapman and Marty Feldman, who also take the credit for having written it (along with possible contributions from Barry Cryer). The top-rated comment on the original black and white sketch on YouTube laments the fact that 'John Cleese has been doing this sketch for forty years and still can't do a Yorkshire accent'. The sketch owes its subsequent fame and legendary comic status almost entirely to its inclusion in this Ball, as well as its earlier appearance on the *Monty Python at Drury Lane* live album of 1974. The Amnesty performance teases out the brilliance of the sketch in a live environment, enabling the performers to hit all the comic beats we know and love.

The undisputed highlight of the final two nights, however, was contributed by one of the stars of the 'old guard', Peter Cook. Stung by an early review, published in the *Daily Telegraph* on Friday 29 June, claiming that the latest production lacked a sharp enough satirical bite, he responded that same morning by writing a parody of Judge Cantley's recent (startlingly biased) summing-up at the Jeremy Thorpe trial. Within a few hours, complete with a judge's wig, gavel and lectern, Cook was ready to perform the routine – still polishing it as he prepared to go on stage.

Michael Palin recalled: 'Peter said to us just before he went on, "I just want one more euphemism for homosexual – any new ones?" And so we all sort of tried them all, and then Billy Connolly came up and said, "Well, in Glasgow there's a phrase called 'the player of the pink oboe'." And then – *boom* – it was time for the sketch to go. Peter goes on, and halfway through it [he adds the line 'a self-confessed player of the pink oboe'], and so Peter, in the time it took to go from the wings to the sketch, had thrown in "self-confessed" – which I thought made the "player of the pink oboe" work!'

INTERESTING FACTS
PETER COOK & JOHN CLEESE

The scene: Cleese, smartly dressed, is sitting on a park bench reading a newspaper. Cook, wearing a brown hat and grey overcoat, is sitting next to him, staring intently.

COOK: Did you know that you've got four miles of tubing in your stomach?

CLEESE: I beg your pardon?

COOK: I said did you know that you've got four miles of tubing in your stomach?

CLEESE: (*Distinctly unimpressed.*) No, no, I didn't know that, no.

COOK: It's a good thing I'm 'ere, then, isn't it? You have, you've got four miles of tubing in your stomach, all coiled up very tightly. It has to be coiled up very tightly, otherwise the people in charge would never be able to cram it all in. Of course, it's not *any* old tubing they use. It's a specialised form of tubing they use. It's called intestines, and it folds up ever so small – and that's how they manage to cram it all in. (*Cleese is doing his best to ignore this irritating little man and refuses to look up from his paper.*) Aren't you interested in your intestines?

CLEESE: (*Brusquely.*) Not particularly.

COOK: Well, you *should* be. You *should* be. Because without your intestines you'd be unable to digest. Then you'd look a bit of a *fool*, wouldn't you? (*Reaches into his pocket and produces a little red notebook.*) Would you like to see a diagram of your intestines? I've got a diagram of your intestines 'ere. Well, it's not actually *your* intestines. Unless it was you what modelled for it. It couldn't have been you what modelled for it because you have to be dead before you can model for intestines.

CLEESE: (*Tetchily.*) Do you?

COOK: Yes. So it's not a very good job to have. Intestinal modelling is not a good job to have. Not much call for intestinal modelling. (*Points to diagram.*) See how far it has to go, the food? See how far it has to go: four miles at one mile an hour. This means none of the food that reaches your stomach is ever really fresh. It's all at least four hours old.

CLEESE: (*Sarcastically.*) Fancy that!

COOK: (*Indignantly*) No, I *don't* fancy that! Thank you very much indeed! I do not *fancy* that at all! I do not *fancy* that in the least tiny bit!

(*Cook realises that Cleese is not paying any attention to his outburst, so decides to change tack.*)

COOK: I'll tell you another interesting fact, though. It's about the whale. Did you know that the whale is not really a fish? It's an insect. And it lives on bananas.

(*Cleese is so rattled he can't resist looking up from his paper.*)

CLEESE: The whale is an *insect*? I've never heard such *rubbish*!

COOK: I know. It's a joke.

(*Quietly fuming, Cleese angrily returns to studying his paper.*)

COOK: But I will tell you an interesting fact. It's about the grasshopper. The interesting fact about the grasshopper is its disproportionate leaping ability due to its powerful hind legs. *Hop hop hop*, it goes, all over arable land. That is land what is

actually tilled by Arabs. And I'll tell you the interesting fact about the Arab. The interesting fact about the Arab is that he can go for a whole year – he can go for a whole *year* – on *one* grain of rice! That's amazing, isn't it? All he needs is one grain of rice a year!

(*Once again too baffled to continue ignoring his tormentor, Cleese looks up again.*)

CLEESE: A whole *year* on *one* grain of *rice*?

COOK: (*Glancing at his notebook.*) No. That's the, er, that's the mosquito. No, I get those muddled up because they're next door to each other in the dictionary.

CLEESE: *What* are?

COOK: Mosquito and mosques.

(*Barely able to contain his anger, Cleese starts noisily turning the pages of his paper, desperately trying to block out Cook's droning monologue.*)

COOK: But the interesting fact, the interesting fact about the giraffe –

(*Cleese seems startled and looks up.*)

COOK: . . . is this: if the giraffe could leap, pound for pound, as high as the grasshopper, they'd avoid a lot of trouble.

(*Cleese sighs heavily and glances menacingly at Cook.*)

CLEESE: Shall I tell *you* something? You're one of the most boring, tedious, uninteresting, monotonous, flatulent, flat-headed, cloth-eared, swivel-eyed, fornicating little *gits* I ever laid eyes on!

(*Cook's expression remains utterly blank.*)

COOK: Is that a fact? How very interesting!

SCHOOL MASTER
ROWAN ATKINSON
(written by Richard Sparks)

A school master arrives to read the register. He looks out at the audience and begins, ticking the register upon each 'Here!' that is shouted back at him.

All right, quiet. Ainsley . . . Babcock . . . Bland . . . Carthorse . . . Dint . . . Ellsworth-Beast Major . . . Ellsworth-Beast Minor . . . Fiat . . . German . . . Haemoglobin . . . Havvernut . . . Jones M . . . Jones N . . . Kosygin . . . Loudhailer . . . Muttock . . . Nancy-Boy Potter . . . Nibble . . . Orifice . . . Plectrum . . . Poise . . . Sediment . . . Soda . . . Taah . . . Taah? . . . Undermanager . . . Wickett . . . Williams-Wickett . . . Williams-Wycherley . . . Wycherley-Wickett . . . Wycherley-Williams . . . and Wycherley-Williams-Wockett . . . Zobb . . . absent.

All right, your essays. 'Discuss the contention that Cleopatra had the body of a roll-top desk and the mind of a duck.' Oxford and Cambridge Board O-level examination, 1976. Don't fidget, Bland. The answer: 'Yes.' Jones M, Orifice, Sediment and Undermanager: see me afterwards. Most of you, of course, didn't write nearly enough. Dint, your answer was unreadable. Put it *away*, Plectrum. If I see it once more this period, Plectrum, I shall have to tweak you. (*Stares.*) Do you have a solicitor, Plectrum? You're lying, Plectrum, so I shall tweak you anyway. See me afterwards to be tweaked. Yes, *isn't* life tragic! Don't sulk, boy, for God's sake. Has Matron seen those boils? (*Mutters to himself.*) Horrid little twerp!

Bland, German, Nancy-Boy Potter, Undermanager: cribbing. Undermanager: answer upside-down. Do you do it *deliberately*, Undermanager? You're a *moron*, Undermanager. What are you? A carbuncle on the backside of humanity.

Don't snigger, Babcock! It's not that funny. *Antony and Cleopatra* is not a funny play. If Shakespeare had *meant* it to be funny, he would have put a *joke* in it. There is no joke in *Antony and Cleopatra*. You would've known that if you'd read it, wouldn't you, Babcock? (*Mutters under his breath.*) Pest!

What play of Shakespeare's plays *does* have a joke in it, hmmm? Anyone . . . ? *The Comedy of Errors*, for God's sake! *The Comedy of Errors* has the joke of two people looking like each other. Twice. It's not that funny, German.

And the other Shakespearean joke is . . . Nibble? *NIBBLE*!! Leave Orifice *alone*! What a lot!

All right, for the rest of this period, you will write about Enobarbus. Undermanager, just try and write 'Enobarbus'. Either way up, boy, I'm not bothered. Usual conditions: no conferring, no eating, no cheating, no looking out of windows, no slang, no slide rules. Use ink only – via a nib if possible. You *may* use dividers, but *not* on each other. Kosygin – you're in charge.

'Put it away, Plectrum. If I see it once more this period, Plectrum, I shall have to tweak you.'

Rowan Atkinson

BALLOON

PETER COOK & ELEANOR BRON

The scene is the living room of a house. A smartly dressed man is sitting in a soft leather chair, reading a newspaper. A woman, who appears to have a large bump beneath her sweater, comes in sporting the smile of someone who has an exciting secret to share.

BRON: Charles?

COOK: Yes, Penelope?

BRON: There's something I've got to tell you.

COOK: Yes, dear?

BRON: I've tried to put it off, hoping against hope that I was wrong, but I've been to the doctor and had all the tests and everything, and there can be no possible doubt about it any longer. I'm . . . going to have a baby!

(Cook rolls his eyes and sighs.)

COOK: For goodness' sake, Penelope, how many times do I have to tell you? It's not a baby, it's a balloon.

BRON: *(Still smiling emotionally.)* Charles, it *is* a baby!

COOK: It's a balloon, Penelope!

BRON: It's a *baby*, darling!

COOK: It's a *balloon*, Penelope!

BRON: It's a *baby*!

COOK: IT'S A *BALLOON*!

(*He reaches over and touches her sweater. There is a loud 'pop' and the bump suddenly disappears. She cries out and looks down, horrified, and then looks at him.*)

BRON: *Prick!*

HOW DO YOU DO IT?
MICHAEL PALIN & TERRY JONES

The scene is the studio set of a cheap and cheerful TV 'infotainment' show. Palin as the cheesy host, is smartly dressed. Jones, as the slightly nervous guest, appears in full sporting attire.

PALIN: Hello, and welcome to another edition of *How Do You Do It?* Tonight, Will Bowes has come along to tell us how to play cricket. Hello, Will.

JONES: Hello, Michael.

PALIN: Now, you've played for Gloucestershire for the last eleven years, Will.

JONES: Sussex, yes.

PALIN: And I'm not too good on cricket facts myself but I believe you've scored over a thousand runs in your career?

JONES: 58,000, yes.

PALIN: And you also bowl ganglies?

JONES: Googlies.

PALIN: How *do* you play cricket, Will?

JONES: Well, Michael, the first requirement is a pitch, which is –

PALIN: Can I stop you there?

JONES: Er, yes?

PALIN: What is a 'pitch'?

JONES: Well, a pitch is a piece of ground, er, preferably flat – although I can think of quite a few that are sloping at all angles!

PALIN: I see, yes, so the pitch needn't be flat?

JONES: Er, well, no, it's better if it *is* flat, yes.

PALIN: What do you *do* on the pitch, Will?

JONES: Well, you have what are called 'stumps' –

PALIN: Sorry, can I interrupt you there, Will? *Who* has the 'stumps'?

JONES: Well, everyone has the stumps.

PALIN: I see. You all have stumps. But what we really want to know now, of course, is: what do you *do* with the stumps when you've got them?

JONES: Well, you stick the stumps in the ground.

PALIN: Ah. Is the 'ground' the same as the 'pitch'?

JONES: (*Beginning to sound exasperated.*) Well, no, the ground is the whole playing area and the pitch is the bit in the middle.

PALIN: I see. So you don't stick your stumps in the pitch?

JONES: Y-yes, y-you do!

PALIN: Ha ha, you're getting as muddled as I am, aren't you, Will!

JONES: No, I'm not, *no*!

PALIN: What happens now, Will?

JONES: Well, you have what are called 'bails'.

PALIN: Balls.

JONES: No, no, no: *bails*.

PALIN: No, Will, I don't know much about cricket myself but I think you'll find they're called *balls* and –

JONES: No! You have one *ball* and four *bails*.

PALIN: I see. So let's just clear this up, Will: so you have four bails in one over, is that right?

JONES: No, no, that's balls. You have six *balls* in one *over*.

PALIN: I see. So you were wrong about the bails?

JONES: No, I *wasn't* wrong about the bails!

PALIN: Ha ha ha, don't worry, Will, I'm always getting it wrong!

JONES: No, I *wasn't* wrong about the bails!

PALIN: What are 'runs', Will?

JONES: I'm still going on about the bails!

PALIN: Tell us about 'runs', Will.

JONES: No, I want to talk about *bails*!

PALIN: You've told us about the bails, Will – tell us about the runs.

JONES: I want to talk about *BAILS*!

PALIN: Are 'runs' the same as 'scores'?

JONES: *I WANT TO TALK ABOUT BAILS!* (*Storms off the stage, shouting.*) *IT'S BAILS, D'YOU HEAR? IT'S BAILS!! THAT'S THE ONLY THING THAT COUNTS IN CRICKET*!!

PALIN: Well, that's all for this week. Next week on *How Do You Do It?* I'll be speaking to the president of the Chinese People's Republic on how to rule 900 million people. Goodnight!

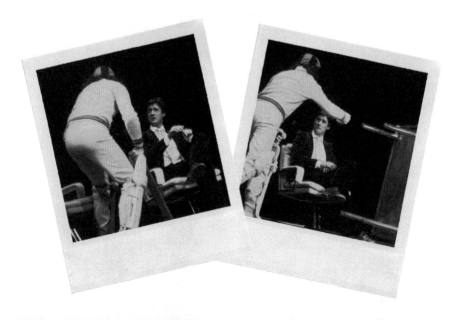

CHEESE SHOP
JOHN CLEESE & MICHAEL PALIN

The scene is in a cheese shop. A man in traditional Greek dress plays the bouzouki while Chris Beetles and Rob Buckman, in dress shirts and bow ties, dance solemnly, both facing forward, with their arms round each other's shoulders. A moustachioed Palin, wearing a white tuxedo and black tie, is standing behind the counter. There are several white china cheese dishes on display. Cleese enters the shop.

CLEESE: Good morning!

PALIN: What can I do for you, sir?

CLEESE: Well, I was just sitting in the public library in Thurmond Street just now, skimming through *Rogue Herries* by Hugh Walpole, when I suddenly came over all . . . peckish.

PALIN: Peckish, sir?

CLEESE: *Esurient.*

PALIN: Eh?

CLEESE: (*Puts on Yorkshire accent.*) I were all hungry, like!

PALIN: Ah, ha ha, *hungry*, sir, yes.

CLEESE: In a nutshell. So I thought to myself, a little fermented curd will do the trick. So I curtailed my Walpoling activities, sallied forth, and entered your place of purveyance to negotiate the vending of some cheesy comestibles.

PALIN: Come again?

CLEESE: (*Yorkshire accent again.*) I want to buy some cheese!

PALIN: Oh, I thought you'd come to complain about the bouzouki player, sir.

CLEESE: Oh, heaven forbid! No, no, I am one who delights in all manifestations of the Terpsichorean muse. Now then, my good man – some cheese, if you please!

PALIN: Oh, yes sir, yes sir. What would you like, sir?

CLEESE: (*Brightly.*) Er – how about a little Red Leicester?

PALIN: I'm afraid we're fresh out of Red Leicester, sir.

CLEESE: Never mind. How are you on Tilsit?

PALIN: Ah – never have it till the end of the week, sir, always get it fresh on Monday.

CLEESE: Tish, tish. No matter. Well, then, stout yeoman, four ounces of Caerphilly, if you please.

PALIN: Ah. Been expecting it for two weeks, sir, it's been on order, er, expecting 'em today, sir.

CLEESE: Ah. It's not my lucky day, is it? Er, Bel Paese?

PALIN: No, sir. Sorry.

CLEESE: Erm – Red Windsor?

PALIN: Ah – *normally*, sir, yes. Today – the van broke down.

CLEESE: Stilton?

PALIN: No.

CLEESE: Gruyère? Emmental?

PALIN: No.

CLEESE: A little Norwegian Jarlsberger, perhaps?

PALIN: No.

CLEESE: No?

PALIN: No.

CLEESE: Liptauer?

PALIN: No.

CLEESE: Lancashire?

PALIN: No.

CLEESE: White Stilton?

PALIN: No.

CLEESE: Danish Blue?

PALIN: No.

CLEESE: Double Gloucester?

PALIN: No.

CLEESE: Leicester?

PALIN: No.

CLEESE: Dorset Blue Vinney?

(*Palin has to think for a moment.*)

PALIN: No.

(*Cleese starts speeding up*)

CLEESE: Roquefort?

PALIN: No.

CLEESE: Pont-l'Évêque?

PALIN: No.

CLEESE: Port Salut?

PALIN: No.

CLEESE: Saint-Paulin?

PALIN: No.

CLEESE: Carre-de-l'Est?

PALIN: No.

CLEESE: Bresse-Bleu?

PALIN: No.

CLEESE: Boursin?

PALIN: No.

CLEESE: Brie?

PALIN: No.

CLEESE: Camembert?

PALIN: Ah, yes! Yes, we do have some Camembert, sir, yes.

(*Taken by surprise, Cleese looks delighted.*)

CLEESE: You do?

PALIN: Oh, yes, sir.

CLEESE: Excellent!

PALIN: It's, ah . . . it's a bit runny, sir.

CLEESE: Ooh, I *like* it runny.

PALIN: Actually, it's *very* runny, sir.

CLEESE: No matter. Fetch hither le *Camembert de la belle France*!
Mmm!

PALIN: I think it's much more runny than you'll like it, sir.

CLEESE: I don't care how fucking runny it is – hand it over with
all speed.

PALIN: Yes, sir, certainly sir . . . (*Peers under counter.*) Ohhhh . . .

CLEESE: What now?

PALIN: . . . The cat's eaten it!

CLEESE: Has he?

PALIN: *She*, sir.

(*Cleese's remarkably ebullient spirits are finally starting to sag.*)

CLEESE: Edam?

PALIN: No.

CLEESE: Gouda?

PALIN: No.

CLEESE: Caithness?

PALIN: No.

CLEESE: Smoked Austrian cheese?

(*Palin thinks for a few seconds.*)

PALIN: No.

CLEESE: Japanese Sage Derby?

PALIN: No.

CLEESE: You *do* have some cheese, don't you?

PALIN: Oh, yes, sir. Cheese shop, sir. We've got er . . .

CLEESE: No, no, don't tell me. I'm . . . I'm keen to guess. Erm . . . Wensleydale?

PALIN: (*Surprised.*) Yes, sir!

CLEESE: Good! Well, I'll have some of that then, please!

PALIN: Oh, sorry, sir, I thought you were talking to *me*, sir. That's my *name*, sir: Arthur Wensleydale.

CLEESE: Greek feta cheese?

PALIN: Not as *such*.

CLEESE: Gorgonzola?

PALIN: No.

CLEESE: Parmesan?

PALIN: No.

CLEESE: Mozzarella?

PALIN: No.

CLEESE: Pippo Crème?

PALIN: No.

CLEESE: Danish Fynbo cheese ?

PALIN: No.

CLEESE: Czechoslovakian Goat's Milk?

PALIN: No.

CLEESE: Venezuelan Beaver Cheese, perhaps?

(*Glancing upwards, Palin has to think for a moment.*)

PALIN: Not *today*, sir, no.

CLEESE: How about . . . Cheddar?

PALIN: I don't have much call for it around here, sir.

CLEESE: Not much *call* for it? It's the single most popular cheese in the world!

PALIN: Ah, not round these parts, sir.

CLEESE: And what, pray, is the most popular cheese 'round these parts'?

PALIN: Ilchester, sir!

CLEESE: *Is* it?

PALIN: Oh, yes, sir. Quite staggeringly popular in the manor, squire.

CLEESE: *Is* it?

PALIN: Yes, sir. Number-one bestseller.

CLEESE: Ilchester, eh?

PALIN: Yes, sir.

CLEESE: All right. I'm game. (*Clears throat.*) Have you got any, he asked, expecting the answer no.

PALIN: (*Ducks under the counter.*) *Ummmmmmmmmmmmmm* . . . . no.

(*Cleese is now clearly very irritated indeed.*)

CLEESE: Not much of a cheese shop, is it, really?

PALIN: Finest in the district, sir.

CLEESE: Explain, pray, the logic underlying that conclusion?

PALIN: Well, it's so clean.

CLEESE: Well, it's certainly uncontaminated by cheese!

PALIN: You haven't asked me about Limburger, sir.

CLEESE: Is it *worth* it?

PALIN: Could be.

CLEESE: Very well. (*Clears throat again.*) Do you –

(*He finally snaps and shouts at the bouzouki player and dancers.*)

CLEESE: *WILL YOU STOP THAT BLOODY NONSENSE?!*

(*Shocked and shaken, the bouzouki player and dancers leave.*)

PALIN: Told you so.

(*Trying to calm himself down again, Cleese closes his eyes, takes a deep breath and resumes his questions.*)

CLEESE: Have you got any Limburger?

PALIN: No.

CLEESE: No, that figures. Should have seen that one coming, shouldn't I? Tell me, do you have *any* cheese here, at all?

PALIN: (*His voice high-pitched and defensive.*) Yes! Yes, sir!

CLEESE: You do?

PALIN: (*His nerve suddenly gone.*) No.

CLEESE: None?

PALIN: (*Sadly.*) No. Not a scrap.

CLEESE: (*Calmly.*) Now, I'm going to ask you again. And if you tell me you don't have any cheese here at all . . . (*He produces a revolver from his pocket.*) . . . I'm going to kill you. Do you have any cheese in this shop?

PALIN: (*Emphatically and fatalistically.*) No.

(*Cleese shoots Palin in the head and then addresses the audience.*)

CLEESE: What a senseless waste of human life. Thank you.

DEAR GOD
(or 'Thou Knowest, Lord')
ELEANOR BRON

There is a single spotlight on Bron. She is wearing a headscarf, and her hands are clasped together in prayer.

. . . And what else? . . . Well, I've been guilty of the sin of anger . . . I shouted at the children several times during the past week. As Thou hast of course seen with Thy all-seeing eye. And no doubt heard, with Thy all-hearing ear. And . . . And then again, I've committed malice on a number of occasions, I was definitely trying to hurt my sister's feelings that time. I mean on Tuesday, when my sister – oh, this is my younger sister, Janice, I'm talking about, the one who lives just outside Watford – oh, well, of course, Thou knowest which sister I mean!

I always forget that with Thy all-knowing mind, Thou knowest perfectly well what I mean – far better than I do, in fact! – anyway, I only went to see her on Tuesday, my sister, because I was over in that direction anyway, visiting mother in the nursing home, which – as Thou knowest – I try to do, at least once a week . . . er, I mean, not that I want to boast about it or anything . . . it's the very least I can do . . . I feel terrible about not having her at home, as Thou knowest – or . . . or was I just . . . slipping that into the conversation like that to make Thee think better of me? Well, *Thou* knowest whether I was or not . . . and if Thou thinks I *was*, I repent it at once, as I try to do with all my unworthy thoughts and actions. Er, I didn't mean that to sound smug.

Oh dear, er – where was I? Before I allowed myself to get sidetracked! – another of my faults incidentally, for which I'm extremely sorry! I was in the middle of repenting something . . . oh, well, Thou knowest what I was going to say. So if I can't remember, perhaps Thou would take it as repented all the same. Oh, I know – my *sister*. Yes!

When she started going on about Mother, and Mrs Weams – who, as Thou knowest, runs the nursing home – and I said, 'Janice, I honestly do not want to sit here and listen to you going on about that woman, who's been so *kind* to mother', and Janice turned round and gave me one of those *looks* of hers – well, of course, Thou sawest the whole incident. And when I told her how clever I thought her children's drawings were, Thou weren't'st fooled for a moment! Neither was she, of course.

Anyway, I'm really and truly sorry about it. In fact, I've been brooding about it ever since. And that's another thing I ought to mention, the way I think about myself all the time – I mean, whenever I'm not thinking about how wrong everything I do is – dost Thou know what I mean? Ha, well, of course Thou dost – this seems to me to be my worst sin of all. I . . . I don't know whether Thou wouldst agree with this assessment – I mean, what am I doing now? I'm talking about myself, but how can I *confess* this sin if I don't?

Wait a minute – am I just thinking that as an excuse for not thinking perpetually about my sins? That's one of the difficulties – knowing for certain *which* sin it is I'm committing here. And whichever it is, I'm really and truly sorry about it.

Aren't I?

STAKE YOUR CLAIM

MICHAEL PALIN
& ROWAN ATKINSON

The scene is a TV studio, with Atkinson as the contestant and Palin as the quizmaster.

PALIN: Hello and welcome to another edition of yet another quiz game and this time *Stake Your Claim*. And first this evening we have with us Mr Norman Voles of Gravesend, who claims he wrote all Shakespeare's works! (*The contestant is brought on.*) Mr Voles, I understand that you claim you wrote all those plays normally attributed to William Shakespeare.

ATKINSON: Ah, that is correct. I wrote all his plays, and my wife and I wrote his sonnets.

PALIN: Mr Voles, these plays are known to have been performed in the early seventeenth century. How old are you, Mr Voles?

ATKINSON: Ah, forty-three.

PALIN: Well, how is it possible for you to have written plays performed over 300 years before you were born?

ATKINSON: Um, yes, well, this is where my claim falls to the ground.

PALIN: Ah.

ATKINSON: There's no way of answering that particular argument, I'm afraid, I was only hoping that you would not make that particular point. But I can see that you're more than a match for me.

PALIN: Right. Thank you very much, Mr Voles. Thank you very much for coming along tonight!

TWO SCOTSMEN IN ROME
BILLY CONNOLLY

This wee thing is about two Glasgow guys who went on holiday to Rome. These two guys were in Rome, and they were going, (*Looking at all the sights.*) 'Aye, look at that, that's fantastic . . . Look at that an' all, fantastic, I'm intae that . . . I wonder who papered that ceiling, that's fantastic . . .'

And the sun was belting down on them: 'Hey, the sun's beltin' doon on me!' 'Aye, we should go an' get a bevvy.' 'Right.' So they shot into a wee bar in Rome.

And they go right up to the bar and say, 'Hey, Jimmy, give us to pints of heavy.' And he says, 'What?' In Italian, like. And they go, 'Two pints of heavy – are you deef or somethin'?' So the barman says, 'Look, we don't have heavy in Rome. We've got all sorts of clever things, but we don't have heavy. But look, (*Pointing at all the different bottles.*) you're welcome to anything you see here . . .' (*Looking suspiciously at all the unfamiliar drinks.*) 'Ah, I don't know about any of these things . . . Hey, tell you what – what does the Pope drink?' The guy says, 'Oh, Crème de Menthe. I've heard he likes a wee glass of Crème de Menthe every now and again.' '*Give us two pints of THAT, then!*'

So their two green pints duly arrive. (*They look at the drink for a moment.*) 'Ah, if it's good enough for the Big 'un, it's good enough for me, okay . . .' (*They pour the whole glass straight down their throats.*) 'Nae bad – it's like drinkin' Polo mints, in't it?' 'When in Rome, eh? D'you get it? When in Rome and that! (*Licks his lips and turns to the barman.*) Give us another two, there you go!'

So they wake up in the morning. They're in a heap in a shop doorway. Their suits are all crumpled up and they've peed their trousers and been sick down their jackets. They've been shouting and hugh-ing all night, right? HEUUEEGGHH!!! RAAAALFFF!!! Hughie and Ralph. *HEUUEEGGHH!!! RAAAALFFF!!!* And it's green. Green Hughie. Hughie Green?

I'll tell you what, though. Just to digress. Talking about being sick. How come – this is a great dilemma – how come *every* time you're sick there's diced carrots in it? I was going to ask somebody here because I reckon I'm the only guy in this building who left school before he was twenty-one. How come? I have *never* eaten diced carrots in my life! You can have lamb madras, a few bevvies, and RAAAALFFF!!! Diced carrots! Every time! And sometimes tomato skins as well! I don't eat bloody tomato skins! *How come?* Now, my personal theory is that there's a pervert somewhere, with pockets full of diced carrots, following drunk guys.

But back to Rome. Back in Rome these two guys are waking up in the morning. (*Rubbing their faces slowly.*) 'Christ Almighty! . . . Ooohhhhh, ma *heid*! . . . I think I'm wearin' an internal balaclava!' (*Starts rubbing his body.*) 'Christ Almighty . . . oohhh, ma body's so sore . . . AAGGHH! *I CANNAE FEEL MA LEG!!!*' 'That's *MA* leg, ya bampot!' 'Oh, thank Christ for that! Jeez, what a fright I got there!'

(*Looks at his friend.*) 'How are *you*?' 'To tell you the truth . . . I feel kind of funny. I think I've had a tongue transplant. This one doesnae seem to fit.'

'Christ . . . and they say the Pope drinks *that* stuff?'

'Aye. Nae wonder they have to carry him about on a chair, eh!'

ENTIRELY A MATTER FOR YOU

PETER COOK

The scene is of a judge addressing his court. The names of several figures from the actual Thorpe case are deliberately mangled here by Cook, so Jeremy Thorpe and his wife Marion become 'Jeremy and Miriam Thrope'; Norman Scott = 'Norma St John Scott'; Peter Bessell = 'Bex Bissell'; Andrew Newton = 'Olivia Newton-John'; Jack Hayward = 'Jack Haywire'; and Nadir Dinshaw = 'Nadir Rickshaw'. Norman Scott did indeed once have a physician called Dr Gleadle.

JUDGE: (*Aside.*) I hope you brought a toothbrush.

(*Aloud.*) Ladies and gentlemen of the jury, it is my duty to advise you on how you should vote when you retire from this court. In the last few weeks, we have all heard some pretty extraordinary allegations being made about one of the prettiest, about one of the most distinguished, politicians ever to rise to high office in this country – or not, as you may think.

We have heard, for example, from Mr Bex Bissell – a man who by his own admission is a liar, a humbug, a hypocrite, a vagabond, a loathsome spotted reptile, and a self-confessed chicken strangler. You may choose, if you *wish*, to believe the transparent tissue of *odious* lies which streamed on and on from his disgusting, greedy, slavering lips. That is entirely a matter for you.

Then we have been forced to listen to the pitiful whining of Mr Norma St John Scott – a scrounger, a parasite, a pervert, a worm, a self-confessed player of the pink oboe. A man, or woman,

who by his, or her, own admission *chews pillows*! It would be hard to imagine, ladies and gentlemen of the jury, a more discredited and embittered man, a more unreliable witness upon whose testimony to convict a man who you may rightly think should have become prime minister of his country or president of the world. You may, on the other hand, choose to *believe* the evidence of Mrs Scott – in which case I can only say that you need psychiatric help of the type provided by the excellent Dr Gleadle.

On the evidence of the so-called 'hit man', Mr Olivia Newton-John, I would prefer to draw a discreet veil. He is, as we know, a man with a criminal past, but I like to think – *ho, ho, ho* – no criminal future. He is a piece of slimy refuse, unable to carry out the simplest murder plot without cocking it up, to the distress of many. On the other hand, you may think Mr Newton-John is one of the most intelligent, profound, sensitive and saintly personalities of our time. That is entirely a matter for you.

I now turn to the evidence about the money and Mr Jack Haywire and Mr Nadir Rickshaw, neither of whom, as far as I can make out, are complete and utter crooks, though the latter is incontestably foreign and, you may well think, the very type to boil up foul-smelling biryanis at all hours of the night and keep you awake with his pagan limbo dancing. It is not contested by the defence that enormous sums of money flowed towards them in unusual ways. What happened to that money, we shall never know. But I put it to you, ladies and gentlemen of the jury, that there are a number of totally innocent ways in which that £20,000 could have been spent: on two tickets for *Evita*, a centre court seat at Wimbledon, or Mr Thrope may have decided simply to blow it all on a flutter on the Derby. That is his affair and it is not for us to pry. It will be a sad day for this country when a leading politician cannot spend his election expenses in any way he sees fit.

One further point – you will probably have noticed that three of the defendants have very *wisely* chosen to exercise their *inalienable* right not to go into the witness box to answer a lot of impertinent questions. I will merely say that you are not to infer from this anything other than that they consider the evidence against them so *flimsy* that it was scarcely worth their while to rise from their seats and waste their breath denying these *ludicrous* charges.

In closing, I would like to pay tribute to Mr Thrope's husband, Miriam, who has stood by him throughout this long and unnecessary ordeal. I know you will join me in wishing them well for a long and happy future.

And now, being mindful of the fact that the Prudential Cup begins on Saturday, putting all such thoughts from your mind, you are now to retire – as indeed should I – you are now to retire, carefully to consider your verdict of 'Not Guilty'.

———————

FOUR YORKSHIREMEN
JOHN CLEESE, TERRY JONES, MICHAEL PALIN & ROWAN ATKINSON

Four middle-aged, prosperous men in white dinner jackets are seated at a table, drinking red wine.

PALIN: (*Looking at his wine.*) Ahh . . . Very *passable*, that, *very* passable.

ATKINSON: Aye, you can't beat a good glass of Chateau de Chassilier wine, eh, Josiah?

JONES: You're right there, Obadiah.

CLEESE: Who'd a thought forty year ago we'd all be sittin' here drinking Chateau de Chassilier?

PALIN: Aye. In them days, we were glad to have the price of a cuppa tea.

ATKINSON: A cuppa cold tea.

CLEESE: Without milk or sugar.

JONES: *OR* tea!

PALIN: In a cracked cup an' all.

CLEESE: We never had a *cup*! We used to drink out of a rolled-up newspaper!

ATKINSON: The best *we* could manage was to suck on a piece of damp cloth!

JONES: But you know, we were happy in those days, though we were poor.

PALIN: *BECAUSE* we were poor. My old dad used to say to me, 'Money doesn't buy you happiness, son.'

CLEESE: 'E was right. I was happier then and we had *nothin'*. We used to live in a tiny old tumbledown 'ouse, with great holes in roof.

ATKINSON: A house? You were lucky to have a *house*! We used to live in one room, twenty-six of us, no furniture, and half the floor was missing. We were all huddled in one corner for fear of fallin'!

JONES: You were lucky to have a room! We used to have to live in *corridor*!

PALIN: Ohhhh, we used to *dream* of livin' in a corridor! Would've been a *palace* to us! We used to live in an old water tank on a rubbish tip. Got woken up every morning by having a load of rotting fish dumped all over us! House!? *Hmph*!

CLEESE: Well, when I say 'house' it were only a hole in the ground covered by a couple of foot of torn canvas, but it were a house to *us*!

ATKINSON: We were evicted from our hole in the ground – we had to go and live in lake!

JONES: You were lucky to have a *lake*! There were a hundred and fifty of us living in *shoebox* in middle of motorway!

PALIN: Cardboard box?

JONES: Aye.

PALIN: You were lucky! We lived for three months in a rolled-up newspaper in a septic tank. We used to have to get up at six in the morning, clean the newspaper, eat a crust of stale bread, go to work down mill for fourteen hours a day, week in-week out, for sixpence a month, and when we got home, our Dad would thrash us to sleep with his belt!

ATKINSON: Luxury! We used to have to get out of the lake at three a.m., clean the lake, eat a handful of hot gravel, work twenty hours a day at mill for tuppence a month, come home, and Dad would beat us about the head and neck with a broken bottle, if we were *lucky*!

JONES: Well, of course, we had it *tough*. We used to have to get up out of shoebox in middle of night, and lick road clean with our tongues. We had half a handful of freezing cold gravel, worked twenty-four hours a day at mill for fourpence every six years, and when we got home, our Dad would slice us in two with bread knife!

CLEESE: Right. I used to get up in the morning at half-past ten at night *half an hour before I went to bed*, eat a lump of *freezing-cold poison*, work twenty-eight hours a day at mill *and* pay mill owner to let us work there, and when we got home, our Dad used to *murder* us in cold blood *each night* and dance about on our graves singing 'Hallelujah'!

PALIN: And you try and tell the young people today that . . . and they won't believe you!

ALL: Nope, nope . . .

PLEASE, PLEASE
ELEANOR BRON & JOHN FORTUNE

The scene: a man and a woman are engaged in a tense and emotional conversation.

FORTUNE: (*Passionately.*) Please! *Please!*

BRON: (*Vulnerably.*) No! You think if you say 'please', you can get anything you want!

FORTUNE: No, I don't. I just think that you're being ridiculously *prudish*, that's all.

BRON: I thought we'd both agreed to *wait*?

FORTUNE: Oh my God, but this *is* the twentieth century! And we are *engaged*, after all!

BRON: Oh . . . John . . . it's just as hard for me to wait as it is for you.

FORTUNE: I know. I mean, are you afraid of . . . you know, what people are going to *say*?

BRON: No! It just doesn't seem *right*, that's all.

(*Fortune becomes even more agitated.*)

BRON: Oh for heaven's sake, John, *listen*: after we're married, you can sleep with anyone you want. *But until then you sleep with ME – understand?*

THE END OF THE WORLD
PETER COOK & CAST

The cast – John Cleese, Rowan Atkinson, Ken Campbell, David Rappaport, Michael Palin, Terry Jones, Eleanor Bron, Chris Beetles, Rob Buckman, Sylvester McCoy and Marcel Steiner – are assembled reverently at the feet of Peter Cook. They are all wearing dark sweaters which are pulled up over their heads, with just their faces poking out through the hole. They are carrying various placards and signs, which read: 'SINNERS REPENT NOW', 'PEARL AND DEAN', 'PROTEIN CAUSES VICE', 'LAST FEW DAYS' and, of course, 'THE END IS NIGH'. The sound of rushing wind is heard, and then an ominous crack of thunder.

CAMPBELL: How will it be, this end of which I once heard you speak, Brother Enim?

ALL: (*Anxiously.*) How will it be? How will it be?

COOK: (*Impassively.*) It will be, as 'twere, a mighty rending in the sky, and the mountains shall sink, and the valleys shall rise, and great shall be the tumult thereof. I should think.

PALIN: Will the veil of the temple be rent in twain?

COOK: Well, the veil of the temple's always rather dodgy, but, er, should be rent in twain about two minutes before we see the sign of the flying manifest dancing on the firmament.

BEETLES: And will there be a mighty *wind*?

COOK: Certainly there will be a mighty wind, if the word of God is anything to go by.

ATKINSON: (*In a strangulated, sub-Mr Bean voice.*) Will this wind . . . be so mighty . . . as to lay low the mountains of the earth?

COOK: Can't hear a blind word you're saying. You're speaking too softly for the human ear. Which is what I'm equipped with. You'll have to speak a little more loudly, please.

ATKINSON: About this wind –

COOK: No better, is it? I asked you to speak more loudly, and you speak more softly. A *strange* reaction from a follower. Or perhaps I'm *very* old-fashioned. Perhaps I'm *very* old fashioned, expecting you to speak louder.

ATKINSON: Yes. You are.

COOK: Come along, come along, we haven't got all day till the end of the world. Get on with it.

ATKINSON: Will this wind –

COOK: We've heard *that* bit. We've *all* heard 'Will this wind . . . ', haven't we? We've heard 'Will this wind . . .' quite enough, thank you very much! '*What* will this wind . . .' is what we want to know. Not 'Will this wind . . .' We don't want to hear 'Will this wind . . .' again. That'd be a very tedious experience! *WHAT* will this wind?

(*Atkinson nods contritely.*)

ATKINSON: Will this wind . . .

COOK: (*Testily.*) Will this wind, yes . . .

ATKINSON: . . . be so mighty . . .

COOK: Be so mighty . . .

ATKINSON: . . . as to lay *low* . . .

COOK: As to lay low . . .

ATKINSON: . . . the mountains . . .

COOK: The mountains . . .

ATKINSON: . . . of the earth?

COOK: Of the . . . ?

ATKINSON: . . . *Earth.*

COOK: (*Summing up.*) 'Will this wind . . . be *so* mighty . . . . as to lay low . . . the mountains of the earth?'

(*There is an expectant pause.*)

COOK: No. It will not be quite as mighty as that – which is why we have come up on the mountain, to be safe, you stupid git! Up here on the mountain we shall be safe – safe as houses.

PALIN: Er – what will happen to the houses?

COOK: Oh, naturally, they'll all be swept away and consuméd by the fire what is dancing on the Jeroboam, and serve 'em bloody well right, as far as I'm concerned.

BUCKMAN: When will it be, this thing of which you have spoken? When?

ALL: (*Excitedly.*) When? Yes, when? When will it be – when will it be?

COOK: (*Looks at his watch.*) Well, in about . . . erm . . . two minutes time, according to the very ancient pyramidic scrolls . . .

BEETLES: P'raps we'd better *compose* ourselves!

COOK: Good idea. (*Supremely calmly.*) Prepare for the End of the World. Thirty seconds . . .

ATKINSON: Have you brought the picnic basket?

COOK: (*Ignoring him.*) Five . . . four . . . three . . . two . . . *one!*

ALL: (*Chanting.*) Now is the end . . . Perish the world!

(*There is an expectant pause. Nothing happens.*)

COOK: It *was* GMT, wasn't it?

(*He checks his watch again.*)

COOK: Well, it's, er, it's not quite the conflagration we'd been banking on. Never mind, lads – same time tomorrow . . . we must get a winner one day!

(*The cast get up and start to disperse.*)

COOK: (*Pointing at Atkinson.*) I think it was *his* fault. This bloke here . . .

(*Marcel Steiner, who is carrying the sign proclaiming 'THE END IS NIGH' walks back onto the darkened stage and tears off the words 'IS NIGH' from the sign.*)

THE
SECRET
POLICEMAN'S
other
BALL

THEATRE ROYAL, DRURY LANE
9–12 SEPTEMBER 1981

AMNESTY INTERNATIONAL

proudly present

THE SECRET POLICEMAN'S OTHER BALL

THEATRE ROYAL
DRURY LANE

THE 1981 AMNESTY
INTERNATIONAL
COMEDY GALA

Directed by John Cleese
& Ronald Eyre

The first of the four shows in 1981 was a shambolic affair which overran wildly, and John Cleese responded by cutting numerous acts and routines and demanding greater discipline from his fellow performers. His intervention worked, although he would still have to contend with the odd crisis during the rest of the run.

Alan Bennett, as always, brought a beautifully literate, but wickedly mischievous, quality to the shows, while John Wells increased the amount of topical satire with his arch impersonations of Ronald Reagan and Denis Thatcher. Probably the most notable performance of this year's production, however, came from the cast's defiantly unclubbable newcomer, Alexei Sayle, who ruffled feathers not only among the audience but also backstage.

He infuriated John Cleese by knowingly overrunning. 'I asked him if he'd take a few minutes out, and on the second night he did longer than he did on the first night, quite obviously deliberately.' Although Sayle was actually very affable off stage, the notoriously truculent nature of his onstage persona also seemed to unnerve Alan Bennett, who ran away soon after the comic tried to engage him in conversation ('He was the only person I'd been really excited to meet,' Sayle recalls. 'I've since cornered him in bookshops and stuff and he's been fine!')

The clash with Cleese, another comedian whom he genuinely held in high regard, rumbled on throughout the run. 'He hated me,' Sayle would say. 'Well, he *kind* of hated me, but his wife – one of his nineteen psychotherapist blonde American wives – *absolutely* hated me. I think she thought I was one of her patients!'

Sayle, however, remained unrepentant. He knew that he was good, that this was his moment, and no one – not even John Cleese – was going to stop him. 'It was the first time I'd encountered that blaze of flashlights, and that degree of interest. I saw it as a rite of passage. It was a great showcase for whoever was hottest at the time. But I'd also been involved in lots of left-wing causes, so there was a real affinity there – it wasn't just a cynical career move!'

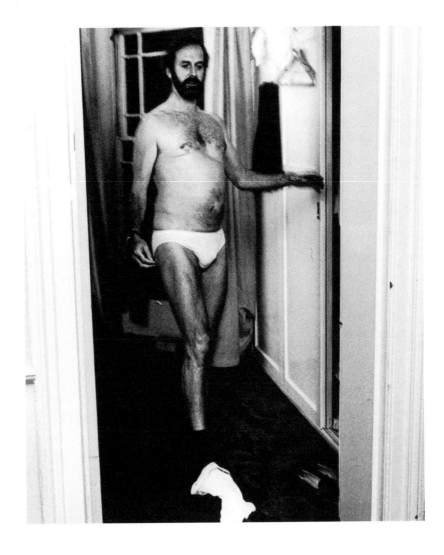

A WORD OF THANKS
JOHN CLEESE & THE CAST

There is a fanfare. The cast (which includes John Cleese, Chris Langham, Tim Brooke-Taylor, John Bird, Pamela Stephenson, Rowan Atkinson, Alan Bennett and David Rappaport) takes to the stage, led by Cleese, who steps forward to address the audience.

CLEESE: Ladies and gentlemen, before we start the show this evening, we do just want to take this opportunity of expressing, on behalf of Amnesty, our sincerest thanks to you for being with us tonight . . . and I am sure that you'll be thrilled to know that tonight's house has raised the truly magnificent sum of seventeen thousand five hundred and sixty pounds. Thank you.

(*Applause.*)

CLEESE: We do, really do, want to thank each and every one of you, even those of you right up the top there who only paid the . . . the – well, the minimum – of six pounds. Thank you.

LANGHAM: Three pounds fifty.

CLEESE: What?

LANGHAM: It's not six pounds, it's only three pounds fifty.

(*Cleese and the cast gaze up in wonder at the balcony seats.*)

CLEESE: You . . . *bastards!* I mean . . . people . . . people being tortured to death, all over the world, and you're prepared to cough up the price of a prawn cocktail! I mean – aren't you ashamed of yourselves? Gatecrashing a . . .

(*Tim Brooke-Taylor grabs Cleese's arm to restrain him.*)

CLEESE: Yes, you're right, never mind, never mind, never mind. We won't spoil the atmosphere. Ladies and gentlemen, I did want to thank all of you – well most of you, anyway – now, on with the show. Ladies and gentlemen, Mr Rowan—

(*John Bird approaches Cleese.*)

BIRD: Let's not forget – let's not forget – that the people up there are the casualties of our society. Students. People gassed in the war. Hospital porters.

RAPPAPORT: . . . Dwarves.

STEPHENSON: . . . Lesbians.

BIRD: . . . So, although they *have* only paid three pounds fifty . . . I mean, let's face it, they've been saving up for this all year, it's their big splash. And they have at least paid for it out of their own pockets. Whereas . . .

(*Everyone looks downwards at the seats in the main arena. There is applause and cheering.*)

BIRD: . . . these people down *here* are, let's face it, writing this off against *tax*.

(*The cast eyes them with disgust.*)

CLEESE: Really?

BIRD: Yes. I mean . . . how many of the people down here have, in fact, paid for their own seats? See? Nobody. There you are! There you are!

CLEESE: (*Counting the raised hands.*) . . . About seven . . . It's incredible, isn't it? Never mind. On . . . on with the show. Ladies and gentlemen, Mr Rowan Atkinson!

ATKINSON: . . . Actually, the people . . . the people who *really* get up my nose are those people who buy the *second*-cheapest seats. And the lot on the second layer down, who'd like to be down here with the rich and influential, but are too flabby to pay top whack – you lot there, the flabby, gutless, indecisive, sitting on every fence—

BENNETT: They're the fucking Social Democrats!

CAST: Fucking Social Democrats!!

(*They leave in disgust.*)

WHAT'S ON IN STOKE NEWINGTON

ALEXEI SAYLE

All right. Good evening. Er, my name's Alexei Sayle. I am actually a journalist – I'm gossip columnist on *What's On in Stoke Newington*. Yeah, you might have seen it, it's a big piece of paper with 'FUCK ALL' written on it, you know?

The lifestyle in Stoke Newington is terribly alternative, you know. (*Middle-class pseud voice.*) Ahahah, it really is, everyone's growing their own denim, you know, and erm, I actually knit me own yoghurt. It's really *'tastic*, y'know?

I've been on my holidays this year, I went to a Greek island, Domestos, y'know? The scene is terribly *alternative*, but there's one thing about the scene I can't get behind, and that is all the people taking drugs. And not giving *me* any, the bastards!

I think, if you wanna get out of your head, what's wrong with going out and having ninety-three pints – of real ale, you know – Scruttock's Old Dirigible – with the twigs and the bits of beak still in it . . . and the chunky jumper, and the suit with a tailored pocket for a calculator, all telling racy stories about commodity investment? (*Miming inane chatter.*) *Anyanyanyanyan! Anyanyaynyanyanyan!* . . . Not called wine bars 'cause of what they drink, it's what they fucking *do*: *whine* all the time . . . *Anyanyaynyanyanyan! Anyanyaynyanyanyan!* . . . 'Ever had a multiple orgasm?' '*Awful*, isn't it?' 'Seen the latest Woody Allen?' 'Yes, *awful*, isn't it?' 'Oh, the *quiche* looks rather nice . . .' (*Mimes the quiche attacking him.*) Bleeargh! . . . 'Right, I'm going to sing a folk song for you now, erm, it's about whale smuggling in the nineteenth century, and it was written by a civil servant, three weeks ago. Here we go now . . .' (*He sticks a finger up his nose*) '*Ringetty*

too! Ringetty too! Ringetty toodle toodle too!' Like, can you imagine the folk songs they're going to be singing in a hundred years time? You know, like – (*Sings in a cod rustic accent, to the tune of 'The Lincolnshire Poacher'.*)

> Oh, I am a computer programmer, from jolly Milton Keynes
> On weekdays I wear a suit and at the weekend Fiorucci jeans
> 'Tis my delight, on a Friday Night to cook some haricot beans
> In my tracksuit with roller skates on
> And one of them stupid fucking Sony headphone units . . .

You do all that, right, and then you round off the evening with a tortoise vindaloo. It's nice, you know what I mean? 'Er, good evening, sir, and what would you like to throw up tonight?' 'Well, fuck, er . . . I think the chicken biryani with the pilau fried rice? Make a nice kind of pointillistic pattern on the floor, don't you think?' I tell you, if you go round New Delhi at closing time, the streets are full of millions of pissed Indians throwing up steak and kidney pies . . .

DENIS ON THE MENACE

JOHN WELLS

Wells walks on stage dressed and made up to resemble Denis Thatcher. He is carrying a glass of G&T in one hand, a cigarette in the other, and is looking and sounding somewhat tired and emotional.

Good evening. I must apologise for being rather late. I have just been entertaining some *frightful*, grubby little left-wing *frog*, one of Margaret's political friends apparently over here on a dirty weekend.

We live, it is true, in a very tense time. The bar to my certain knowledge has been shut for the last hour, and I am probably unique among you in having had my retirement entirely buggered up by my wife becoming Prime Minister of Great Britain and *parts* of Northern Ireland.

A recent popularity poll suggests that Margaret is marginally less popular than the Black Death. I've advised her to reshuffle the Cabinet as soon as possible. My advice was: Prior to Northern Ireland and Sir Keith Joseph to Broadmoor.

I blame it on the Chancellor of the Exchequer, that little fellow Howe. I don't know whether you know him – curly hair, specs, brothel-creepers? He was quoted in public as saying: 'We are coming to the end of the recession.' He didn't in fact say any such thing. I was standing beside him at the time – a little champagne-and-Twiglets do. He had admittedly had a tincture or twain. What he *actually* said was, 'We are coming to the end of the reception.'

Our main failure in my view is failing to come to grips with the unions. We came in with a rock-solid mandate, as I have frequently explained to Margaret, to club the bloody unions back into the Stone Age. And who does she wheel out the moment it comes to any kind of confrontation, but Pinko Prior – who is, in my humble opinion, about as much use as a one-legged man at an arse-kicking party! She really ought to take a leaf out of old Hopalong's book in Washington – buy manacles and leg irons for every member of the TUC.

Margaret and I saw him in Washington. There he was standing at the top of the steps, bold as brass, six inches deep in make-up, holding *hands* with his *wife*. Doesn't that strike you as very *rum* in a man of his age?

Meanwhile we are still threatened with the spectre of unemployment, and I myself am absolutely in favour of it. It's an

old wrinkle from army days: if the lower ranks are getting stroppy about doing fatigues, march them out into the snow, leave them out there for a couple of nights, and they're only too grateful to come back and scrub out a nice warm shithouse.

I mean, what has unemployment ever done to you or me? *I've* been unemployed to all intents and purposes for the last fifty-eight years. I don't go around setting fire to public vehicles and lobbing Molotov cocktails at the constabulary!

One critic blamed all our present troubles on mindless hooligans bent solely on personal greed. Well, that *may* be true, but it's no way to talk about President Reagan and my wife!

Goodnight to you all!

THE ROYAL AUSTRALIAN PROSTATE FOUNDATION
DAME EDNA EVERAGE

Dame Edna enters, wearing a sparkling blue dress modelled after the Sydney Opera House. Behind her, her pianist sits at a grand piano.

My name is Dame Edna Everage, housewife, superstar, mother, megastar and Melbourne millionairess. I wasn't sure about this little Amnesty night, because I generally support my own special pet little charity, which is the very, very wonderful Royal Australian Prostate Foundation.

My husband Norm – well, he hasn't been a well man. I've had his prostate hanging over my head for many, many years. And for a very long time, the poor darling, he's had a rumbling prostate, but he never let on. He kept it under his hat, particularly at the pictures. But it had to leak out in the end, it did. And, you know, there is a wonderful new operation which, thanks to my munificence, we have been exploring in Australia. It's a part of the branch of cyronics [sic] where they snap-freeze the prostate in the hope that one day a doctor or a wonderful surgeon will be born who can perform a miracle operation. And of course, this is cold comfort to my husband in more ways than one.

Oh, Silly Billy me! I had to take it home from the hozzie – in a thermos on the back seat of my car, and I can assure you that

I haven't had Norm's organ there for many moons. And then I got it home and I've tucked it into the freezing compartment of our fridge. It's there on the left at the back. I've got all the barbie meat on the right . . . my worry, of course, is that my marvellous old bridesmaid, Madge Allsop, will get a little bit peckish in the middle of the night. She could be in the mood for a scrummy old shish kebab, couldn't she, darlings? I could come home from one of these lovely shows that I do and find my husband's organ halfway down her throat. That's a worry.

But it is lovely for me to be here, because I am a believer in Amnesty. You know, in Australia, half the population are behind bars, they are, and the other half are leaning on them, my darlings.

This little frock, of course, the little smart trendsetters in the audience will be up all night copying, I know that. They will be, they will be. Little Thea Porter will be huddled over her Singer all night, won't she, copying this lovely frock of mine, which is inspired by the Sydney Opera House Casino. Can you see it? It's just dawned on you, you poor little things, saturated with satire that you are. A little bit of naturalness comes as a bit of a shock to you, I suppose – does it?

But to me, when I do my little sharing shows, it's not just me, it's you as well. I know that sounds a sentimental, silly old thing, but that's the kind of person I am. I'm a bit of an old softy – I'm an old *softy* from way back, darlings, and it's the public that mean such a lot to me and I feel a little song coming on . . .

(*Sings.*)

A cheering crowd at my stage-door,
An audience crying out for more
That's what my public means to me.
The loyal fans who queue for hours
The cards, the telegrams and all those lovely flowers
Yes, and that's what my public means to me.

You need to have a pretty humble attitude
When you see little faces looking up, grotesque with gratitude,
But from tiny tots to grannies
I love all your nooks and crannies
That's what my public means to me.

The Queen's birthday honours list
This lovely Cartier on my wrist,
That's what my public means to me.
A limousine, a sable coat,
The lump that's rising in my throat,
That's what my public means to me.
Superstars may come and go but there's no other
The folks identify with their own mother.
To think there's people in this room
Who wished they'd sprung out of my womb,
That's what my public means to me.

The Royal visitors who call
A concert in the Alfred Hall
That's what my public means to me.
All those requests I get to stay
With famous folk in St Tropez,
That's their idea of fun for me.
But you can keep Roman Polanski and Bianca
It's for the company of nobodies like you I hanker.
You're my shelter from the storm,
You're as precious as my Norm,
That's what my public means to me.

And now the time has come to pass,
I feel a lump inside my heart
That's what my public do to me.

The little know-alls squirt their poison
I can feel my eyelids moisten
But I know that my public still stands true to me.
I may be forced to live in a tax haven
But I know I'm poor when I see all those gladdies waving,
And how could I forsake them
When they raise their stalks and wave them,
That's what my public means to me.

Thank you, darlings, thank you!

CHEKHOV & THE GORILLA

JOHN BIRD, JOHN FORTUNE & CHRIS LANGHAM

It is 1904, and a meeting of the board of directors of the Moscow Art Theatre is taking place following the first preview of The Cherry Orchard. *Present are the playwright Anton Chekhov, the director Constantin Stanislavski and the financial director Sergei Nemirovich.*

STANISLAVSKI: I thought, you know, that *Cherry Orchard* went pretty well, Anton.

CHEKHOV: Not bad, not bad.

STANISLAVSKI: I mean, especially, you know, for a first preview. I think, you know, you've really answered the critics who say you can't write a happy ending.

CHEKHOV: Oh, yeah, yeah.

STANISLAVSKI: I mean, the characters always end up in despair or shooting themselves or whatever. I think you certainly got away from that with the big production number at the end. Very upbeat. I just have this worry at the back of my mind that when all the characters come on at the end –

CHEKHOV: Yeah?

STANISLAVSKI: . . . and go into the song. (*Sings.*) 'The orchard is saved –'

CHEKHOV: Yeah, yeah. Good number.

STANISLAVSKI: . . . then go into the big dance number and throw the streamers into the audience –

CHEKHOV: And the bubble machine.

STANISLAVSKI: . . . I just have this slight feeling that it doesn't quite gel with the general atmosphere of what's gone before. Do you know what I mean?

CHEKHOV: I know what you mean. Yeah, there is a bit of a change of gear at that point.

STANISLAVSKI: Right. I mean, I wouldn't like to lose any of the sort of *pizazz* or the *optimism* or sending the audience home in a *happy* mood. I just wondered if we could do a bit of fine tuning at the end of the play.

CHEKHOV: Well, I was thinking about this last night, actually, Constantin, and I've come up with something which might just fit the bill. Now, this is all off the top of my head, a bit rough and all that. But let's say, for the purposes of argument, that the orchard isn't saved.

STANISLAVSKI: *Isn't* saved?

CHEKHOV: Isn't saved.

STANISLAVSKI: Now, don't forget what the critics say about your doomy endings.

CHEKHOV: No, hang about. So all the characters are a bit pissed off about that, they all come in, and the old lady comes on and she's a bit tearful, like we all would be. Looks around and says 'Goodbye house, goodbye chairs, goodbye light fittings, goodbye fire extinguisher', you know, 'goodbye whatever'. And she goes off and the stage is empty. Now you remember that bloke who was on in the first two acts, the old servant, what was his name?

STANISLAVSKI: Firs.

CHEKHOV: Firs. That's the fellow. Now he went down well, a very lovable eccentric character.

STANISLAVSKI: Dynamite.

CHEKHOV: Got a lot of laughs. Now the audience hasn't seen him for, what, half an hour? So he's been locked away in a cupboard somewhere, he comes out, has a look round the stage, goes about muttering to himself about they've all gone off and left him and his life's passed him by without him noticing and all that caper, and he sits down, twanging noise and the curtain comes down. How about that?

STANISLAVSKI: I like it, Anton. I think it could work.

CHEKHOV: I mean, what you've got there, Constantin, you've got your humour . . .

STANISLAVSKI: You've got your humour, you've got your pathos going on. You've got the best of both worlds. What do *you* think, Sergei Nemirovich?

SERGEI NEMIROVICH: Yes, yes, I think I see what you're driving at there. It sort of rounds off the play more. Yes, I go along with that.

STANISLAVSKI: Good, good, right.

SERGEI NEMIROVICH: There is one slight suggestion that I would make. It's just a small point, really.

STANISLAVSKI: What's that, then, Sergei Nemirovich?

SERGEI NEMIROVICH: It is only a suggestion. Shoot me down in flames if you think I'm barking up the wrong tree here. How would it be, during – as an example, sort of thing – during the time that the old servant was off stage and locked in the cupboard or wherever he happens to be . . . how would it be if, during that intervening period of time, he could have been somehow, by some means or other – don't ask me exactly how – sort of . . . *changed* . . . transformed into something *different*, if he could be changed . . . into a . . . gorilla?

CHEKHOV: I knew it. I *knew* it would be something like that. Jesus wept!

STANISLAVSKI: Calm down, Anton.

CHEKHOV: For Christ's sake! That's all I get! That's all he *ever* wants! Gorillas, gorillas, gorillas! 'Why can't we have a gorilla in the play?' 'Why can't two gorillas be at the dinner party?' 'Why can't a gorilla bring on the samovar?' *What the fuck's he talking about?* Changing a servant into a gorilla? What's he trying to *do*?

SERGEI NEMIROVICH: Pardon me for breathing! I'm only the financial director!

CHEKHOV: What the fuck's the matter with him? Let me just remind you what we're trying to *do* in this theatre. We're trying to create a new revolutionary, naturalistic kind of drama, where the audience can come in, they can sit in the audience, they can look at the stage and they can identify with the characters on the stage, they can see their own ordinary, humdrum lives being portrayed with honesty, truthfulness, with *realism*. Let me just ask you this *one* simple question: how many, exactly what proportion of the audience that comes to the Moscow Art Theatre every night, are in fact gorillas?

SERGEI NEMIROVICH: Well, *I* come every night, for one!

CHEKHOV: Of course *you* fucking come, you're the financial director! You get free bloody seats!

SERGEI NEMIROVICH: Well, of course I get free seats! Where am I going to put a ticket stub?

CHEKHOV: The same place you put your banana!

SERGEI NEMIROVICH: Oh, that's *very* nice! I see the way the conversation is sliding now! I wondered when you'd come out from under your stone, Anton! Let's face it: you don't actually *like* gorillas, do you?

CHEKHOV: I wouldn't say that. I've got nothing against gorillas. I just don't think the *stage* is the right place to have a gorilla, actually!

'I've had it up to here, with sex, those nylon vests and hairy necks.'

Victoria Wood

HAD IT UP TO HERE
VICTORIA WOOD

I've had it up to here with men,
Perhaps I should phrase that, again;
Been wearing pretty dresses – floral . . .
Taking contraceptives – oral . . .
Since I don't remember when.

I've had it up to here, with blokes,
And all their stupid dirty jokes,
It's not a lot of fun,
To hear the one about the nun,
The marrow, the banana, and John Noakes.

It's not that I expect true love,
Or gazing at the stars above,
If as a person they'd acknowledge me,
Not just bits of gynaecology,
Or if they'd just take off the rubber glove!

To start your evenings off in Lurex,
Finish them with biscuits
Doesn't really turn me on!
I'll stay at home in my pyjamas,
Watch a programme about llamas,
I won't need any lip gloss,
I won't need any Amplex,
Just Ovaltine and buns for one!

I've had it up to here, with sex,
Those nylon vests and hairy necks,
They expect you to be flighty
And they act like God Almighty
'Cause they've got a cock and they can mend a flex!

And when they proudly strip and pose,
I want to say, 'What's one of *those*?'
They tend to feel a failure
If you don't love their genitalia,
Though why you should, Christ only knows!

No more nights of drinking,
Nodding, smiling, thinking,
'Jesus, when can I go home?'
No more struggling in taxis,
In Vauxhalls, Imps and Maxis,
With stupid little bleeders with all the charming manners
Of the average garden gnome!

And when they're down to socks and grin,
You know it's time to get stuck in;
Full of self-congratulation,
They expect a combination,
Of Olga Korbut, Raquel Welch, and Rin-Tin-Tin!

I've not had an encounter yet,
That didn't leave me cold, and wet;
I'd be happier, I know,
If we could only go –
From the foreplay –
Straight to the cigarette!

I'll finish and just say, again,
I've definitely had it – well,
Very nearly had it, had it nearly up to here
With men!

TOP OF THE FORM

JOHN CLEESE, ROWAN ATKINSON, JOHN FORTUNE, GRIFF RHYS JONES, TIM BROOKE-TAYLOR, JOHN BIRD & GRAHAM CHAPMAN

The scene is a TV quiz show for school children. John Cleese is the quiz master. The Boys' Team comprises Brian (Rowan Atkinson), Kevin (John Fortune) and Stig (Griff Rhys Jones). The Girls' Team comprises Tracey (Tim Brooke-Taylor), Arthura (John Bird) and Cynthia (Graham Chapman).

QUESTION MASTER: Hello, good evening and welcome to another edition of *Top of the Form*. And this week we're at the semi-final stage and tonight's contest is between the boys of King Arthur's Grammar School, Podmoor, and the girls of the St Maria Kangarooboot the Second County High School and a Half. (*A quick burst of canned applause.*) And so, without further ado, let's go straight on with round two. Brian, what is the name we give to the meat we get from pigs?

BRIAN: Pork.

QUESTION MASTER: Good, that's two marks to you. Tracey, what is the name of the metal alloy we get from zinc and copper?

TRACEY: Brass.

QUESTION MASTER: No, no, I'm afraid not. The answer's pork. Kevin, what is the capital of Australia?

KEVIN: Sydney.

QUESTION MASTER: No, no, the capital of Australia is pork. Now, Arthura, who wrote *A Tale of Two Cities*?

ARTHURA: Pork?

QUESTION MASTER: Good. It's two marks to you. And so on to Stig's question. Stig, what was the date of Captain Cook's discovery of Australia?

STIG: (*Quickly.*) Pork!

QUESTION MASTER: Good. Two marks to you. And the last question in this round goes to you, Cynthia. Can you recite the first two lines of Thomas Gray's 'Elegy Written in a Country –'

CYNTHIA: Pork!

QUESTION MASTER: Good. Two marks to you. That's the end of round one and the score is four points each. (*Another burst of canned applause.*) And straight on to round two. Brian, what is the name we give . . . to the meat . . . we get from pigs?

BRIAN: (*Stuttering with excitement.*) P-P-Pork!

QUESTION MASTER: What?

BRIAN: (*Less confidently.*) Pork?

QUESTION MASTER: No, no, you're guessing, aren't you? The meat we get from pigs is called . . . Baghdad.

(*Both sets of contestants have begun looking at each other with a growing sense of bewilderment.*)

QUESTION MASTER: Tracey, your question next. Tracey, what is the capital of Iraq?

TRACEY: (*Bemused, she consults her teammates before answering.*) Baghdad?

QUESTION MASTER: No, nearly. No, the capital of Iraq is Rome. Kevin, what is the capital of Italy?

KEVIN: (*Utterly baffled.*) Paris?

QUESTION MASTER: No, no, the capital of Italy is Tokyo. Arthura, what is the capital of Japan?

ARTHURA: Washington?

QUESTION MASTER: Good, two marks to you. Stig, what is the capital of the United States of America?

STIG: (*Anxious, he consults his teammates.*) Sydney!

QUESTION MASTER: Well . . .

BRIAN: Canberra!

QUESTION MASTER: Jolly good – two marks to you. And finally, Cynthia, what's the capital of Australia?

CYNTHIA: Pork?

QUESTION MASTER: Well done, well done indeed! And at the end of round two the score is, um . . . (*Another burst of canned applause.*) And straight on with round three. Brian, what is the difference between a mongoose and a monsoon?

BRIAN: A mongoose is a long white plastic pole . . . that you hang out of your window to frighten the birds away . . . and a monsoon is a . . . medieval Hungarian stomach pump.

QUESTION MASTER: No, I can only give you a half for that.

BRIAN: Oh, um, Brussels, Brussels!

QUESTION MASTER: No. No, no, a monsoon is a wind, and a mongoose isn't. Well, that's enough of that round and the score is . . . (*Another burst of canned applause.*) Now on to round four, which is all about butterflies. Tracey, here's your question, and they're all about butterflies, okay? Your question on butterflies: who wrote *Jane Eyre*?

TRACEY: Red Admiral? Cabbage White? Fritillary?

QUESTION MASTER: No, no, you're on the wrong track here.

TRACEY: Pork!

QUESTION MASTER: No, no, the answer is the Taj Mahal.

(*By this stage even the Question Master is baffled and he tries to double check his cards.*)

QUESTION MASTER: No, I'm sorry, I got a bit muddled there. The answer is, in fact, Brussels. But I can give you one for Cabbage White. Well, that makes the scores even and there's only time for one more question, so whichever school gets this will go through to the final next week.

TRACEY: Pork!

BRIAN: Rangoon!

ALL: *PORK!*

QUESTION MASTER: No, no, wait for the question. Here it is, and it's quite a hard one. Ready? Can you tell me: who shuffled my question cards just before transmission?

BRIAN/STIG/KEVIN/ARTHURA/CYNTHIA: TRACEY!!!

PRESIDENT REAGAN'S BIG ONE
JOHN WELLS

We hear a blast of 'The Star-Spangled Banner'. John Wells enters as President Ronald Reagan, dressed in a garish cowboy outfit, complete with gun and holster.

My Republican producers told me, 'Ronnie, you are going to be a model president.' I said, 'Does that mean I have some kind of big key in my back, wound up by a bunch of rich hooligans?' They said, 'No, if we'd needed that, we'd have got the old Abraham Lincoln dummy out of Disneyland. Why, he talks just like you do, he has a considerably wider range of facial expressions . . . (*Grins fixedly.*) No, we need a live ac-tor . . . and, failing that, Ronnie Reagan.'

That does not mean I intend to be written out of my big scene. I'm not talking about some localised nuclear conflict between two crazed tinpot demagogues, like Haig and Weinberger . . . but if it comes to real gunplay, I intend to demonstrate, as a mature statesman, that I have a bigger one . . . (*He reaches for his crotch, then his gun, which he holds aloft.*) . . . than any crazed commie in Pakistan, or wherever it is they come from. So we burn up a couple of billion. That's show business!

Finally, as a conservative – and I do not give a shit about conservation – I intend to conserve, to cleanse, tone and moisturise that face of America that will, under God, strike terror into friend and foe alike.

(*He grins cheerily and waves, while 'The Star Spangled Banner' plays again.*)

MEN'S TALK

ALAN BENNETT & JOHN FORTUNE

Bennett and Fortune, playing two donnish middle-aged types, are standing on the stage, already immersed in conversation.

BENNETT: . . . And did you have to go through that tedious charade, sexual intercourse?

FORTUNE: (*Eagerly.*) Oh, yes, from A to Z.

BENNETT: (*Sounding horrified.*) Z!? Oh, *B* is the furthest I've ever wanted to go!

FORTUNE: Oh, no. A, B, C, D . . . – the whole alphabet of love.

BENNETT: What *form* did it take?

FORTUNE: (*Dreamily.*) Oh . . . myriad forms.

BENNETT: Put it in and jiggle it about a bit, did you?

FORTUNE: Well, ultimately, yes, but it was a long and winding road.

BENNETT: (*In a world-weary tone.*) That's all it comes down to in the end, though, isn't it? Put it in and jiggle it about a bit? I said to my wife on the last occasion, I said, 'You know, I've lost count of the number of times I've done this.' She said, 'Well, think about somebody else for a change.' 'Course, I *was* doing – *desperately*. (*He looks strained at the memory of it.*) How old was she . . . your, ah, . . . sex partner?

FORTUNE: Seventeen.

BENNETT: *Seventeen*?

FORTUNE: With pert young breasts that I oh-so tenderly cupped and kissed, before fondling my loving way around all the sweet highways and byways of her fresh young body.

BENNETT: And then you put it in and jiggled it about a bit. How long did it take?

FORTUNE: Oh, I did a real text-book job: foreplay, afterplay, all the trimmings. I don't suppose we had much change left out of three hours.

BENNETT: Three hours! Jesus *Christ*! You could have been in *Leeds* in that time! Did she enjoy it?

FORTUNE: Oh, yes, she enjoyed it all right. (*Chuckles.*) Oh yes, she enjoyed it all right.

BENNETT: How do you *know*?

FORTUNE: Oh, the infallible sign. She started moaning. Moaning and crying, pleasure and pain inextricably mingled.

BENNETT: (*Dismissively.*) I take all that with a pinch of salt.

FORTUNE: Oh, no, those cries were wrenched from her very being. (*Moans.*) '*Oh ah ah oh!*' It was as though her very soul was speaking: '*OH AH OOOH AH OH!!*' You know, it was almost as if she was being stabbed. In fact, I honestly *did* think she was being stabbed.

BENNETT: Well, she *was* being stabbed. By you.

FORTUNE: Oh, no, no, no. From *underneath*. I thought there was somebody under the bed stabbing her through the mattress. '*Oh,*' she was crying, '*Oh oh oh!!*' In fact I was so certain that there was somebody under the bed stabbing her that I leaned right over to see if there was somebody there.

BENNETT: While you were still, ah – ?

FORTUNE: While I was still, ah, yes.

BENNETT: And what happened?

FORTUNE: She started moaning twice as much as before. She kept begging me to look under the bed again because it was so wonderful. I mean, for her.

BENNETT: (*Sceptically.*) I think that's all put on, you know. I think probably, once upon a time, somebody, a Mrs Wendy Barraclough, say, was laid up with a fractured pelvis and *il suo marito* arrived home and rather callously insisted on having his marital rights, you know.

FORTUNE/BENNETT: Putting it in and jiggling it about a bit.

BENNETT: And, of course, if you *have* fractured your pelvis in three places, putting it in and jiggling it about a bit is *acutely* painful, and the hapless Wendy, of course, started moaning, you see – '*Oh ah ah oh!'* – and found that hubby, who was normally a reticent chartered accountant of modest sexual pretensions, was transformed into a crazed animal. So as soon as practicable she gets herself down to flower arrangement, or whatever it is they do on an afternoon, and said, 'Listen, girls, gather round, drop the macramé – big news. If you moan, they like it more; besides which, it gets them to the point a lot quicker, which will leave us more time for making chutney!' Since when it's gone round, you see. One's passed it on and they're all at it now, you know: *OOOH! OOOH!*

FORTUNE: Yes. (*Crestfallen.*) I thought she moaned because she liked me.

BENNETT: Oh, no. How old did you say she was?

FORTUNE: Seventeen.

BENNETT: Oh, no, no, no, no.

FORTUNE: (*Wistfully.*) I didn't think anyone was seventeen any longer.

BENNETT: Well, I . . . more or less scored with somebody seventeen the other day.

FORTUNE: (*Surprised.*) Oh, *did* you?

BENNETT: Oh, yes, yes.

FORTUNE: Oh, really?

BENNETT: Yes.

FORTUNE: Tell me about it.

BENNETT: Well, I will. I was at home. It was a beautiful evening, very crisp, clear, just a *hint* of autumn in the air, and I thought, it's a crime to stay *indoors* on a night like this, so I'll just take a turn along to the lavatory at the end of Ladbroke Grove and get a breath of fresh air.

FORTUNE: (*Puzzled.*) Lavatory?

BENNETT: The lavatory, yes, at the end of Ladbroke Grove.

FORTUNE: But you *live* in Ladbroke Grove.

BENNETT: I do, yes. I live in Ladbroke Grove, yes, yes.

FORTUNE: Was there some kind of *malfunction* with your own toilet?

BENNETT: No, no, at last flush it was in tip-top condition. No, do you know that lavatory at all?

FORTUNE: Well, yes. I mean, I . . . I . . . I have been there on occasion, I mean, you know, purely for functional reasons.

BENNETT: Yes, yes, of course. Well, that's why most people visit it, you know, they go for absolutely legal, moral and . . . and . . . functional reasons, you know. They use it for the purpose for which it is designed, you see. I don't. *I* go for . . . ancillary reasons.

FORTUNE: (*Trying not to sound shocked.*) I . . . I . . . I didn't know that.

BENNETT: (*Slightly awkwardly.*) No, well, you wouldn't know that, you see, because I haven't, um, well, I haven't, um, er, come out of the closet.

FORTUNE: In Ladbroke Grove?

BENNETT: No, I've gone *into* the closet in Ladbroke Grove.

FORTUNE: Oh, *into* it. Well, I see.

BENNETT: I was speaking metaphorically, you see. But it's a very *reliable* sort of place, really. It's not three-star, but it's quite definitely two crossed knives and forks. It's got a very eclectic clientele; you get a very good social mix. There's the usual groundswell of Spanish waiters, one or two BBCs, a sprinkling of Foreign Office, and, God bless Our Lady of Downing Street, many, many unemployed youths.

FORTUNE: Unemployed youths?

BENNETT: Yes, yes, many of them. Great pity, but there they are.

FORTUNE: Tragic.

BENNETT: It *is* tragic, yes, yes. Anyway, I've stood, you see, in the toilet for about, ah, twenty minutes, purporting to have a Jimmy Riddle.

FORTUNE: *Twenty* minutes?

BENNETT: Yes, twenty minutes, yes.

FORTUNE: Is that what you have to do?

BENNETT: Oh, yes, you have to do that. It's a real RSC award-winning performance, really. I mean, in any other context it would get you a Tony or an Oscar. And indeed in that context occasionally gets you a Tony, less often an Oscar. Anyway, I'm stood there, you see, and meanwhile various good citizens come and go, having emptied their honest bladders, but very quiet, nothing happening, not a nibble. Probably a Bette Davis movie on the television, or something like that. Then suddenly, the doorway is darkened by the massive form of Mr Right.

FORTUNE: Mr Right?

BENNETT: *Mr Right.* Oh, six foot tall, bronzed, blonde, crisp hyacinthine curls, built . . . like a brick shithouse and, biggest plus of all, never says a word.

FORTUNE: Never says a word?

BENNETT: Never says a word. You see, the beauty of which is . . . it allows me free play with all my fantasies.

FORTUNE: Of course.

BENNETT: Yes, and I thought, is he a Hungarian truck driver, fresh from driving his juggernaut across the motorways of Europe and to hell with the environment? Is he, ah, a member of the SAS, with his balaclava dangling nonchalantly from his back pocket? Ah, is he – ?

FORTUNE: Is he the Wayneflete Professor of Moral Philosophy in the University of Oxford?

BENNETT: No, no . . . *that* hadn't really occurred to me.

FORTUNE: No, no.

BENNETT: It wasn't anyway, I don't think, no. Anyway, dissolve to half an hour later. We're back at my place, my wife is upstairs somewhere, making her four hundred and thirty-seventh quiche of the day, and we're downstairs in the snug.

FORTUNE: The rumpus room?

BENNETT: The rumpus room, yes. We're just about to cross the start line. I've eased down his nether garments with practised skill and he has done the same for me with a clumsiness I found rather endearing. It's at this point that doubts begin to creep in, because, to begin with, he seems totally – ah – unfamiliar with the geography of the area in question and, while what I've got to offer is *respectable*, it's not *remarkable*, but he's gazing upon it with all the wonder of an Eskimo gazing at the Eiffel Tower.

FORTUNE: Silent upon a peak in Darien.

BENNETT: Exactly, yes, yes. And it's then that the thought strikes me, *la pensée* – and it's a *pensée* that certainly never occurred to Pascal, or if it did, he certainly didn't publish it – 'This bugger is a policeman.'

FORTUNE: So what did you do?

BENNETT: Well, I taxed him with it. I said, 'You've seen one of these before, I suppose? Ha, ha.'

FORTUNE: Irony?

BENNETT: You're not familiar with it.

FORTUNE: Litotes.

BENNETT: Exactly, and I said to him, 'Are you a policeman?' And he said, 'No, actually, I'm more familiar with feet. I'm a chiropody student at Richmond Polytechnic.' So I went right off it, really. Not my cup of tea at all.

FORTUNE: And he didn't . . . moan?

BENNETT: Oh, no, no, no, no. Boys don't *moan*, you see. Well, I mean, they moan about not having a job or not having anywhere to sleep or, you know, not having enough money, but they don't moan about that. A little grunt is the most you'll ever get.

FORTUNE: Well, I suppose it is all in the mind.

BENNETT: Oh, yes. And sometimes, these days, not even there.

DIVORCE SERVICE

PAMELA STEPHENSON, GRIFF RHYS JONES, JOHN FORTUNE AND ROWAN ATKINSON

(written by John Cormack)

Solemn organ music is heard.

MINISTER: We are here to celebrate the holy sacrament of divorce. Dennis, wilt thou leave this woman, who is they wedded wife? Dost thou dislike her, despise her, has thou told her a thousand times if thou've told her once to squeeze the toothpaste tube from the bottom and not from the top, and dost thou despise her brother, the chartered surveyor, who invites himself to dinner and then drinks thy Scotch after ye have gone to bed? Dost thou dislike her mother, hate her cooking, get irritated that she picks her toenails in bed, and that the clippings somehow find their way into that little crack in the side of the duvet, and wilt thou forsake her for as long as ye both shall live?

DENNIS: I will.

MINISTER: Muriel, wilt thou leave this drunken shit who is thy wedded husband? Didst thou dislike the brevity and infrequency of his lovemaking and wert thou so sick of having to lie to him about how it's not size that's important and that you may as well be sleeping with one of those seaside collection boxes made out of a mine? Wert thou driven to distraction by the fact that he uses saucers as ash trays and the fact that when he said he was going to

his mother's for the weekend he was in fact in Ipswich with Elsie Maynard, and will you, if given half a chance, cheerfully wring his neck?

MURIEL: I will.

MINISTER: Who taketh this woman away from this man?

FRANK: I do.

MINISTER: Just say these words with me: 'I take thee from thy wedded husband.'

FRANK: I take thee from thy wedded husband.

MINISTER: 'To have and to hold, from this day forth.'

FRANK: To have and to hold, from this day forth.

MINISTER: 'For I am Frank Hodgkiss, the lounge lizard from accounts.'

FRANK: For I am Frank Hodgkiss, the lounge lizard from accounts.

MINISTER: 'And thereto I plight thee my troth.'

FRANK: And thereto I plight thee my troth.

MINISTER: Those whom I have put asunder I bet no man can join together. Dearly beloved, divorce is an honourable state and is not to be taken in hand lightly, inadvisedly or wantonly to satisfy men's carnal lusts, although that's a pretty good reason, and for as much as Dennis and Muriel have consented to abandon holy wedlock and instead pledge their troth to whomsoever tickles their fancy, I pronounce that they be man and woman apart and henceforward shall be free to be swingers and frequent singles' bars that have been approved by the Archbishop of Canterbury, perhaps dancing cheek to cheek. Amen.

MURIEL: Amen.

'Muriel, wilt thou leave this drunken shit who is thy wedded husband?'

HOW TO GET OUT OF YOUR HEAD
ALEXEI SAYLE

It's a load of old toss, innit, eh, *mime*? Ain't it a load of old *wank*, mime, eh? I mean, who in their right minds, right, would pay good money to see a real man sew his fingers together, walk into a high wind, and get shut in a fucking glass box? But some French fucker called Bip or Snot or something, he *pretends* to sew his fingers together, walk into a high wind, and get shut in a fucking glass box, and people travel from Guildford to see him! (*Cockney accent.*) It's a funny old world, really, innit, eh? (*Mimes punching.*) Sorry, sorry, I thought I was Alan Minter there for a minute, sorry. (*Does a fascist salute, then, shocked, pulls his hand down as if it has a life of its own.*) Oh, fuck it! Right, okay . . .

I went round to some friends' flat the other night, right . . . I got up to the flat, right, talking about drugs, I got up to the flat, right, and I noticed the sickly sweet smell. (*Yorkshire accent.*) Sickly sweet bloody smell! I thought, 'Aye, aye', I thought, 'Aye, aye – Spam for tea!' And then I saw them – the extra-long nine-skin Gauloises *dick compensators* they was rolling . . .

(*Puts on middle-class pseud voice.*) I said, 'Byron . . .' I said, 'How did you manage to get the Spam in *there*?!'

And then I realised what was happening, I said, 'I'm hip to this groove, daddy-o, 23 Skidoo, rock around the crocodile, man!' So they all ignored me, you know? I sat down on the Habitat pine scatter cushions, and they all settled down for a good alternative night in, you know? Lentil fondue bubbling away on the hot plate . . . (*Pseud voice.*) 'Oh, yes, I got this recipe out of a book called

A Thousand and One Things to Do with Cling Peaches – or a thousand and two, if you eat the fuckers . . .' And they put the child into its Victorian night smock – made it look like an extra from *Tess of the D'Urbervilles* . . . and they're all sitting there, right, with tea cosies on their heads, telephone cord wire coming out of them . . . they're all weekend white Rastafarians! They all live on the front line in *Hemel Hempstead!*

And they lit up the joints, right, lit up the joints . . . (*Mimes taking a toke, then goes into pseud voice again.*) 'Ooh, fucking hell, yeah . . . oh, wow . . . did you strip those floorboards yourself? . . . Oh, it's like fucking *Norway* in here, man . . .' And this one guy says, 'Oh, this is really amazing dope, you know, I mean it's really *incredi-bubble*, you know? I mean, It's really *amaaaaayyyzing*,' he said. 'But let me tell you about some dope *I* had the other week. It was really good stuff, it was Swedish Leb, you know . . . I had one toke of this dope, right, just one toke, I was paralysed from the waist down, I lost the use of my fingers, and I developed every single symptom of typhoid! It was fucking *amaaaaayyyzing* . . .' And they're all going 'Ooh, fucking amazing, ooh, fucking fantastic . . . ooh, *SAVE THE SHRIMP, MAN* . . .'

So this second guy, right – another civil servant – says, 'Well, actually, I've been taking coke – you know, cocaine – only, no, it's really good stuff, it's only about nine-fifths Harpic.' He said, 'Like, it's TFM, you know? It's Too Fucking Much. So I had one snort of this coke, right, just one snort, and I went *blind* for a fortnight! It was fucking *amaaaaayyyzing* . . .' And they're all going 'Ooh, fucking amazing, ooh, fucking fantastic, ooh, *SAVE THE MORRIS MINOR, MAN*, yay . . .'

A Morris Minor's like being inside a fifties radio, isn't it? See 'em all, pedalling away . . . 'Look, look, it's Noddy the Social Worker . . .' (*Mimes waving and pedalling.*) . . . Cunt!

So this first guy's a bit pissed off, so he says, 'Okay, stakes are raised, well, erm . . . I've been taking, er . . . napalm. I've been roasting the phone in the oven and then taking it through my

kneecaps . . .' He said, 'I've been taking acid, you know? I dropped a couple of tabs round at Kenny and Dave's, you know, round the squat, you know? It's really nice, they're making an effort . . . they're using a pig on a string as an air freshener. It was really amazing acid, this, you know, I mean it was much better than Sainsbury's tinned cream magic mushrooms!' He said, 'And, like, we dropped these two tabs, you know, and our brains started to throb – and I didn't think Kenny and Dave *had* any brains left after Knebworth . . .'

Well, who fucking would have – nine hours of Santana? Eighteen quid for a fucking lentil burger? God! It was like the First World War! Of course, they had heavy metal then, but it was called shrapnel in those days . . .

Oh, actually, it was wonderful though, wasn't it, Knebworth? I don't know if you remember that wonderful climactic moment, you know, when we all struck a match and held it aloft, you know . . . yeah. Suddenly, there was fifty thousand people going . . . (*Mimes burning his hand.*) 'Ow, fucking *hell*!'

 ' I'm hip to this groove, daddy-o, 23 Skidoo, rock around the crocodile, man! '

Alexei Sayle

THE

Secret

POLICEMAN'S

THIRD

BALL

THE LONDON PALLADIUM
26-29 MARCH 1987

The Secret Policeman's Third Ball

THE COMEDY

Lenny Henry ▪ **Phil Cool**
Ben Elton ▪ **Mel Smith &**
Griff Rhys-Jones ▪ **Emo**
Phillips ▪ **French &**
Saunders ▪ **Hale & Pace**
Spitting Image ▪ **Andrew**
Sachs ▪ **Chris Langham**
Warren Mitchell ▪ **Rory**
Bremner ▪ **Mike Hurley**

AMNESTY INTERNATIONAL &
in association with
THE INDEPENDENT

INSPIRING THE AGE OF LIVE AID
AN INTRODUCTION

When *The Secret Policeman's Ball* returned in 1987 after a six-year break, it was to a rather different cultural, and commercial, landscape – a landscape that, ironically, had been changed largely by the success and influence of the previous Balls. Earlier productions had inspired so many other charitable ventures to follow suit that Amnesty now found itself in a much more crowded and competitive marketplace.

Bob Geldof had initially been dismissive of the very idea of *The Secret Policeman's Ball*, reportedly saying: 'There's no point in doing a fucking charity show. They never make any fucking difference . . .' But, after being persuaded to participate in the 1981 show, he changed his mind dramatically – and followed in its footsteps. 'He took the Ball and ran with it,' as Sting would put it, to launch Live Aid in 1985 and raise some £150 million for Ethiopian famine relief. U2's Bono – another Amnesty participant – would credit the same 1981 show with inspiring him to use similar means to promote the same kind of causes: 'It became a part of me,' he said of the event. 'It sowed a seed.'

Even particular strands within the productions, such as the regular acoustic musical sets that began so memorably with Pete Townshend in 1981, started being credited with sparking their own spin-offs, such as MTV's *Unplugged*. Among the many other *SPB*-influenced campaigns and projects that were launched during this time were *The Prince's Trust* gala concerts (1982); the London-based *Evening for Nicaragua* comedy night (1983); *Comic Relief*, *USA For Africa* and *Farm Aid* (all 1985); and Dublin's *Self Aid* and the *Hands Across America* concert (both 1986).

More parochially within the UK, there were periods when the sheer number of worthy-sounding benefits, spread out over a short space of time, could appear overwhelming – in 1985, for example, it was possible to attend three separate events in two days in aid of the striking miners – and listings magazines were now covering so many different charity shows that they started running a 'Best Benefit' annual award. Not only were countless organisers borrowing the tried and tested format of *The Secret Policeman's Ball*, but there were also a few who were adapting its famous name, too – such as a fund-raising show in 1984 for London's Gay Switchboard which was entitled *The Pretty Policeman's Ball*, and a 1986 event jointly in aid of the Campaign for Press and Broadcasting Freedom and the Campaign for Freedom of Information that was called *Censorama: The Official Secrets Ball*.

Amnesty itself had added to the burgeoning range by starting a number of other (non-comic) consciousness-raising projects, such as the high profile 1986 *Conspiracy of Hope* tour (comprising six concerts staged across America, featuring such musicians as U2, Sting and Peter Gabriel) and the very ambitious series of twenty-eight rock concerts entitled *Human Rights Now!* presented worldwide in 1986.

The challenge facing *The Secret Policeman's Ball* upon its return, therefore, was to compete not only with the high standards that its previous shows had set, but also with the many other events that they had spawned. 'Charity fatigue' was now a phrase in popular circulation. 'There's something about these fundraising spectaculars,' wrote one jaded critic, 'that sucks the fun out of the room', and it was becoming hard to make out the distinct causes for the multiplicity of concerts.

Amnesty's first response to the situation was to concentrate on supplying more of the same, but making it seem bigger and better than ever before. It already had the distinctive brand, and already had the illustrious history, so now the aim was to reclaim the initiative from all of the many pretenders through the application of superior experience, expertise and professionalism.

A suitably grand venue – the London Palladium – was booked, and arrangements made for the shows to be shot for a theatrical/cinema release. John Cleese was approached to help organise the show, but said he was unable to take part. He did, as it turned out, relent at the last moment and agreed to make a surprise appearance on one of the nights, good-naturedly being the butt of a rather cruel Fry and Laurie sketch called 'The Silver Dick Award', in which he was mocked for everything from his recent hair-weave to his apparent reluctance to take part in charity shows.

Two significant developments in terms of the composition of the cast were the increased presence of women (apart from the efforts of French and Saunders, Ruby Wax filmed some comic inserts backstage, and Kate Bush and Joan Armatrading provided some music) and, in the person of Lenny Henry, the event's first black comedian ('For the first time,' he reflected wryly, 'there's a black guy on stage being funny rather than having people talk about him being in jail'). These changes, combined with the introduction of several other young performers associated with a brasher 'alternative' style, helped the shows seem more closely attuned to their times.

'Suddenly,' Henry recalls, 'you had this very attitudinal stance that alternative performers could take. The idea of the privileged classes coming onto the stage and being funny in an intellectual way had been slowly subverted by other folks, from the redbrick universities and the secondary moderns, who also had something funny to say and also believed that the abuse of human rights was wrong. So suddenly this thing started to become a broader church.'

The production as a whole served Amnesty's ambitions well. The many 'pop people' included Lou Reed, Peter Gabriel, Kate Bush, David Gilmour, Mark Knopfler, Jackson Browne and Duran Duran, and among the comedians were Ben Elton, Fry and Laurie, French and Saunders and Emo Philips. The shows were again spread over four nights – but, unusually, split as two music nights and two devoted to comedy. The event generated a range of money-spinning merchandise, including a film and a book.

Amnesty decided to consolidate on the return of the *SPB* by tying its next event, *The Secret Policeman's Biggest Ball*, which took place in 1989, even more tightly to its own tradition – and differentiating it further from its many music-heavy competitors. John Cleese was again firmly at the helm – and he and Amnesty once again decided to create something unique by approaching Jennifer Saunders to be co-director, to ensure that a younger generation of performers was also represented. In terms of impact, however, with several stars from the era of *Beyond the Fringe* and *Monty Python* back at the top of the bill, and some of the younger performers co-opted into sketches that originated in the 1960s or '70s, it was Cleese's signature that was stamped most clearly

on the show. The highlight for many – and yet another coup for Amnesty – was the appearance of Peter Cook and Dudley Moore on a London stage for the first time in sixteen years. The audience reaction was both deafening and affectionate.

Strongly reminiscent of the very first event back in 1976, and at times quite emotionally nostalgic, it was an apt way for Amnesty to end a decade in which the seeds sown long ago had grown and blossomed so brightly. From *A Poke in the Eye* to *Live Aid*, from one good cause to a multitude of them: never before had so much good come from such a lot of balls.

REAGAN AND THATCHER
SPITTING IMAGE: CHRIS BARRIE & STEVE NALLON

A Ronald Reagan puppet appears from behind a bank of filing cabinets.

REAGAN: My fellow . . . things . . . Now, I haven't got much left but I can offer you this little turkey . . . (*Produces a revolver.*) I know it's not much – I cannot expect a *whole* hostage for it – but I'll give it to you if you just have any *small* hostages – say under five feet one – or perhaps a *young* hostage . . .?

(*The Thatcher puppet appears.*)

THATCHER: My dear Mr Reagan, what on earth are you doing? (*Indicating the audience.*) You mustn't deal with these people!

REAGAN: Why not, Nancy, old honey bun?

THATCHER: Because they're *communists*.

REAGAN: Communists! Where?

THATCHER: (*Pointing.*) There!

REAGAN: That's your hand. You mean your hand's a communist?! You've been *infiltrated*?

THATCHER: (*Indicating the audience.*) No, no, no, no. *Those* people.

REAGAN: Oh, come on, Nance. How do you know?

THATCHER: Because they want to free dissidents.

REAGAN: Er . . . sorry, Nance – I'm confused – could you go back a bit?

THATCHER: The . . . the people in this theatre . . .

REAGAN: Erm, perhaps a little *further* back?

THATCHER: How much further?

REAGAN: Well, I remember making that movie with the monkey, but after that, everything's a bit of a blur . . .

(*Reagan laughs in a contented manner.*)

THATCHER: Now look, please – these people would like to see dissidents freed –

(*Reagan, distracted by most other things in the theatre, continues chuckling.*)

THATCHER: Please pay attention when I'm talking down to you. Now, these people – *these* people – would like to see dissidents freed. Now – who *else* is freeing dissidents at the moment?

REAGAN: Er . . . er . . . what was the question again?

THATCHER: *GORBACHEV!*

REAGAN: Gorbachev? That's not much of a question!

THATCHER: No, no, no – that's the *answer!*

REAGAN: Okey dokey – so the question must have been: 'Who's the president of Russia?' (*Laughs again.*) That's one in the eye for those who call me an asshole, Nance! Okay – my turn. Who played the lead in . . . *The Dawn Patrol?*

(*Thatcher slaps Reagan about.*)

THATCHER: Listen, you boring old fart: *Gorbachev* is releasing dissidents, *these* people want to release dissidents, so *these people* are *communists!* Got it?

(*She head-butts him.*)

REAGAN: Nope. As a matter of fact, I think it was William Holden.

THATCHER: Aaaaaargh!

(*She bangs her head on the table in frustration.*)

THE HEDGE SKETCH
STEPHEN FRY & HUGH LAURIE

The scene is inside a shop. There is a long wooden counter. Laurie, dressed as the customer, arrives from one side of the stage; Fry, dressed as the shopkeeper, from the other. They both walk to the front of the stage and acknowledge the audience.

FRY: Thank you. Thank you very much, ladies and gentlemen. Um, we'd like to do a sketch for you now. It's called 'The Hedge Sketch'. And it's set in a shop. 'The Hedge Sketch' – thank you very much indeed.

(They move back to their positions on either side of the counter and prepare to commence the sketch.)

LAURIE: Hello, I'd like to buy a hedge, please.

FRY: Good morning, sir, how can I help you?

LAURIE: Well, what sorts have you got?

FRY: A hedge? Certainly, sir, what sort would you like?

LAURIE: Could I have a look at the Imperial, please?

(Both start to realise that something has gone wrong, making their delivery increasingly hesitant.)

FRY: Well, we have three sorts, sir. We have the Royal, the Imperial and . . . the Standard hedge.

LAURIE: No, no, it's a present.

FRY: Certainly, sir. Um . . . may I ask, is the hedge for you?

LAURIE: I'm not married.

FRY: F-For your wife . . . perhaps?

LAURIE: N-Not at all, I'm in no hurry.

FRY: Well, if you wouldn't mind waiting, I'll just . . . ring down to the Stock . . . (*Whispers.*) *Start again, start again!*

(*They leave the stage and return again to start afresh.*)

FRY: Good morning, sir, how can I help you?

LAURIE: Hello, I'd like to buy a hedge.

FRY: A hedge? Certainly, sir, what sort of hedge would you like?

LAURIE: Well, we have three sorts, sir. We have the Royal, the Imperial (*He realises they've gone wrong again.*) . . . or the Standard hedge.

FRY: (*Sounding very worried.*) Can I have a look at the Imperial, please?

LAURIE: (*Sounding equally worried.*) Certainly, sir. May I ask is the hedge for you?

FRY: Um, no, it's a present.

LAURIE: Ah. Er, for your wife, perhaps?

FRY: I'm not married.

LAURIE: Well, if you wouldn't mind waiting, I'll just ring down to the Stock Room.

FRY: N-Not at all, I'm in no hurry.

(*They look at each other for a moment, then Fry gestures awkwardly for them to switch sides. Disoriented, Laurie complains there's no telephone; Fry whispers that it's under the table. Laurie picks it up and pretends to make a call.*)

LAURIE: Hello, Stock Room? Have we got any Imperial hedges left?

(*An embarrassing silence is ended when Fry puts his fingers on his nose and furtively tries to supply a voice from the other end of the phone.*)

FRY: I'll just go and have a look.

LAURIE: Thanks. (*To Fry.*) He's just having a look.

FRY: (*Once again disguising his voice.*) You've got one left, sir.

LAURIE: Right, I'll take it, then!

(*Yet again, they look at each other and realise they've gone wrong. After a moment of barely suppressed panic, they decide to switch sides again.*)

FRY: Ah, you seem to be in luck, sir – Stock Room tells me we've got one left!

LAURIE: Cash, if you don't mind.

FRY: Certainly, sir, how would you like . . . to . . . pay?

(*They are visibly distraught at what is happening, and quickly decide to go off and start yet again. They return, however, looking somewhat shell-shocked and desperate to get it all over with, and so they start racing through their lines at breathtaking pace.*)

FRY: Good morning, sir, how can I help you?

LAURIE: Hello, I'd like to buy a hedge.

FRY: A hedge? Certainly, sir, what sort of hedge would you like?

LAURIE: Well, what sorts have you got?

FRY: Well, we have three sorts, sir. We have the Royal, the Imperial and the Standard hedge.

LAURIE: Can I have a look at the Imperial, please?

FRY: Certainly, sir. May I ask is the hedge for you?

LAURIE: No, it's a present.

FRY: For your wife, perhaps?

LAURIE: No, I'm not married.

FRY: Oh, well, if you wouldn't mind waiting, sir, I'll just ring to the Stock Room.

LAURIE: Not at all, I'm in no hurry.

FRY: Er, hello, Stock Room? Do we have any –

(*Laurie realises Fry has forgotten to pick up the phone and gestures impatiently for him to do so.*)

FRY: Er, Stock Room? Um, do we have any hedges left? (*To Laurie.*) He's just checking, sir. You're in luck, we have one left.

LAURIE: Right, I'll take it then!

FRY: Certainly, sir, how would you like to pay?

LAURIE: Cash, if you don't mind!

FRY: Cash would be perfectly convenient, sir!

(*Both men fall silent. Laurie looks at Fry expectantly. Fry looks at him the same way. Suddenly, both of them realise they don't know how to go on. Laurie looks at his shoes. Fry gazes at his fingers. Laurie looks up at the ceiling. Fry scratches his head. Fade out.*)

'A hedge? Certainly, sir, what sort of hedge would you like?'

LOW-DOWN LEFT-HANDED DIRTY HOUND DOG

LENNY HENRY

A blues guitarist at the rear of the stage plays a slow and languorous riff. Lenny Henry, as the veteran blues singer Low-Down Left-Handed Dirty Hound Dog, strolls into vision, dressed in a pale zoot suit and dark glasses. He speaks slowly and deeply.

Good evening to you. My name is Low-Down Left-Handed Dirty Hound Dog . . . I'm a *blues* singer. I been singin' the blues for sixty-five years. That's a mighty long time. Especially when you want to go to the toilet.

I was, I was, I was born . . . I was *born* with the blues. I was an unlucky chiiiiild . . . I was abandoned on a doorstep. By my foster parents. They made, they, they, made sure I was safe, they put me in a black plastic bag . . . and they tied that sucker real *tight*. And you know, I *love* oxygen.

Yes, sirree, oxygen helps to stimulate the, er . . .

(*Long pause.*) . . . When I was nine years old, I drifted, ah, ah drifted, I drifted – (*Does Frank Bruno voice.*) – you know what I mean Harry? – I . . . I . . . I drifted. I drifted all the way *dowwwwwn* to New Orleans, and I joined my first band. There was me, singing, on vocals . . . Rico 'Hogface' Ravenshaw on drums . . . Mikey 'No Fingers' McGinty on piano . . . and a guy called Joe 'Hunchback' Williams. Joe didn't actually play nothing, he just used to kind of make this weird sort of cracking noise with his hump. Used to go – *Pmmmmf!*, scared the shit out of me. He kind of filled out the rhythm section a little bit.

We were called 'The Beautiful People'. And we to – we-we-we to – we-we-we-we to – we-we-we- – Chaka Khan – we-we-we toured – we-we-we-we – (*To himself.*) talk *sense*, Godammit, they paid good money – we toured all the way round the Deep South. And there was a lot of segregation going around. We weren't allowed to play in the same room as white folks. Used to have to play in a little broom cupboard down the hall. They used to send the applause back in a little envelope.

But you know, a lot of people say, 'What *is* the blues?' We-e-e-ell, the blues is when you meet a beautiful woman. And she's wearing a shimmering white dress. And you take her home. And you make love all night long. And next day, you find out it's the Pope.

But you know, I *luuurve* women. I love women all the time, man . . . (*Dances.*) . . . ah-eh-oh – one more time – ah-eh-oh – again – ah-eh-ooh – ho-hey-ho-hey . . .

(*Breaks into song.*)

> You're a cabbage patch for me, baby.
> I'm your gardener
> And I've got a big hose for ya . . .
> You're a cabbage patch for me, baby.
> I'm your gardener
> And I've got a big fat wobbly nasty stick o' hose for ya,
> I sure do like your vegetation
> But your caterpillars get right up my nose.
>
> I'm a blues man, baby,
> I sing the blues day and night.
> I'm a blues man, baby.
> I can love you right.
> I'll love you any way you want, girl,
> Just as long as you turn off the light.
> Play the blues for 'em, Miles . . . Miles Seabrook on guitar . . .

(*Guitar solo while he dances.*)

I'm a hound dog, baby,
I'll follow you to the world's ends (*Howls.*)
I'm a hound dog, baby,
I'll follow you to the world's ends.
I'll howl for you all night long,
And scratch my goolies in front of your friends.

I'm a blues man, baby,
I sing the blues day and night, and night and day, and day and
     night and night and day and day and night, uh
You know I'm a blues man, baby, yeah
I can love you right, I can love you all night.
I'll love you any way you want, girl,
But I got a headache tonight.

. . . and that's the blues!

'We weren't allowed to play in the same room as white folks. Used to have to play in a little broom cupboard down the hall. They used to send the applause back in a little envelope.'

Lenny Henry

THE SILVER DICK AWARD

STEPHEN FRY, HUGH LAURIE & JOHN CLEESE

Fry and Laurie walk onto the stage. Fry is carrying a small metallic object that looks rather like the base of a table lamp.

FRY: Ladies and gentlemen, we now come to the part of the evening where we make our special award in the gift of this Academy, the life achievement award in recognition of outstanding services to comedy.

LAURIE: This fellowship in our exclusive gift honours an individual who, in the opinion of the Academy, has used his skill and judgement in an apt and entertaining and original way. The award, of course, is named after Dick Emery.

FRY: Past winners of the Silver Dick include the wild punster Mr Richard Whiteley, the presenter of TV's cult programme *Countdown*; Mr Gus 'Right to Reply' Macdonald; and the woman who does the Shake n' Vac commercial.

LAURIE: How can we describe in just a few words the winner of this most prestigious of awards? A man whose humanity shines through absolutely everything he does. Certainly a very great personal hero of ours –

FRY: One of the most lovely, fluffy, pink, moist and super people in show business – I think I can speak for all us here when I say that I'm desperate to develop a close sexual relationship with this man.

LAURIE: This *thrillingly* lovely elder statesman of comedy – for heaven's sake, you all know who we are talking about now. He had

his own TV show which ran for, I think, twelve whole programmes
before being taken off –

FRY: Yes, which was a mistake, I think.

LAURIE: *I* think it *was* a mistake.

FRY: Yes, they shouldn't have done that. Nonetheless, with no further
ado, let's announce him – the winner of this year's Silver Dick. Ladies
and gentlemen, the shudderingly gorgeous – Mr Jim Cleese!

(*Enter John Cleese, resplendent in smart black evening dress. The
audience applauds and cheers.*)

FRY: Jim, Jim, I want to go to bed with you! Oh, Jim! Jim Cleese!

LAURIE: So, Jim, let's talk about you now. They took your highly
entertaining, heart-warming comedy classic *Fawlty Towers* off the
air after only twelve episodes. Well, what was that all about?

FRY: It was really beginning to get *good*, Jim.

LAURIE: *I* thought so.

FRY: It had the *makings* of something.

CLEESE: Yes, there were only in fact supposed to be the twelve episodes.

LAURIE: And the twelve were *fine*, Jim. You know, there was *lots* in there which I thought may have turned into something –

FRY: Yes, I mean, one minute you're a rising star and then some TV executive decides to make you a nobody with a flick of his pen.

LAURIE: Just cuts you off.

CLEESE: (*Bemused.*) I don't think that that –

FRY: It was around that time, wasn't it, Jim, when you were in the middle of rather a messy divorce with the woman who was chiefly responsible for writing your scripts? And it was from then on that things started really to go wrong for you.

LAURIE: Now, they tell me, Michael Barrymore doesn't even bother to *do* you any more.

FRY: Do you feel bitter? Regrets?

CLEESE: No, no – none at all!

LAURIE: Oh, surely – just a few, Jim?

CLEESE: No . . . no.

LAURIE: Oh, Jim, for heaven's sake, I hate to see a *very* old man cry. I mean, *we* still love you, we want to see you come back –

FRY: Oh, yes, I'm sure I speak for the ladies and gentlemen when I say we'd like to see more of his amicable hotelier. Wouldn't we? (*The audience applauds.*) Yes, yes! You see, Jim? *Plenty* of people remember you! We *all* want to see Basil Brush back on television!

CLEESE: (*Now utterly baffled.*) It's not Basil Brush!

FRY: Oh, Jim, dry those eyes and tell a few warming thoughts to some of the public.

CLEESE: Yes, yes – I would . . . I would just like to say—

LAURIE: What was it that finally finished you off, Jim?

CLEESE: I do not . . .

LAURIE: Was it the *hair-weave* or was it the move to the SDP – which was it, do you think?

(*Embarrassed, Cleese tries to hide his hair.*)

FRY: Was it growing that rather odd beard, I wonder, or perhaps it could have been those strange psychiatric group therapy sessions?

(*Feeling humiliated, Cleese pulls out a handkerchief and starts to sob. Neither Fry nor Laurie appear to notice.*)

FRY: Did you find, Jim, that once you stopped being mad, you stopped being funny?

LAURIE: And then, of course, you let down Amnesty by refusing to do their annual charity show.

(*Cleese cries out and falls to his knees, sobbing uncontrollably.*)

LAURIE: Until, of course, you caved in at the last minute because the press kept ringing you up.

(*Cleese, still on his knees sobbing loudly, gestures desperately to Laurie to shut up.*)

FRY: (*Disgusted.*) Look, he's got nothing to say for himself . . .

LAURIE: Nothing.

FRY: Without his dead parrot, he's nobody. It's tragic! This is the wreck of a once noble comedian. He's a nothing, a nobody. Come on – get off stage, Jim, get off!

LAURIE: You're finished!

(*Cleese starts crawling off the stage.*)

FRY: Oh, Jim, Jim . . . (*Cleese crawls back.*) Don't forget your Silver Dick . . . There you are, Jim, there you are . . .

(*Cleese takes the award and crawls off sobbing from the stage.*)

MANUEL AND ALF GARNETT

ANDREW SACHS & WARREN MITCHELL

Sachs enters in character, dressed as the Barcelona-born waiter Manuel from Fawlty Towers. He is waving a small union flag.

It's very nice to have you with me today! (*Sings:*)

> Of all the countries in the world
> There's only one for me
> Where a man can live and work and play,
> A country of the free.
> I speak of England's green and pleasant land
> Just next door to France,
> I've been here a long long time
> Not days, not weeks – but months.
> England! My England,
> I sing of you with pride,
> And Scotland which is at the top
> And Wales on the left-hand side,
> And there's Ireland . . . .

(*Sitcom Cockney bigot Alf Garnett enters, wearing an overcoat and a West Ham scarf, shouting at Manuel to stop.*)

Get orf out of it! Go on, clear orf, load of bloody rubbish! (*Manuel flees.*) Never mind about bringing foreigners over here, eating us out of 'ouse and 'ome! If anyone out there's got anything to give away, they should be giving it to us old-aged pensioners in need!

Never mind about *children* in need – give it to them when they're old! They'll appreciate it more! Yeah, start giving children everything they need and you turn 'em into bloody cadgers, crying and whining for something for nothing!

You'll all be old, all youse lot one of these days. Yeah, and you'll know what it's like, struggling to get out of bed in the mornings, all crippled wiv arthritis and old age, and, when you *do* get up, find out there's nothing worth getting up for! No bloody breakfast, no coal for the fire, no tobacco for your bloody pipe . . . *Then* you'll find out what life is all about!

Sitting there waiting for it all to end. Oh, yeah. They'll spend millions on bloody AIDS, oh yeah. 'Don't die of ignorance,' they say. What about dyin' of old age, eh? No one wants to spend a penny on *that*, do they? Oh, no! Fornicating and buggery, that's all right, innit? Oh, yes, catch a packet sticking your John Thomas where you didn't ought to stick it, where no decent *respectable* man would stick it – unless he's married and then only into the woman he loves.

Catch a nasty dose and the government wants to look after you, don't they? Give yer nice clean needles on the National Health, prescriptions for your heroin and your Valiums and yer Mogadons – they hand 'em out like bloody *sweets*! Cor blimey, yer sex maniac, he gets French letters on the National Health now!

But when you're poor and starving, ain't got nothing, nobody wants to give you nothing, do they? Not even AIDS!

The bloody National Health Service! Sod 'em! I went to my doctor last week there in Wapping and I said, 'Doctor, I've got a terrible pain in my leg.' He said, 'It's old age.' I said, '*OLD AGE*? The other leg's all right and that's the *same* age!' I said, 'What am I gonna do?' And he said, 'Limp.' I said, 'Just a minute . . .' and he said, 'What are you going on about, Garnett? You're all right. You'll live to be sixty-five!' I said, 'I *AM* sixty-five!' He said, 'Well, there you are – I told you!' I said, 'All right, all right, clever dick, can I ask you a question, doc?' I said, 'What about that bottle of pills you gave me last month, to make me feel strong?' He said, 'What about them?' I said, 'I can't get the lid off!'

And I said, 'And another thing . . .' I said, 'Are you aware that you've got a suppository stuck behind your ear?' He had a bloody suppository stuck behind his *ear*! He said, 'Christ Almighty, what's that bloke done with my fountain pen?'

Bloody doctors! I don't trust 'em. I came out that doctor's surgery, walked through the waiting room – it's gospel, this – I see a nun, a real nun, sitting there waiting, crying her eyes out. So I rushed back into the surgery and I said, 'Doctor, excuse me, you've got a nun sitting in your waiting room, she's crying her eyes out.' He said, 'Yeah, I know. I've just told her she's pregnant.' I said, 'Is she?' He said, 'No, but it's cured her hiccups!'

Anyway, I wouldn't have been the least bit surprised if she had've been, all this permissible society. I was walking through

Soho last week, and outside the cinema it says, 'If you are a sporting gentleman, come in and see the midnight game.' Well, I thought it was floodlit football. It was one of them filthy Swedish films! I went in and sat down and this fella in the seat next to me, he's laying over the back of the seat, looking up at the film, and he's going, 'Oh! Oh! Oh!' I said, 'Shut up, be quiet! What's the *matter* with yer?' He's layin' there and he's going, 'Oh! Oh! Oh!' I had to call the manager. The manager came over and he said, 'What's your name?' He said, 'John – John White.' He said, 'Where do you come from?' He said, 'Balcony.' (*Groans and laughter from the audience.*) It's a *joke* – a joke, wasn't true!

But I went to the film. I sat there and I never seen such *filth* in all my life! I nearly walked out! In this film, right, there's a fella and a girl laying on the beach – and they were *doing* it! Doing it in *broad daylight*, y'know! He's whispering in her ear what he's gonna do to her. I looked down at the subtitles, and by the time I looked up again, he had bloody well *done* it! So I kept my eyes glued to the film! I missed the next subtitle and never found out if he enjoyed it or not! She's lying there – enormous, great . . . You know, you could see the pimple, everything, you know, she was naked. Well, she wasn't *entirely* naked, 'cause the producer of the film had a bit of decency to put a bit of seaweed down *there*, you know. Well, I *think* it was seaweed.

Anyway, by the time the film was finished I wished it *had* been football! What about that, banning us out of Europe? Isn't that a diabolical liberty, just the year West Ham were gonna do it, weren't they? (*The audience laugh and boo.*) Yes, we bloody *was*! And now we're banned out of Europe! I notice they didn't want us banned out of Europe when Hitler was around, eh? It was all 'voulez-vous, avec et moi, ce soir'. Come-and-liberate-us time! Now it's all piss-off time, innit? We should've left 'em to Hitler, he'd have given 'em bloody soccer hooligans, all right!

I could bloody starve. Bloody *starve*, yeah! Supposed to be Christians, love thy neighbour – there's not one of them comes

knocking on *my* door to see if I've got any bloody dinner. Oh, no! They give money to Ethiopia, send things to Oxfam, they're busy rushing 'em off to Africa, ain't they, looking for starving bloody natives, but no one comes knocking on *my* door to see if I've got any dinner to eat! Bloody Bob Geldof, never been down *my* road . . .

FREEDOM
FRENCH & SAUNDERS

French and Saunders take to the stage wearing dark and sober clothes. They look very serious as they prepare to address the audience.

SAUNDERS: Freedom – a state of being free. Liberty – particular privilege, facility of doing anything.

FRENCH: If I have freedom in my life and in my soul, and free angels alone that soar above enjoy such liberty . . .

TOGETHER: The answer, my friend, is blowing in the wind. The answer is blowing in the wind.

SAUNDERS: Jennifer Saunders – Actress.

FRENCH: Dawn French – Younger Character Actress.

SAUNDERS: Ladies and gentlemen, I'm afraid it's rather down to us to do the serious part of the evening. Judi Dench and Anna Massey were going to do this part this evening, but unfortunately, and very sadly, they're working.

FRENCH: We, however, are not working at all, and are completely available, so we can be here.

SAUNDERS: Of course, it's wonderful to be involved in wonderful causes when we are lucky enough not to be working, 'cause there is a wonderful feeling of camaraderie on stage.

FRENCH: Oh, yes!

SAUNDERS: It's very, very wonderful.

FRENCH: Yes!

SAUNDERS: One has the opportunity to work with people whom one wouldn't really want to work with ever again.

FRENCH: And, honestly, backstage – it's just marvellous, marvellous. It's just great.

SAUNDERS: Marvellous, marvellous feeling of camaraderie.

FRENCH: Yes.

SAUNDERS: Wonderful moments . . .

FRENCH: Yes, yes. Right, well, I'd like to read some Polish writing now –

SAUNDERS: Actually, the wonderful thing about actors and actresses is we always have a fund of very, *very* funny stories to tell.

FRENCH: Oh yes, yes we do! But now I'd like to read some Polish writing.

SAUNDERS: Actually, there's one particular story I can think of actually at this moment. I'll just tell you quickly. It actually happened to me when I was in a play.

FRENCH: Ah . . .

SAUNDERS: And I was in a play and there were a lot of other actors and actresses also in the play with me, and this one particular night I'm thinking of happened, and I had to come on stage in the play, and all the other actors and actresses were also on stage, and this one night I'm thinking of –

FRENCH: Yes . . .

SAUNDERS: . . . in a hat, I'd come on in a *hat* – I'd forgotten about that hat.

FRENCH: In a hat.

SAUNDERS: I had come on in a hat, and this one particular night I'm thinking of, I'd come on, and I'd *forgotten* to put on my hat! *Somehow* we managed to carry on, I don't know how!

FRENCH: Oh, that's funny. That's *very* funny.

SAUNDERS: I don't know how, I don't think the audience realised, but it was wonderful, wonderful –

FRENCH: Marvellous –

SAUNDERS: . . . funny moment.

FRENCH: Marvellous . . . So what – did you have a hat on because somebody else didn't have a . . . ?

SAUNDERS: It doesn't matter now.

AN AMERICAN IN LONDON
EMO PHILIPS

Well, if someone would have told me ten years ago that I'd be here at the Palladium . . . I just would have stared at him. 'Cause I was on medication at that time.

I'm finally getting the hang of your city . . . How about those bus drivers, huh? I chased a bus three blocks the other day. Finally, he opens the door, you know . . . and I get my coat out. And the Underground . . . I'm on the . . . I'm on the platform, and it's so loud! And I put my fingers in my ears . . . (*He puts his fingers in his ears, but realises that he can't talk into the mic. He grabs the mic stand and puts the mic in it, and continues.*) Ha – seem to have overestimated the number of my limbs . . . I put my finger in my ear, and this guy bumps my elbow, and it gets stuck in the eardrum, you know, and everyone's staring at me . . . so, to save face, I go . . . (*Puts other hand on hip and dances.*) 'I'm a little teapot, short and stout . . .' . . . and I was able to leave with *some* dignity.

Speaking of dignity, there's nothing like Amnesty International! The worst thing in the world is being locked up when you're innocent. Once I was driving down the highway, and I'm swerving all over 'cause I'm trying to change the radio, you know? And just as I get the old one taken out, this police officer pulls me over – (*He makes a siren noise and wheels around.*) – well, I shouldn't make fun of his speech impediment.

He says, 'Can I see your licence?' So I hand him my wallet. He says, 'Kindly remove it from the wallet.' I thought, 'Oh, great,' and sure enough the rubber snake pops up in *my* face, you know?

He said, 'Haven't I seen you on TV?' And I say, 'I don't know, you can't see through the other way.'

He says, 'Walk a straight line.' So I do. He said, 'You call *that* a straight line?' Now, you know how you can never think of a clever reply until after the guy's gone? I mean, I wished I had said – I *wished* I had said . . . 'Yeah.'

But I was nervous, and all I could think of to say was: 'Well, Officer Pythagoras, the closest *you* could ever come to achieving a straight line would be by making an electroencephalogram of your own brain waves!' (*Shrugs.*) I was under *pressure*, you know?

Anyway, he takes me to the police station. They said, 'You get one phone call', so I call my house, and my sister answers, I thought, 'Oh, great . . .' I said, 'Hello.' I said, 'I need a thousand dollars for bail.' She said, 'Where am I gonna get that money this time of night?' I said, 'I don't know, is the naval base still open?'

And they throw me in this cell, and I was scared. I have never been locked up before, without my family . . . And there's a real big guy in this cell, smoking a cigarette. Now I don't care how big someone is, when it comes to my health I think of my body as a temple – or at least as a relatively well-managed Presbyterian youth centre, you know? I said, 'Put that out,' and he says, 'No,' so I flicked it out of his mouth. He said, 'I'm gonna mop the floor with your face!' I said, 'You do, and you'll be sorry.' He said 'Why?' I said, 'Well, you won't be able to get into the corners,' you know?

And he comes at me. I prayed, 'Lord, if you rescue me, I'll go to church every Sunday for the rest of my life!' Just then the guard comes to tell me my mom had posted bail and I was free to go. So I prayed, 'Thanks anyway,' and I got out of there. And *you* could help innocent people everywhere get out by supporting Amnesty International!

ON SEX
BEN ELTON

Since it's late, and we do not have the constrictions of television . . . let us indulge in a little . . . *liberation sexuality*. Wouldn't it be nice . . . if you could . . . give yourself a blowjob? 'Cause – be honest – only *you* understand your own body. Only the individual knows *exactly* what their individual body needs. It doesn't matter how good a relationship – a caring, monogamous, one-to-one relationship, lots of Marxism – very nice! – but only *you* understand your *own* body. So every time – 'Oh nearly, oh nearly, you got it, no *that's* good, oh no, a little bit *too* much, oh you're *biting*, you're biting, no, more – no, *less*, no, that's it, that's perfect, no, you fu – no, no, *no* . . . oh for, oh fuck it, I'll do it myself!'

Women thinking . . . 'He's been down there half an hour and he *still* hasn't found it!' Men thinking . . . 'Found *what*?' Few men out there thinking, 'Hang on a minute – am I wrong? But has he overstepped the mark here? He's talking about clitorises, is he? That's a bit fucking *rude*, isn't it? Clitor – . . . I don't wanna hear about this! Come on, Doris, we don't wanna hear about clitorises, you might find out you've got one, come on, let's go!'

The words are wrong . . . Sexuality is . . . the reason the world is so messed up is because sex is made *brutal*, it's made a *secret*, every effort to try and liberate is called 'leftyism', you know, it's brutal . . . all the words, you learn 'em behind the bike shed. They mean nothing. '*Blowjob*'. '*Blow job*' . . . I may not know much about sex, but I *do* know one thing . . . you're not supposed to *blow*. *Pffffff*! *Pffffff*! Watching your partner inflate before your very eyes! You come up for air, they shoot across the room like a balloon – *pffffff*!

We need new words! Words that describe the act! Words that give kids an idea what they're taking on! 'Suffocate job'. That'd about sum it up, wouldn't it? 'Desperately try to be sensitive even though your neck's half-broken job'. Ha ha . . . few fifteen-year-olds pretending they've got it down the front there. Because it's very, very difficult. Creative sex is not easy, and I don't care about all the books and diagrams, you try and fit into 'em. If God had wanted us to have oral sex, he wouldn't have given us *elbows*. 'I know you're trying to be deeply sensitive to my every bodily need, but could you get your elbow out of my arsehole?'

I mean, sex is abusive. People use it for what they can get, it's outrageous. Maybe some of the heterosexual women in the audience will remember, perhaps, that first time, and last time, that you allowed him to persuade you to *do it for him*. Oh, what a magical star-spangled night of romance that was! (*Sighs deeply as he mimes disinterestedly masturbating a man. Then mimes looking at a watch.*) 'Oh, sorry.' 'Do you promise you're thinking about me? Well, why d'you keep shouting "Madonna", then?'

And then slowly that realisation that only the individual understands their own body, as a slightly larger, sweatier hand, clamps on top of hers and takes over control of the ship. 'Bollocks – I'll make the tea, you do it yourself!' Because nobody *understands* . . . people should *talk* more, in a loving relationship, they should *communicate*! After sex, you should *chat*. You don't just roll over and start farting. (*Points into audience.*) Ah, there's a ring of light . . . no, I can see, there's a fledgling fresher couple there . . . yeah, broken *that one* up. '*You* do that! *You* do that, you should *listen* to him, *you* bloody do that. You *do*, you – fart, fart, *fart*, you!' Women fart too, remember that. Let's have cool politics, but let's be realistic!

You should *talk* after sex! You should talk politics, take the opportunity, current affairs . . . I always chat current affairs after making love. Well, last time I can remember, anyway . . . I er, think we were going through the Falklands War at the time. But even that – tiny little bit of liberation, that tiny bit of sensitivity, between two human beings . . . is ruined. By oral sex. 'Cause it is *extremely* difficult to have an in-depth Marxist dialectic on the nature of international materialism when you've got a pubic hair stuck in the back of your throat.

You can't shift it! (*Mimes coughing.*) Got any tea, love? (*More coughing.*) I mean, you don't wanna say, do you? Romantic evening, ending up saying, 'Sorry, love, you've got loose pubes.' (*Mimes further coughing.*) You can't clear it! They come out your balls easy enough, why can't you get them out the back of your neck?

Actually – ain't they funny old things, pubes? No, really . . . (*Does Kenneth Williams voice.*) Aren't they funny old things? They're not *happy* where they are, are they? They like to get about a bit. Oh, yeah, I'm not surprised, staring at a pair of sweaty old pants: 'Fuck this, I'm off!' (*Dances across stage.*) You know, sometimes I think what a strange job it is, I *do* you know . . . I just mimed a pubic hair to 2,000 people . . . My mum thinks I work in a bank!

They get everywhere! There is no area of human life that a pubic hair has not colonised. Open a book – wallop, there's a pubic hair. Brand new copy of *Trivial Pursuit*, take off the cellophane – boom. Pubic hair. The bar-of-soap-seeking pubic hair . . . is a wonder of creation. How'd they *get* here? You've got a new bar of soap, put it on a basin, watch it, wait for the pube to form. I think they put 'em in at the factory. 'What do you do?' 'I work at Palmolive.' 'Oh, make soap, do you?' 'No, I put the pubes in.' (*Mimes putting a single hair in each bar of soap.*) 'Pays well. Fucking *hurts*, but you know. Gotta go where the work is. Thatcher's Britain.'

Oh! *Politics!* Let's *lever* it in at the very end! No! There has been very little politics tonight. Because, of course, we've come together for a very good cause. But I think, not to disappoint, I ought to say, that there is a great deal to be respected about Mrs Thatch – no, she has a *bad* side, but she has a *good* side, and I think it's important, that we should show her good side, 'cause she's a strong woman, she keeps her word. She never lies. Last general election, she said she would not touch the National Health Service,

she kept her word. When she had a hand operation done, she did it in a private hospital. I respect that. (*Looking out at the audience.*) Ooh, politics goes down like a turd in a water strike! No, but she did. She had a very, very, very sore hand. Do you remember? Mrs Thatcher's hand? Awwww. She had a sore hand – awwww. Four million unemployed, but awwww. Yeah. 'cause the tendons were constricting. That's true. In her hand, the tendons were constricting. And drawing in the fingers. *To form . . . a claaaaaw*!

And the doctors tried to reverse this! They tried to undo what God has done! You cannot do it! First, the claw, then the horns, *then the forked tail* . . .

We're gonna leave it here, ladies and gentlemen, it's been a long night, thank you for coming, my name's Ben Elton, goodnight!

'If God had wanted us to have oral sex, he wouldn't have given us elbows.'

Ben Elton

THE
SECRET
POLICEMAN'S
Biggest
BALL

THE CAMBRIDGE THEATRE, LONDON
30 AUGUST–2 SEPTEMBER 1989

THE SECRET POLICEMAN'S BIGGEST BALL, 1989

In contrast to its predecessor's somewhat strained efforts to appear cheekily à la mode, the 1989 *Secret Policeman's Ball* seemed rather elegiac in tone. With a valedictory appearance by Peter Cook and Dudley Moore, and John Cleese and Michael Palin returning for one final reprise of some Python routines, the show exhibited a special emotional resonance.

When Cook and Moore – the much-loved double act who were back on a London stage together for the first time in sixteen years – first walked onto the stage together to perform their 'Frog and Peach' sketch, they looked both surprised and moved by the warmth (and length) of the ovation they received, with Moore glancing over nervously at Cook while his erstwhile partner smiled shyly back at him as the applause continued. Once they had started the sketch, it only took a matter of seconds before Pete (ad-libbing at whim as usual) was causing Dud (whose script was stuck to his clipboard) to corpse all over again, and the magical dynamics of their relationship were fully re-established. Moore (whose participation had been kept a surprise) was even happier when hopping about as the hopeful unidexter in their 'One Leg Too Few' routine: 'Pete wrote the Tarzan sketch when he was eighteen,' he said admiringly, 'and he's been going rapidly downhill ever since!'

Cleese and Palin, who had started the very first Amnesty event back in 1976, also seemed genuinely pleased to be reunited, with the two of them lapping up the sense of anticipation as they launched into a revised version of the 'Dead Parrot' sketch, as well as a similarly doctored 'Cheese Shop' sketch that went unfilmed. Cleese's intrusions into Palin's 'Biggles Goes to See Bruce Springsteen' were another highlight of each night. Even the younger performers, such as Lenny Henry, Dawn French, Adrian Edmondson and Robbie Coltrane, seemed happy to engage with the air of nostalgia as they helped revive other favourite routines from an earlier time. When the entire cast gathered at the end to accompany Cook and Moore for one final and joyously chaotic rendition of their trademark song 'Goodbye-ee', it really did seem like a fond farewell to some very special performers.

```
                              JENNIFER SAUNDERS
                              20 Park Road
                              Richmond
                              Surrey
                              TW10 6NS
                              Tel: 01-948 4944

        1st June 1989


        Hello.  I'm writing to give you more information about the
        Amnesty International show this year.  You may or may not
        have already been approached - either way I hope you can
        be involved.

        Yes (incredible but true) I am co-directing the show with
        John Cleese and hope to make it a very funny and spontaneous
        evening with the emphasis strongly on comedy rather than
        music.

        The dates of the show will be 30 & 31 Aug, 1 & 2 Sept. and
        we're hoping it'll be an 11 O'clock start.  We cannot
        reasonably expect everyone to do every night - although
        that would be brilliant - but hope that realistically people
        will be able to commit to one or two nights.

        In either event we're not looking for a definite yes or no
        now.  Either John or myself will be in  contact two weeks
        before the show and, out of interest, there will be a
        rehearsal on the Sunday before the show at the venue, which
        looks like being either Her Majesty's or The Palladium.

        The event will be filmed but any person can veto their piece
        if they choose to.  We would like the show this year to be
        truly original as well as exciting and enjoyable for the
        performers themselves.  If there's anything unusual you
        want to do or if you want to link with any of the other
        performers, then just liase with myself or John some time
        before August.

        I really hope you'll be able to take part.

        Yours
```

THE PARROT SKETCH (REVISED EDITION)

JOHN CLEESE & MICHAEL PALIN

The curtain rises to reveal a shop counter. Michael Palin enters, dressed in an overall and smoking a cigarette. At the other side of the stage, John Cleese walks on, holding a parrot cage with a dead parrot in it.

CLEESE: I wish to register . . . a complaint.

(Palin ducks down behind the desk.)

CLEESE: Hello, Miss?

PALIN: What d'you mean, '*Miss*'?

CLEESE: I'm sorry, I have a cold. I wish to make a complaint about this parrot what I purchased not half an hour ago from this very boutique.

PALIN: Oh, yes, the, er, the Norwegian Blue?

CLEESE: The Norwegian Blue.

PALIN: What's wrong with it?

CLEESE: I'll tell you what's wrong with it, my lad – it's dead, that's what's wrong with it!

(He plonks the cage, complete with dead parrot, on the counter. Palin bends down and scrutinises it.)

PALIN: . . . So it is.

(There is shocked laughter and applause. Palin reaches into a drawer and removes some cash. Cleese looks stunned.)

PALIN: Right, here's your money back, and a couple of holiday vouchers. Thank you.

(Palin takes the cage and leaves. Cleese walks away, dazed.)

CLEESE: Well, you can't say Thatcher hasn't changed *some* things.

THE FROG AND PEACH
PETER COOK & DUDLEY MOORE

The scene is The Frog and Peach restaurant. Moore is smartly dressed and holding a clipboard. Cook is wearing a deerstalker hat and a tweed suit. The audience applauds them as they sit down opposite each other.

MOORE: I'm talking tonight to Sir Arthur Greeb-Streebling.

COOK: Oh, no, you're not!

MOORE: What?

COOK: No, no, you're not at all. You're talking to Sir Arthur Streeb-Greebling.

MOORE: Oh . . .

COOK: You're confusing me with Sir Arthur Greeb-Streebling.

MOORE: Ah, right, yes.

COOK: Yes, my name is Streeb-Greebling. The 'T' is silent, as in 'fox'.

MOORE: Right, I'm so sorry.

COOK: Quite all right.

MOORE: (*To the audience.*) I would like to ask Sir Arthur something about his very unique restaurant, The Frog and Peach.

COOK: Well, this seems like an ideal opportunity, really, what with me being here and, ah, you being there.

MOORE: Yes, indeed, yes.

COOK: A wonderful opportunity.

MOORE: Yes, indeed.

COOK: Seize it!

MOORE: I . . . I certainly will. How did the idea of The Frog and Peach actually come to you?

COOK: The idea for the Frog and Peach came to me in the bath. I suddenly thought to myself, 'Where can a young couple, with not too much money to spend, feeling a bit hungry, feeling a bit peckish, where can they go and get a really big frog and a good fine peach?' And answer came there none. And so on this premise I founded the restaurant.

MOORE: On these premises, in fact.

COOK: (*Looking around at his restaurant.*) On *these* precise premises, yes, I founded The Frog and Peach.

MOORE: How long ago did you actually start this venture?

COOK: God, that's a tricky one. Ah . . . certainly within living memory. I believe it was shortly after World War Two.

MOORE: Ah, yes.

COOK: Do you remember that? Absolutely *ghastly* business!

MOORE: Yes, yes.

COOK: I was completely against it.

MOORE: I . . . I think we all were.

COOK: Yes, well, *I* wrote a letter.

MOORE: Getting back to The Frog and Peach . . .

COOK: Of course, yes.

MOORE: How has business been?

COOK: Let me answer that question in two parts. Business hasn't been, and there hasn't been any business. The last forty-five years have been rather a lean time for us up at the old F&P.

MOORE: But don't you feel you're somewhat at a disadvantage, being stuck out here in the middle of a bog in the heart of the Yorkshire Moors?

COOK: I think the word 'disadvantage' is awfully well chosen here, yes. But I thought at the time, rightly or wrongly, or possibly both . . .

MOORE: Yes?

COOK: That people in this country were crying out for a restaurant without a parking problem. And here in the middle of a bog in the heart of the Yorkshire Moors there is no problem parking the car. A little difficulty extricating it, but the parking here is a joy.

MOORE: But don't you feel, though, that you're at a slight disadvantage with regard to the menu?

COOK: Have you seen it?

MOORE: Oh, very briefly.

COOK: That's the only way to see it. It's so . . . so . . . what's the word? So *limited*. There are only two items on the menu. First of all, there is *Frog à la Peche*, which is basically a large frog is brought

to your table covered in boiling Cointreau and with a peach stuck in its mouth. One of the most disgusting sights I've ever seen. The only alternative to *Frog à la Peche* is even worse: *Peche à la Frog*. *Peche à la Frog*. A peach is brought to your table by the waiter, again covered in boiling Cointreau –

MOORE: The waiter?

COOK: Very often. Very often the waiter is covered in boiling Cointreau. But the policy here is to aim the Cointreau at the peach.

MOORE: Ah, yes.

COOK: That's the policy. The peach is then sliced open to reveal 300 squiggling black tadpoles. It is *the* most nauseating sight I've ever seen. Enough to put you off your food. Which is a damned good thing, considering what the food is like.

MOORE: Yes. This is fascinating stuff, of course, but I would say that the whole *venture* of The Frog and Peach has been, ah, a little disastrous.

COOK: (*Thoughtfully.*) I don't think I'd use the word 'disastrous' here.

MOORE: No?

COOK: I think 'catastrophic' would be nearer the mark. The whole thing has been a gigantic failure and a huge catastrophe.

MOORE: Yes, but do you feel that you have learned from your mistakes?

COOK: Oh, certainly. Certainly. I have learned from my mistakes, and I am sure I could repeat them exactly.

MOORE: Thank you, Sir Arthur Greeb-Streebling.

COOK: Streeb-Greebling!

THE ROYAL FAMILY'S POLL TAX

SPITTING IMAGE

The Royal Family Spitting Image puppets – Prince Philip, the Queen Mother, the Queen and Prince Charles – are seated around a banqueting table, having breakfast. A royal lackey lurks in the background.

QUEEN: One must say how nice it is to be sitting down to a nice quiet breakfast.

PHILIP: PULL!

(*Prince Charles throws a piece of toast into the air. Prince Philip fires a blunderbuss at it.*)

QUEEN MUM: Ooh! Is it my birthday again?!

LACKEY: (*Obsequiously.*) Erm, Ma'am . . . ?

QUEEN: Ah, good – the Royal Mail's arrived! (*To lackey.*) Thank you, Lickbottom.

LACKEY: Ma'ammmm.

QUEEN: This one's for you, Mummy.

QUEEN MUM: Oooh, I wonder what it can be?

QUEEN: Ah . . . and this one's addressed to . . . 'Theo Cupier'. Some Greek friend of yours perhaps, Philip?

PHILIP: No, no, no, you silly souvlaki! That says 'The Occupier'!

QUEEN: Oh, I *see*. Oh, me again, is it?

CHARLES: Well, it has been for the last thirty-six years, dammit.

PHILIP: (*Throwing a banana at him.*) Stop whingeing, boy! You green berk. Go on, Liz! *Open* it!

QUEEN: Very well. I now declare this envelope . . . open.

PHILIP: What is it, Liz?

QUEEN: Oh. It says 'Community Charge'.

QUEEN MUM: Oooh, smashing! I like a nice game of Monopoly! Bags I'm the old boot!

CHARLES: No, no, no, no, no, Granny – it's the poll tax! Complete within twenty-one days or you get fined fifty pounds!

QUEEN MUM: (*Playing with her shoe.*) Fifty pounds? Oooh – I haven't even passed 'Go' yet!

PHILIP: What exactly does the form *say*?

CHARLES: It says we have to list all our other homes.

QUEEN: What, you mean Sandringham, Windsor?

PHILIP: . . . Kensington Palace, Clarence House?

QUEEN MUM: . . . Park Lane, Mayfair, the Old Kent Road!

PHILIP: Oh, blimey! This is going to cost us a *fortune*!

QUEEN: Ah.

CHARLES: One could always . . . flee the country?

QUEEN: (*Looming over him.*) Oh, *Charles*!

CHARLES: Sorry – sorry – just an idea, Mama.

QUEEN MUM: Oooh, no, he's right, you know – we could all run away to Balmoral! They'd never think of making us pay the poll tax in Scotland!

(*Philip bangs his head on the table.*)

THE ARGUMENT CLINIC

JOHN CLEESE, MICHAEL PALIN, DAWN FRENCH & CHRIS LANGHAM

There are three desks on the stage, with, left to right, Dawn French, Chris Langham and John Cleese seated behind them. Enter Michael Palin stage left.

PALIN: Ah – good morning. I'd like to have an argument, please . . .

FRENCH: Right. Now, are you sure you wouldn't prefer a lengthy moist rogering?

PALIN: Um, no, just an argument, please.

FRENCH: Righty-o . . . Now, do you want the single argument, or can I offer you a course?

PALIN: Ah, well, what is the cost?

FRENCH: Well, it's two pounds for a five-minute argument, but only fifteen pounds for a course of ten.

PALIN: Oh, well, I think I'll just take the five minutes and see how it goes from there.

FRENCH: All right, all right. Now, let's see who's free. Mr Wobble is free, but he's a bit conciliatory, Mr Wobble.

PALIN: Oh. Nice name.

FRENCH: Erm, now what about Mr Nicholls, room 12?

PALIN: Thank you very much, thank you.

(*Palin approaches Room 12, opening the door.*)

LANGHAM: What do you want?

PALIN: What?

LANGHAM: Don't give me that, you snotty-faced heap of parrot droppings!

PALIN: Well, I was told outside –

LANGHAM: Shut your festering gob, you *tit*! Your type makes me puke! You scrofulous, toffee-nosed, vacuous *pervert*!

PALIN: Look, I came here for an argument! I didn't –

LANGHAM: *Oh*! Oh, I'm *sorry*! This is Abuse.

PALIN: Oh, I see! That explains it!

LANGHAM: (*Warmly.*) Yes. You want, erm, 12A – it's next door. Yes.

PALIN: Oh, I see! Thank you very much! Sorry.

LANGHAM: No, it's okay, it's okay.

(*Palin exits the room.*)

LANGHAM: . . . Stupid git.

(*Palin opens the door of Room 12A.*)

PALIN: Er – is this the right room for an argument?

CLEESE: I've told you once.

(*Palin looks puzzled.*)

PALIN: Er – no you haven't.

CLEESE: Yes, I have.

PALIN: When?

CLEESE: Just now.

PALIN: No, you didn't.

CLEESE: Yes I did.

PALIN: You didn't!

CLEESE: I did!

PALIN: You didn't!

CLEESE: I'm telling you I *did*!

PALIN: You *didn't*!

CLEESE: (*Suddenly sounding very business-like.*) I'm so sorry – is this the five-minute argument or the full half hour?

PALIN: Oh! Just the five minutes.

CLEESE: Just the five minutes.

PALIN: (*Sitting.*) That's right.

(*Cleese fills in a form.*)

CLEESE: Thank you. Anyway: I did.

PALIN: (*Good-humouredly.*) You most certainly did not!

CLEESE: Now, let's get one thing quite clear. I most definitely told you.

PALIN: No, you didn't.

CLEESE: Yes, I did.

PALIN: No, you didn't.

CLEESE: Yes, I did.

PALIN: No, you didn't.

CLEESE: Yes, I did.

PALIN: No, you didn't.

CLEESE: Yes, I did.

PALIN: No, you didn't.

CLEESE: Yes, I did.

PALIN: No, you didn't.

CLEESE: Yes, I did.

(They degenerate into just repeating these phrases at each other rapidly for a few more seconds.)

PALIN: Look, this isn't an *argument*!

CLEESE: Yes, it is!

PALIN: No, it isn't! It's just contradiction!

CLEESE: No, it isn't!

PALIN: It *is*!

CLEESE: It is *not*!

PALIN: You just contradicted me!

CLEESE: No, I never!

PALIN: You *did*!

CLEESE: No, no, no, no, *no*!

PALIN: You did, just *then*!

CLEESE: Nonsense!

PALIN: Oh, this is futile!

(There is a brief pause.)

CLEESE: No, it isn't.

PALIN: Yes, it is. I came here for a *good* argument.

CLEESE: No, you *didn't*. You came for an *argument*.

PALIN: An argument isn't just contradiction!

CLEESE: Well. It can be.

PALIN: No, it *can't*! An argument is a connected series of statements intended to establish a proposition.

CLEESE: No, it isn't.

PALIN: Yes, it is! It isn't *just* contradiction!

CLEESE: Look, if I *argue* with you, I must take up a contrary position!

PALIN: Yeah, but that isn't just saying, 'No, it isn't.'

CLEESE: Yes, it *is*!

PALIN: No, it *isn't*!

CLEESE: Yes, it is!

PALIN: No, it isn't!

CLEESE: Yes, it is!

PALIN: No, it isn't!

CLEESE: Yes, it is!

PALIN: No, it *isn't*!

CLEESE: Yes, it *is*!

(*They degenerate once more into just rapidly saying these phrases to each other for a few more seconds.*)

PALIN: (*Slamming his hand on the desk.*) LOOK! Argument is an intellectual process! Contradiction is just the automatic gainsaying of anything the other person says –

CLEESE: No, it isn't!

PALIN: It *is*!

CLEESE: It is *not*!

PALIN: Now, *look* –

(*Coolly and very abruptly, Cleese rings a bell on the desk.*)

CLEESE: Thank you, good morning.

PALIN: W-What?

CLEESE: That's it. Good morning.

PALIN: Oh. I was just getting interested.

CLEESE: Ah. I'm sorry. The five minutes is up.

PALIN: That was never five minutes just now!

CLEESE: I'm afraid it was.

PALIN: (*Enthusiastically.*) Oh, no, it wasn't!

(*Cleese just stares at him.*)

CLEESE: I'm sorry. I'm not allowed to argue any more.

PALIN: *What?*

CLEESE: If you want me to go on *arguing*, you'll have to pay for another five minutes.

PALIN: (*Spluttering.*) What?? That was *never* five minutes just now!

(*Cleese whistles to himself.*)

PALIN: Oh, come *on!*

(*Cleese continues whistling.*)

PALIN: This is ridiculous!

CLEESE: (*Calmly.*) If you want me to go on *arguing*, you'll have to pay for another five minutes.

PALIN: Oh, all right. (*He hands over another five-pound note.*) There you are.

CLEESE: Thank you.

(*Although Cleese pockets the money, he continues to ignore Palin and just stares into space.*)

PALIN: Well?

CLEESE: Well what?

PALIN: . . . That was never five minutes –

CLEESE: Look, I just told you. If you want me to go on *arguing*, you'll have to *pay* for another five minutes.

PALIN: Yeah? Well, I just paid!

CLEESE: No, you didn't!

PALIN: *I did!*

CLEESE: *You did not!*

PALIN: *I did!*

CLEESE: *You never did!*

PALIN: *I did!*

CLEESE: *You never did!*

PALIN: *I did!*

CLEESE: *You never did!*

PALIN: Look – I don't want to argue about it –

CLEESE: Right, well, I'm very sorry, but you didn't *pay*!

PALIN: *Aha!* If I didn't *pay*, why are you *arguing*? *A-haaah*! Gotcha!

(*Cleese ponders this for a moment.*)

CLEESE: No, you haven't.

PALIN: Yes, I have. If you're *arguing*, I must have paid.

CLEESE: Not necessarily. I *could* be arguing in my spare time.

PALIN: Oh, this is ridiculous!

CLEESE: No, it isn't.

PALIN: *YES, IT IS!*

(*They degenerate into contradicting one another again. The lights fade out.*)

IMPROVISATION
FRENCH & SAUNDERS

Dawn French and Jennifer Saunders walk onto the stage and address the audience directly.

SAUNDERS: Thank you very much. We're French and Saunders, and we're going to do something a little bit *different* this evening. Er, it's called . . . 'Improvisation' –

FRENCH: And it's very, very dangerous!

SAUNDERS: Now, some of you –

FRENCH: *Very* dangerous.

SAUNDERS: Shut up. Some of you may have seen this . . . somewhere else, on television, somewhere like that . . . Ah, for those of you that *don't* know, what it involves is Dawn and I making up a –

(*French embarks on some ludicrous 'warm up' exercises.*)

SAUNDERS: . . . Do that in a minute. Do that in a minute, when I've finished.

FRENCH: I'm just . . . I'm warming up.

SAUNDERS: I *know* . . . Erm, what it actually involves is Dawn and I making up a sketch on stage, as we go along. In a minute, I'm going to ask for some help from *you* – I want *you* to shout out just some names of some famous people. We will pick two people, and *become* those people, on stage, in a situation. Like, for instance, er . . . steam bath, steam ship . . . something like that. Steam bath. Let's say steam bath, for this evening.

FRENCH: Steam bath . . .

SAUNDERS: Okay? So, can you just shout out some names and we'll pick a couple? Thank you.

(*The audience shout out names.*)

SAUNDERS: Claire Rayner?

AUDIENCE MEMBER: Linda Lovelace!

SAUNDERS: All right.

FRENCH: Thank you. Thank you.

SAUNDERS: All right. We've got Claire Rayner and you've got . . .

FRENCH: Linda Lovelace.

SAUNDERS: Okay. So, Claire Rayner, Linda Lovelace, in a steam bath. All right?

FRENCH: How will we know exactly when to go into character?

SAUNDERS: Because I'll clap my hands.

FRENCH: Oh, I see.

SAUNDERS: So when I clap my hands . . . sorry, when I've *clapped* my hands, we're in character. Okay? Are you ready?

FRENCH: Right, right.

SAUNDERS: Here we go . . . One, two, three – (*Claps hands.*)

FRENCH: (*Approaching Saunders.*) Actually, can I just ask you about Linda Lovelace?

(*Rattled, Saunders hisses something to her.*)

FRENCH: What? Oh! Sorry! (*She retreats back to her original position.*) Sorry!

(*They do nothing for a short while, unsure of how to proceed. After a couple of seconds, French starts to mime 'sexily', touching her breasts,*) *and completes the effect with strange facial expressions. Saunders looks exasperated.*)

SAUNDERS: (*Sternly.*) Have you got a problem?

FRENCH: Erm . . . *Oh*, I know! I know something she does!

(*French adopts a strange stance, then gallops around the stage. Saunders looks bewildered.*)

SAUNDERS: Sorry, I didn't know she did that. You threw me then. I didn't know she did that.

FRENCH: No, she *doesn't* do that.

SAUNDERS: Well, what did *you* do it for?!?

FRENCH: I made it up.

SAUNDERS: Well, *don't* just make things up like that! That's just *stupid*!

FRENCH: But I thought –

SAUNDERS: Don't just make things up like that! It just ruins it if you do that!

FRENCH: I thought that's what this was supposed to –

SAUNDERS: (*Abruptly.*) Got to do another one now.

FRENCH: You're supposed to –

SAUNDERS: God! We were doing *so* well! Sorry, ladies and gentlemen. Will you shout out a couple more names? We'll do another one quickly.

(*The audience shout more names.*)

SAUNDERS: Sorry? Gloria Hunniford? Gloria Hunniford and . . . Nanette Newman, thank you.

FRENCH/SAUNDERS: . . . Gloria Hunniford and Nanette Newman . . .

SAUNDERS: . . . in a steam bath.

FRENCH: Oh, all right.

SAUNDERS: I'd better be Nanette, I think. Gloria – ready?

FRENCH: I can't *do* Gloria!

SAUNDERS: (*Ignoring her protestations.*) Ready?

(*French looks panicked. Saunders claps her hands.*)

FRENCH: Oh, *no*, I'm not ready, I'm *not* ready!

SAUNDERS: I've done it. I've done it!

FRENCH: I'm not *ready*!

(*As Nanette Newman was advertising washing up liquid at the time, Saunders duly mimes washing up some dishes.*)

FRENCH: (*In terrible Irish accent.*) That's good. That's good . . . what you're doing.

SAUNDERS: (*Annoyed.*) Thank you. Thank you very much.

FRENCH: Oh – I know! I know what she does!

(*Once again, French adopts a strange stance, then gallops around the stage in a demented fashion. Saunders looks on, aghast.*)

SAUNDERS: (*Beside herself with irritation.*) I told you *not* to do that, didn't I?

FRENCH: Yeah, but Gloria Hunniford does do that!

SAUNDERS: *SHE DOES NOT DO THAT*!

FRENCH: She does!

SAUNDERS: I have NEVER seen her do that!

FRENCH: She does! She . . . you don't –

SAUNDERS: You've just ruined it *again*!

FRENCH: . . . You don't even know Gloria!

SAUNDERS: She does not do that!

FRENCH: I know Gloria, and she does that all the –

SAUNDERS: You've got *one* more chance!

FRENCH: That's not fair –

SAUNDERS: ONE MORE CHANCE!

FRENCH: That's really not fair!

SAUNDERS: *FRANK BOUGH AND JUDITH CHALMERS. IN A STEAM BATH. NOW!*

FRENCH: All right, all right – well, which one am I?

SAUNDERS: Frank Bough.

FRENCH: I KNOW *THAT!* (*Storms back to her position.*) Right. Frank Bough. Right.

(*Saunders claps her hands.*)

FRENCH: No – I'm not fu –

SAUNDERS: I've done it!

(*A tense silence as they fume at each other. After a couple of seconds, French gets ready to gallop across the stage again. Saunders looks furious. French gears up to gallop, but at the last minute breaks off.*)

FRENCH: Ooh, look! There's something just *there*, look! Something on the stage, *look!!*

(*Saunders examines the stage. French walks away, grinning broadly, then prepares to do the gallop again.*)

SAUNDERS: Don't do that. If you're thinking of doing that –

(*French giggles and launches into her gallop. She gets about three paces away before Saunders grabs her ear and tweaks it, hard.*)

FRENCH: (*Screaming.*) Ow! *Oww!*

SAUNDERS: I *told* you not to do that, didn't I?

FRENCH: *Ow!* You hurt my ear! (*Addresses someone in the wings.*) Is my ear bleeding? My ear's bleeding!

SAUNDERS: You've just ruined that now!

FRENCH: My ear's bleeding, apparently!

SAUNDERS: You've just *ruined* that!

FRENCH: You bitch!

(*French storms off stage.*)

SAUNDERS: Sorry about that, ladies and gentlemen! Complete fiasco! There's something else for you now. Sorry about that . . .

(*She leaves the stage, humiliated.*)

BIGGLES GOES TO SEE BRUCE SPRINGSTEEN

MICHAEL PALIN

There is chair in the centre of an empty stage. Michael Palin enters, carrying a book, walks over to the chair and sits down.

PALIN: *Bedtime Story* tonight comes from the prolific pen of Captain W.E. Johns. It's one of the later Biggles books – it's called *Biggles Goes to See Bruce Springsteen*, 1976.

(*He reads from the book.*)

Biggles was tired. He lit a cigarette and exhaled, slowly and thoughtfully. He gave a little cough. Then, a slightly bigger cough. Then, an enormous, rheumy, wheezing wrench of a cough which nearly flung him off his chair. He gasped, for one brief, gravelly intake of breath, but was cut short by a retching, wracking, heaving, spume-ridden roar that seemed to split his chest like a sledgehammer.

Ah. That was better.

Suddenly, the rough wooden door of 'E' Hut was pushed aside, and Algy entered, brandishing a newspaper. He was clearly very stoned. He climbed up onto Biggles' desk, and began dancing provocatively.

'Hey, Algy, for bally heck's sake, watch out for those meteorological charts!' cried Biggles.

'Hey, man, I'm so happy!' warbled Algy, his fleshy white body cavorting crazily in the flickering light of Biggles' hurricane lamp. 'Look, man, *look!*' grinned Algy, jabbing his finger at a copy of the *Midshire Advertiser*.

Biggles' eye was drawn to a large advert, beneath an article by Paul Johnson called 'Lighting Fires with Communists': 'Finally, Midshire is ready for Bruce Springsteen!' he read. 'Who the bally heck is Bruce Springsteen?' queried Biggles, testily.

'Who is Bruce Springsteen?! Where have you been all these years, man – under a *rock*?!'

Biggles hated Algy when he was like that. He would talk all hip, and come out with silly suggestions, like getting Bob Marley to play the Royal Tournament. On this particular day, Squadron Leader Bigglesworth was in no mood for Algy's little games.

'Look, Algy, go and lie down. We've got some heavy flying tomorrow.'

Biggles' remark seemed to send Algy into paroxysms of helpless laughter, and he fell back against the wall, grabbing at

Biggles' huge 'WE RULE IT' map of the world. A crack appeared just outside Barcelona, and running across Europe, down through the Caucasus, and was accelerating into Southern Assam, when Algy toppled helplessly off the filing cabinet onto the floor.

He lay there shaking, the Southern Hemisphere draped across his stomach.

'Oh, that's good, man, that is so good! Ha ha ha! Oh, you're beautiful, man!'

Biggles could stand it no longer. In a couple of strides, he was beside Algy. Well, actually, he was a little beyond him. One stride would probably have been enough in that small room. He turned, and took half a stride back. But that took him too far the other way, and when he bent down he couldn't quite reach Algy. So he stood up, and went back to where he'd originally started from, and this time did only one stride. It brought him right up beside Algy. In fact, a little too close this time . . . he'd over-compensated, and now could hardly bend down at all. He took half a stride back, and tried again. This time, he found himself in quite an interesting position, astride Algy's body.

The rough wooden door of 'E' Hut was suddenly pushed aside, and Ginger entered.

'*Oh*, I'm sorry, Biggles!' he declared, quickly.

'No, no, come in, old chap, you can help me!' He motioned him to a chair. Biggles sat down and lit a cigarette.

'Well, spill the gen, Ginger!' He drew heavily on the thin blue smoke.

'Bruce Springsteen's coming to the Midshire Odeon, sir!'

Biggles exhaled slowly. He coughed. Involuntarily at first, then, with a quick throat-clearing rumble, which developed into an uncontrollable, shattering, rasping, sepulchral rattle of mucus and phlegm, which nearly turned his lungs inside out. Oh, God, what a cough!

The Midshire Odeon had never seen anything like it. Their previous highest attendance had been ten – when Michael

Dennison and Dulcie Gray toured in 1927, with the Arthur Spendlove Partially Nude Aerial Ballet. Who were arrested during the performance.

'I'm so bally excited I can hardly keep this kite on course!' shouted Algy, as the twin-engine filtered Morgan bi-plane headed for Midshire International airport. Ginger was –

(*Suddenly, John Cleese appears, half in his underwear and half dressed as the Pope.*)

CLEESE: Have you got the dressing-room key again?

PALIN: Now?

CLEESE: Come on!

PALIN: *Now?*

CLEESE: Yes. *Now.* Oh, come *on!*

(*Palin roots in his trouser pocket and comes up with some keys. Cleese leaves, muttering to himself. Palin resumes reading from the book.*)

. . . Ginger was reading: '*Born to Run* is a work of complete and unadulterated genius. It makes the Sistine Chapel look like the toilets of Millwall Football Club.' He had in his hands a huge book called *6,423 Wonderful Things about Bruce Springsteen*, and he was navigating with his feet.

Suddenly. Ginger lowered his book, and a trace of anxiety crept into his otherwise quite un-anxious voice.

'You *have* got the tickets, haven't you, Algy?'

'Sure thing, Ginger! I've tucked them into my flying suit, where no one'll find them!' shouted Algy above the roar of the two seventeen-horsepower Spenger and Cotteswoode single-cam engines.

Ginger grimaced. Algy always put the tickets down there, and, though they were safe, they were nasty and sweaty by the time they got to the concert.

'I say, Algy!' he shouted. 'D'you think I could have my ticket now?'

'Okay, I'll have a go!' bellowed Algy, and, leaning back, he began to undo his flying costume. Biggles looked up in alarm. 'Put it away, Algy, for God's sake!'

'Just looking for the bally tickets, old bean!' reassured Algy.

Biggles ruminated on how much nicer Algy was when he talked like that . . . when suddenly, Algy turned, a dawning look of horror settling across his handsome –

(*From the wings, some keys are thrown. They tinkle to the floor by Palin's chair, and he stoops to pick them up.*) Thank you, love – er, John! (*Looks embarrassed.*) Goes back a long way. Erm – well, not that far . . . about halfway.

Anyway, er . . . A dawning look of horror settled across his handsome, non-spotty features. That's Algy, who I was talking about, the minute before the . . . erm, keys were thrown on by my, erm, 'room partner' . . . chum.

'Oh, shit!' conjectured Algy.

'Wash your mouth out!' ordered Biggles, dropping his sewing.

'*Shee-it!*' repeated Algy. 'They've gone! The fucking tickets have *gone!*'

Biggles slapped Algy hard across the face. 'Don't you dare use language like that aboard this twin-engine Hillter-Morton bi-plane!'

Algy turned and gave Biggles six left jabs, and a swinging right to the jaw. Biggles hurtled towards the back of the plane, hit his head a glancing blow on the first-aid kit, and slumped into unconsciousness.

'I gotta see Bruce!' screamed Ginger, hysterically. 'I gotta see him! I gotta see the rock sensation of the seventies! I'm gonna jump!'

'Don't be a fool!' yelled Algy. 'There's only one parachute!'

'And I'm wearing it!' roared Ginger in triumph, pushing Algy aside and hurling himself out of the plane.

'No, you're not!' screamed Algy above the roar of the seven-horsepower engines. Ginger paused in mid-fall. Algy was right.

What he had thought was a parachute ripcord was only his hearing aid. He pulled it hopefully, but it just came out of his ear.

'Don't worry! I'm coming after you! We'll get to see Springsteen!' yelled Algy, as he clambered out of the plane and dropped towards Ginger.

'Don't forget the parachute!' screamed an accelerating Ginger.

'Ohhhhhhh . . . .*SHIT*!' ejaculated Algy.

When Biggles came round, he realised he was the only one left on the plane. He grabbed the joystick, and eased himself behind the controls.

He looked down at the frozen countryside below him. Algy and Ginger were awfully close to the fields. It was a pity, really. He'd liked them both. But what were two rather stock fictional characters compared to the greatest white musical talent to emerge in America this decade?

Biggles set course, north north-east for Midshire. It was eight-thirty. The concert should have started at eight, but Biggles knew the roadies would still be bringing the guitars on. He settled into his seat, and smiled to himself as he felt the cool, crisp assurance of the two front-circle tickets in the lining of his old flying jacket.

Finally, Biggles was ready for Bruce Springsteen.

'Don't you dare use language like that aboard this twin-engine Hillter-Morton bi-plane!'

Michael Palin

SPECIAL BRANCH
CHRIS LANGHAM

There is an empty stage with the curtain down. Chris Langham shuffles awkwardly on, covered head to toe in thick foliage. He turns – and we see he's holding a mobile phone and is in the process of making a call. He is completely unaware of the audience.

Red Baboon, this is Blind Mullet. Red Baboon, this is Blind Mullet. Red . . . hello? Hello, is that Special Branch? Yeah, I was trying to contact, er, Red Baboon, actually. No, no, I don't know the extension . . . erm, could you look it up? 'Nothing under Red Baboon?' Er, no . . . er, could you try 'Derek'?

Er, obviously for security reasons, we don't use last names here. Would you? Thank you. 'Derek in catering'? No, no, I don't think that would be him. 'Derek in records'? No. 'Derek the secret agent'? Yes, that would *probably* be him, yes! Well, could you page him in the bar? Thank you!

Red Baboon, this is Blind Mullet. Red Baboon, yes, this is . . . Blind Mullet? Bli – . . . Trevor, the new bloke, from Purley. Yes!

Well, erm, daybreak found me in position, in the suspect's front garden. Oh, you're absolutely right, er, the camouflage outfit was an absolute stroke of genius on your part. From my vantage point behind the rockery, I could keep an eye on his every move, while at the same time blending effortlessly in with my herbaceous environment.

Yes, but at that point, er – as these anarchists are notoriously prone to do – er, our man did the unexpected . . . Well, Derek, he went out. Yes, and at that point, my fiendishly clever disguise became something less of a help and I must say more of a hindrance, to be honest. Well, erm, from the point of view of being the only man dressed as a tree on the District Line, Derek.

Well, there then followed a nightmarish journey across the park, on what I must say appeared to me to be 'National Rottweiler Incontinence Day' . . . And he then joined forces with a whole crowd of subversives who seemed to have gathered for an event. And that's where I am now. I found a quiet place to speak to you unobserved.

(*At that moment he turns and moves some of the foliage away from his eyes. This allows him, for the first time, to see the audience.*)

Er, Derek? Everyone's looking at me! No, I'm not being paranoid, they really *are* looking at me! Ah, I think you'd better get over here right away – I will try and keep their attention occupied, okay?

(*He whips off the headpiece of his disguise, revealing his face.*)

Hello! Um, I know that, erm, appearances are against me, but I'm not a secret, er, civil servant. I'm just like the rest of you. Er . . . a communist. And a homosexual, probably. How well I remember that first day when I first succumbed to the lures of Janus . . . It was, erm, during my medical, as it happens. I suddenly found myself overwhelmed by a great surge of emotion for the doctor. Went home, found myself pining by the phone. Lost my appetite. Couldn't stop thinking about the man. And suddenly, it occurred to me . . . 'My God! You're a latent homosexual!' Well, I thought, better latent than never.

And, under the pretext of a fraudulent haemorrhoidal attack, I made a second appointment. I went back for another examination. As he probed the most intimate recesses of my body, I was in seventh heaven, when suddenly the doctor said, 'Jesus Christ!' I said, 'What is it?', he said 'Hold still.' (*Mimes pulling something.*) He said, 'You've got a dozen red long-stemmed roses up your bum!' I said, 'Read the card, read the *card*!' So embarrassing!

(*A man in a security uniform walks onstage.*)

Ah! Derek! These are the people I – Er, what are you doing?

(*The man grabs Langham and bundles him off.*)

These are the people I was telling you about!!

HEADMASTER AND PUPIL

STEPHEN FRY & HUGH LAURIE

The scene is the headmaster's office. Fry, as the headmaster, is sitting behind the desk. Laurie, as the pupil, enters looking very meek.

FRY: Ah, Terry, Terry, come in, come in.

LAURIE: Yes, sir.

FRY: Ah, do you know why I've sent for you, Terry?

LAURIE: Er, not really, sir, no.

FRY: (*Ponders the response.*) 'Not really, not really.' Well, er, Terry, first of all, congratulations on winning the school poetry prize.

LAURIE: Thank you, sir.

FRY: Mr Drip tells me that it is the most mature and exciting poem he has ever received from a pupil. Don't suck your thumb, boy.

LAURIE: (*Bemused.*) I . . . I'm not, sir.

FRY: No, that was just a piece of general advice for the future. Now, er, Terry. Terry, Terry. Terence. It's about this poem, really . . . I read it, Terry. I can't pretend to be much of a judge of literature – I'm an English teacher, not a homosexual – but I have to say it worried me.

LAURIE: Oh?

FRY: Yes, it worried me. I have it here, in fact. (*Looks at it.*) Er, 'Inked Ravens of Despair Claw Holes in the Arse of the World's Mind'. I mean, what kind of title for a poem is that?

LAURIE: Well, er, it's *my* title, sir.

FRY: 'Inked Ravens of Despair Claw Holes in the *Arse* of the World's Mind'? Are you *sickening* for something?

LAURIE: Well, you know, I think that's what the poem explores.

FRY: Oh, it *explores*, does it? I see. Explores. Right, well, let's have a look at this, then. (*Reads again from poem.*) 'Scrotal threats unhorse a question of flowers'. I mean, is it a *girl*? Is that the problem?

LAURIE: Well, er, it's not something I can explain, sir, you know, it's all in the poem.

FRY: It certainly is 'all in the poem'! (*Reads again.*) 'I asked for answers and got a head full of heroin in return'. Now, Terry, listen to me. Who's been giving you heroin?

LAURIE: No one, sir.

FRY: No, no, Terry, I must insist – *it's in the poem*! 'I got a head full of heroin in return'. This is a police matter, Terry, you *must* tell me!

LAURIE: Sir, no one has given me heroin!

FRY: Oh, I see, so this poem is just a fiction, is it, a fantasy, a lie?

LAURIE: Oh, no, it's all true, it's autobiographical.

FRY: Well, then, Terry, I *must* insist you *tell* me!

LAURIE: No, it's a metaphor.

FRY: Metaphor? *How* metaphor?

LAURIE: (*In a self-admiring tone.*) It means, 'I came to school to learn, but all I got was junk instead of answers.'

FRY: Junk? But the GCSE syllabus is rigidly adhered to in every –

LAURIE: You know . . . it's just an opinion.

FRY: I see. And is this 'just an opinion', too? (*Reads again.*) 'When time fell wanking to the floor, they kicked his teeth'. 'Time fell

wanking'? I mean, is it just put in to shock? 'Time fell wanking' –
what does it *mean*?

LAURIE: It's a quotation.

FRY: Quotation? A quotation? Who from? It's not Milton, and I'm
pretty sure it can't be Wordsworth!

LAURIE: It's Bowie.

FRY: Bowie? *Bowie?*

LAURIE: David Bowie.

FRY: Oh! And is this David Bowie, too? (*Reads again.*) 'My body
disgusts, damp grease wafts sweat balls from sweat balls and thigh
fungus'. I mean, do you *wash?*

LAURIE: Er, yeah, of course!

FRY: Well, then, why does your body disgust you? It looks perfectly
all right to me – why can't you write about *meadows* or something?

LAURIE: I've never seen a meadow.

FRY: Well, what do you think the *imagination* is for, hmmm? (*Reads
again.*) 'A girl strips in my mind, squeezes my last pumping drop
of hope and rolls me over to sleep alone'. You're fifteen years old,
Terry, what's going on?

LAURIE: Well, I think that's what the poem –

FRY: 'Explores', yes. I don't understand any more, I *don't*
understand!

LAURIE: Well, sir, you were young once.

FRY: Well, in a sense, yes.

LAURIE: Well, didn't you ever feel like that?

FRY: You mean did I ever want to 'fireball the dead cities of the
mind and watch the skin peel and warp'? Then, thankfully, I can
say no, I did not. I might have been unhappy from time to time, if

I broke my penknife or lost my stamp album, but I certainly didn't write it down and show it to people.

LAURIE: (*Loftily.*) Huh, perhaps it might have better if you had!

FRY: Oh, *might* it, oh, *might* it, young Terry? (*Reads again.*) I am one of 'the unhappy bubbles of anal wind popping and winking in the mortal bath', am I? Oh, I *see*, your silence tells me everything! I am! I *am* an unhappy bubble of anal wind!

LAURIE: Well, y'know, that's just how I see it – that's valid.

FRY: *Valid*? You're not talking about a banknote! You're calling *your* headmaster 'an unhappy bubble of anal wind'!

LAURIE: Well, I'm one, too!

FRY: Oh, well, as long as we're *all* unhappy bubbles of anal wind popping and winking in the mortal bath then I suppose there's no problem! But I don't propose to advertise the fact to parents. If this is poetry, then every lavatory wall in England is an anthology. What's happened to the *Book of English Verse*? Where's *that* in all this, hmm?

LAURIE: (*Smugly.*) Huh, that's the lavatory paper!

FRY: Is that *clever*?

LAURIE: (*Awkwardly.*) I don't know.

FRY: I suppose it's another quotation from Derek Bowie, is it? I *don't* understand any more, I *do not* understand!

LAURIE: Well, it's not surprising, sir, you know, you're frustrated, perhaps. After all, it's a lonely job.

FRY: You're right, I *am* frustrated. And it *is* a lonely job. I am assailed by doubt and wracked by fear.

LAURIE: Well, then, write it down.

FRY: Hmm?

LAURIE: Write it down – get it out of your system. 'Assailed by doubt / Wracked by fear'.

FRY: Yes . . . yes! (*Picks up pen.*) 'Assailed by doubt . . . wracked by fear . . . er . . . tossed in a wrecked mucus foam of . . . of . . .'

LAURIE: Hatred?

FRY: Good, good! What about 'steamed loathing'?

LAURIE: Better – you're a natural!

FRY: Excellent! 'Steamed loathing . . . Snot trails of lust perforate the bowels of my intent. Is there life on Mars, Major Tom, put on your red shoes . . .'

(*Laurie starts slipping away as his headmaster is engrossed in his writing.*)

FRY: '. . . and dance the flunky . . . my China girl . . .'

(*Fade out.*)

'I can't pretend to be much of a judge of literature – I'm an English teacher, not a homosexual . . .'

Stephen Fry

CRUNCHY FROG
ROBBIE COLTRANE, LENNY HENRY & JIMMY MULVILLE

The scene is inside a sweet shop. The owner, Mr Hilton – played by Robbie Coltrane – is sitting idly behind the counter, reading a newspaper and smoking a cigarette. Two policemen enter: Inspector Praline (Lenny Henry) and Constable Parrot (Jimmy Mulville). Praline is carrying a box of chocolates. Parrot is holding his helmet and looking rather queasy.

PRALINE: Mr Hilton?

HILTON: Yes?

PRALINE: You are owner and sole proprietor of the Whizzo Chocolate Company?

HILTON: (*Cagily.*) I might be.

PRALINE: Constable Parrot and I are from the Hygiene Squad. We'd like a word with you about your box of chocolates entitled: 'The Whizzo Quality Assortment'.

HILTON: (*Smiling brightly.*) Ah, yes?

PRALINE: (*Producing box of chocolates.*) To begin at the very beginning. First of all, there is the Cherry Fondue. This is extremely nasty, but we can't prosecute you for that.

HILTON: (*Smugly.*) That's very true.

PRALINE: Next, there's number four, 'Crunchy Frog'.

HILTON: Ah . . . .

PRALINE: Am I right in thinking there's a real *frog* in here?

HILTON: A little one.

PRALINE: What *sort* of frog?

HILTON: A *dead* frog.

PRALINE: Is it *cooked*?

HILTON: No.

PRALINE: What, *raw* frog?

(*Constable Parrot looks increasingly queasy.*)

HILTON: (*Indignantly.*) We use only the finest *baby* frogs, dew-picked and flown from Iraq, cleansed in the *finest* Crown spring water, *lightly* killed and then sealed in a *succulent* Swiss quintuple smooth full-cream treble-milk chocolate envelope and lovingly dusted with glucose.

PRALINE: Well, don't you even take the *bones* out?

HILTON: If we took the bones out it wouldn't be crunchy, would it?

PARROT: Would you excuse me for a moment, please? (*He exits hurriedly.*)

HILTON: It says quite clearly on the box: 'Crunchy Frog'.

PRALINE: Look, the general public will *not* be expecting a *real* frog to be in this chocolate. The constable thought it was an Almond Whirl! People are bound to think it's some kind of mock frog!

HILTON: (*Insulted.*) *Mock* frog? *MOCK FROG?* How *dare* you! There are absolutely no artificial flavourings or additives in our products whatsoever!

PRALINE: Nevertheless, I advise you in future to replace the words 'Crunchy Frog' with the legend 'Crunchy Raw Unboned Real Dead Frog', if you wish to avoid prosecution!

HILTON: But what about my sales?

PRALINE: I have no interest in your *sales*! I have to protect the *public*! Now, what about this next one. (*The constable returns.*) It was number five, wasn't it, Constable? (*The constable nods.*) Yes, number five: Ram's Bladder Cup. (*Exit the constable once again.*) What kind of confection is this?

HILTON: We use only the choicest juicy chunks of fresh Cornish ram's bladder, emptied, steamed, flavoured with sesame seeds whipped into a fondue and garnished with lark's vomit.

PRALINE: (*Examining the box.*) It doesn't say anything about *lark's vomit* here!

HILTON: Yes, it does, just beside 'sodium benzoate'.

PRALINE: (*Squinting.*) Well, I hardly think this is good enough! I think it would be more appropriate if the box bore a large red label: '*WARNING – LARK'S VOMIT!*'

HILTON: I think our sales might well plummet.

PRALINE: Well, why don't you move into more *conventional* areas of confectionery? Like Praline and Lime Cream – a very popular flavour, I'm led to understand. Or Strawberry Delight. (*White-faced, the constable re-enters.*) I mean, look at these, look at these: 'Cockroach Cluster', 'Phlegm Cream' –

HILTON: That's the wife's favourite!

PRALINE: . . . 'Anthrax Ripple'. (*The constable's cheeks puff out and he is close to vomiting all over again.*) What's this one all about, 'Spring Surprise'?

HILTON: (*Proudly.*) Ah . . . now, that's the *crème de la crème*, that's our speciality – you just pop the wee choccy in your mouth and two steel bolts spring out and pierce both cheeks.

(*The constable vomits into his helmet.*)

PRALINE: *Pierce both cheeks*? Where's the pleasure in *that*?

HILTON: Well, watching, of course.

PRALINE: This is an inadequate description of the sweetmeat. I shall have to ask you to accompany me to the station.

HILTON: (*Getting up from desk and being led away.*) It's a fair cop.

PRALINE: And don't talk to the camera!

HILTON: I'm sorry.

PRALINE: Constable, would you deliver the punchline, please?

(*Constable Parrot salutes as Inspector Praline and Hilton leave. He then turns to the audience and puts his helmet back on, thus showering his head with sick. He leaves the stage.*)

ONE LEG TOO FEW

PETER COOK & DUDLEY MOORE

The scene is a theatrical producer's office.

COOK: (*Calling off-stage.*) Miss Rigby! Stella, my love! Would you please send in the next auditioner, please? Thank you, my darling.

(*Enter Moore, hopping energetically on one leg. He shakes hands with Cook.*)

COOK: How d'you do, nice to meet you. Er, Mr Spigott, is it not?

MOORE: Yes – Spigott by name, Spigott by nature. (*Keeps hopping.*)

COOK: Settle down. (*Spigott props himself on the edge of a chair.*) Now, Mr Spigott, you are auditioning, are you not, for the role of Tarzan?

MOORE: Yeah, right.

COOK: Now, Mr Spigott, I couldn't help noticing, almost immediately, that you are a one-legged man.

MOORE: You noticed that?

COOK: When you've been in the business as long as I have, Mr Spigott, you get to notice these little things almost instinctively.

MOORE: Yeah, well, you're bound to.

COOK: Yes, you're bound to. Now, Mr Spigott, you, a one-legged man, are applying for the role of Tarzan –

MOORE: Yes, right.

COOK: . . . a role traditionally associated with a two-legged artiste.

MOORE: Er, yes.

COOK: And yet you, a unidexter, are applying for the role.

MOORE: Yes, that's right.

COOK: A role for which two legs would seem to be the minimum requirement.

MOORE: Yes.

COOK: Well, Mr Spigott, need I point out to you with undue emphasis where your deficiency lies as regards landing the role?

MOORE: Er, yes, yes, I think you ought to.

COOK: Need I say with too much stress that it is in the leg division that you are deficient?

MOORE: Oh, the leg division?

COOK: Yes, the leg division, Mr Spigott. You are deficient in the leg division – to the tune of one. Your right leg I like. I like your right leg. It's a lovely leg for the role. As soon as I saw it come in, I thought: 'Hello! What a *lovely* leg for the role!' I've got nothing against your right leg.

MOORE: Ah!

COOK: The trouble is – neither have you. You fall down on the left.

MOORE: You mean it's inadequate?

COOK: It is inadequate, Mr Spigott. And, in my view, the British public is not yet ready for the sight of a one-legged Tarzan swinging through the jungly tendrils shouting, 'Hello, Jane!'

MOORE: I see.

COOK: However great the charm of the performer may be. They are not ready for it. Mind you, you score over a man with no legs at all.

MOORE: Oh!

COOK: If a legless man came in here demanding the role, I'd have no hesitation in saying, 'Go away. Hop off!'

MOORE: So there's still hope?

COOK: Yes. There *is* still hope, Mr Spigott. If we get no two-legged artistes in here within the next, say, eighteen months, there is every chance that *you*, a unidexter, are the very type of artiste we shall be attempting to contact at this agency.

MOORE: Oh, well . . . thank you very much!

COOK: Sorry I can't be more definite. (*He shows the hopping Spigott out.*)

ON HEALTH AND THE ENVIRONMENT

BEN ELTON

We're all depressed about the environment at the moment, and I see little hope in some ways, because how can we look after the world if we can't even look after our own bodies? We can't even develop foresight about our own experiences, you know?

Let me tell you – take drinking, for instance. Most people like a drink, and they equate drinking with having a good time.

They think, 'Have a drink, have a good time,' 'I'm gonna get pissed, I'll have a good time' . . . 'I'll pass my exams, I'll get pissed' . . . 'I've got a new job, I'll get pissed, I'm gonna have a really, really good time.' So! The next time it's midnight, and you're kneeling in a bathroom (*Drops to his knees.*) face down the toilet, desperately trying to be sick, remind yourself what a good time you're having, eh?

'Oh, this is marvellous, this is. This only cost me fifteen pounds!' Desperately trying to connect your fingers with that little flap of flesh that hangs at the back of your neck! That's God's sick trigger, that is. It's a marvellous bit of the anatomy. Fantastic – you touch it, wallop, there you go. It serves no other purpose, it has got no other point, it is a sick trigger. Wonderful thing. But why has it got to be out of reach? It could be on the end of your nose, couldn't it? Be all right, wouldn't it? No messing around, fifteen pints of lager, click, *wallop*, I'm off to bed, fair enough. Instead, it's half an hour, probing, with a teaspoon. What's that about?

How can we protect the world? We don't even understand ourselves, our own bodies. The body is a highly sensitive piece of natural engineering, it is a highly complex machine! You should respect it! I mean, you wouldn't pour seven points of lager in your stereo, would you? You wouldn't buy a camera that spent every New Year's Eve unconscious on the toilet floor. 'Ah, the old body, bollocks, not gonna live forever, am I, come on, here we go, course I can drive, wallop, what's that? An old lady? Who cares!'

People have got to learn. I mean, you live in a strange, strange reversed world when you're drunk. A strange parallel universe where good is bad, and bad is good. 'What a *fantastic* night we had last night, eh? It was brilliant! We could not *walk*! We couldn't *talk*! It was marvellous!' – You get the same effect when you break your spine. Throw yourself under a bus, it's a lot cheaper . . . *lasts . . . for . . . ever*!

You've got to get out of it. It's a drug. I mean, it's all right taking the mick, but it *is* a drug, booze, it's like any other drug. *I* can't get off it. I tried cold turkey. Didn't work! Too pissed to keep it down . . .

You know . . . intelligent audience – the first pun gets a smattering of applause, love it to death! So, there we were, you see – having a goad at the hand that feeds it, brave stuff, yeah, dangerous tonight! So, ladies and gentlemen, we're going to bring down the government, no question at all there!

So, you get a terrible thing about being drunk, 'cause there's no phase that's good: the drinking's no good, the throwing up's no good . . . The hangover? You get no sympathy. It's the only illness where you get no sympathy. You're poisoned – but you get no sympathy. 'You brung it on yourself!' 'You never had to do it! I've got no sympathy, you brung it on yourself, you never had to do it!'

Well, what about the hang glider who breaks his or her legs jumping off a cliff, eh? Does anyone force them to entrust their lives to a sheet of polythene? No! But they get plenty of sympathy when they're puréed on the rocks below, don't they? I'm saying, 'You never had to do it, you stupid basket! Should have been down the pub with me! I've got a headache! You can't flipping *walk*!'

You see, the world is full of useless things. We're consuming our environment in order to have things we don't need, the things we don't want. I mean – my fridge is the most useless thing in my life. Not just because it's got CFCs in the back, d'you know that? Your friendly old fridge? It's going to kill you one day. When you trash it, all the CFCs float up into the environment, we get skin cancer, that's nice. Your little fridge with the rubber carrot stuck on for the kiddies . . . that's gonna kill you.

My fridge . . . is entirely useless. I pay twenty-four hours' worth of electricity every day, so that when I open the door . . . it will light up my face. There is never any food in my fridge . . . I buy plenty of food, I always seem to be down the shops, I spend twenty-five quid, 'I've got no food in here, where's the food?' I think my fridge is eating my food. It *eats* my food, and then . . . wets itself. It hates me, my fridge, it thinks 'Umnumnumnum, I'll eat his food then I'll piss on his floor.'

There's never any food in the house! And you can never buy food when you want it. When are they gonna have open all-night shops round the town? You don't want shops open on a Sunday, you want 'em open in the middle of the night. That's when you need food! After a few pints of lager, that's when you'll eat anything . . . You go home – there's nothing in the fridge, there's nothing to eat . . . 'I'm pissed, I've got to *eat* something, must be something . . .' Always ends up the same. *Corn Flakes*! With . . . *water*! Because it's *slightly* preferable to squeezing a tube of neat tomato purée down your neck!

People will eat anything when they're pissed, anything! I mean, why do you think Kentucky Fried Chicken stay open all night? Be honest. I mean, what's that about? They give you a 'lemon clean-up square'. That's nice, isn't it? A lemon clean-up square. It's scarcely adequate when you've thrown it up on a carpet, is it, eh? (*Mimes mopping up sick with a tiny hand towel.*) Bit of mime, Rowan Atkinson, love it to death . . . No! They should give you a *bucket*, shouldn't they? Maybe that's what the party buckets are for. Eat the chicken, throw up in a bucket – very convenient! I'll tell you why they give you a lemon clean-up square – because it's the only edible thing in the fucking box!

Fast food? The world – we've been conquered, we've given up our culture, ladies and gentlemen. Across the world, cultures and civilisations, languages that have stood for myriad civilisations, they've been destroyed in a decade. Napoleon could not hold Moscow. Ronald McDonald just danced in. Richard the Lionheart was stopped at the gates of Jerusalem. Ronald McDonald? No problem, in he goes . . .

Fast food is gonna get faster. No one's got any work, no one's got anything to do, the one last pleasure is eating – make it *fast*, make it *fast* . . . get 'em out the restaurant, have them lovely plastic shiny seats shaped like ski slopes, burp once, *wallop*, you're under the table . . . Fast food? I wonder why they don't just flush it straight down the toilet, cut out the middleman, eh? That'd speed things up, wouldn't it? You go in your local Big Mac Whopper McDog Burger . . . 'Er, flush us a couple of Big Mac and fries down the toilet, will you, John? Make it quick, I've got a bus to catch.' He says, 'Sorry, sir, no can do. The U-tube's blocked up with diced gherkin . . .' Why'd they put that gherkin in, eh? Everyone lifts the lid off, takes it out and puts it on the table, some other bastard puts their elbow in it . . . 'The U-tube's blocked,' he says. 'We're only serving liquids.' Have you seen fast-food versions of liquids? A triple-thick shake? A *liquid*? You need an industrial suction pump to get it up the straw! Everybody sucks at once, the windows of the shop cave in.

What are we doing to our children, our environment? The kid's drinking this damn thing, his intestines are going, 'No, not *again* – it took two years to digest the last one!'

But when you're drunk . . . 'Oh I could just fancy a McDonald's . . .' *Wallop!* 'Oh Gawd, I wish I hadn't done that . . .' You get home, you've got to eat something, there's no McDonald's, they were closed, the Kentucky was full of yobs and you respect their right to be yobs but you don't wanna go in there while they're being it . . . and there, you're going, 'There's nothing to eat, there's no cornflakes . . . *Ah!*' Suddenly! That casserole dish you put in to soak a month ago looks like a culinary delight. 'I'll just get a knife and chip all the crispy bits off . . . ah, lovely crisp, lovely crispy bits . . .' You don't realise you're so pissed you've done this three nights in a row, you've got through to the enamel!

People will eat *anything* when they're drunk . . . I mean, ladies and gentlemen, if there's any young parents out there in the audience tonight, who've got little kids . . . who won't eat their food . . . get 'em pissed!

Little Johnny, three years old . . . couple of vodkas . . . 'Fuck me, those Brussels sprouts look nice!' I mean, all right, you've got to put up with him lying face down in a bathroom in a puddle of vomit singing, 'Maybe It's Because I'm a Londoner' . . . but he's eaten his *greens*.

So many useless things in the world . . . my fridge, I'm talking about . . . but those telephones? I remember in the old days, before they sold off Telecom, it was marvellous. Them telephones used to be one shape, didn't they? Now it's any shape and size. It's got confusing! You remember how in the old days, if you heard a ringing in your sitting room, you knew what you had to look for, didn't you? The big telephone-shaped lump of plastic. These days it could be *anything* – I'm picking up the toaster, listening to the cat . . . they got Mickey Mouse-shaped phones, Snoopy-shaped phones . . . It's a serious instrument, we don't need all these trashy non-biodegradable bits of plastic nobody fucking wants . . . I mean, what, a Snoopy-shaped phone? You ain't supposed to take it seriously. You're having a business conversation, and you're talking to Snoopy's bollocks!

All this selling-off of the private stuff . . . I think perhaps the most useless thing of all is the advertising industry. They are excelling themselves at the moment. Ooh – they're advertising all the new electricity companies – Powergen – and telling us how wonderful – streak of lightning: 'Powergen is Marvellous!' I mean, what are they trying to tell us? Are we supposed to read the advert and go, 'Oh, I bet those are fucking good, I'll switch on another light!' You know? I mean, what's the *idea*? Powergen are promising they're going to have the most efficient and the *cheapest* form of electricity. Well, frankly, I think it might be a little bit *cheaper* if there wasn't a private company making a *profit* out of it, but perhaps I'm being old-fashioned, I don't know.

Whoah! Power to the people, little bit of politics, dangerous night tonight!

So . . . Ladies and gentlemen, do not trust the advertising industry, no! They do not have a good track record, they have no morals, they have no principles, no! Do you know that up until recently, it was against the rules of the advertising standards to advertise, on the telly, tampons? That's nice, innit? What an enlightened bit of legislation. What were they doing in Parliament when they thought that one up? Did they think, 'Ooh, what shall we do today? Er, put the unemployed back to work, feed the Third World . . . No! Let's have a rule about advertising tampons!' Now, we can have tampon adverts! We're all grown up and squiggly, and we have tampon adverts . . . only on Channel 4, and as an experiment, a couple of years ago, 'cause of course you've got to have O-levels to understand the stark reality of menstruation, you know? Got to have the tampon ads on the telly on Channel 4 in the middle of the Polish films, so no fucker watches 'em, you know, 'cause it would really mess up *Bruce's Big Night*, wouldn't it, a tampon ad in the middle of it? You don't want that on channel one.

I saw this ad. I saw . . . I could not believe it, when they were experimenting with tampon ads. They started with this woman, she was like, she was lovely. Oh, she was so *pretty*, she was a lovely blonde, pretty woman, she was all pretty and lovely, 'cause that's a relief, innit, girls? Pretty girls have periods, too! Cor, bet you're relieved, eh? And she's feeling all . . . she's in this advert, it's true, she's looking through her diary, and she's reading all her letters, which are all feminine and all done up in a little pink bow, and there's a bit of gloss on the filter, and she's all blonde and pretty, and she's feeling all wistful. She's kind of got little, little thoughts in her mind about love, and being a girlie, and all feminine and gooey and squidgy and moist and lovely and wistful, she's going all soft and drippy and wistful . . . Well, that's exactly how you feel when you have your periods, isn't it, girls, eh? 'Never mind stomach cramps – fuck me, I'm feeling wistful, I must be on!'

'Hello, boss? I won't be in for work today, I'm feeling a bit wistful, all right?' 'If you don't do your share of the washing up, I'm feeling so *wistful*, I'll *knife* you!' Pre-Wistful Tension.

On comes the voiceover, I kid you not, for the brand name, the voiceover – (*Does a deep, caring, voice.*) It's a lovely voice that goes, 'Ladies.' *Lay*-dies. Yeah, 'cause ladies have periods as well! Gawd, there you go – Felicity Kendall, the Queen, yeah, they *do*, yeah! People are going, 'Hang on, that's going *too* far! Say what you like about the Queen, but leave Felicity Kendall out of this, all right?'

It goes, 'Ladies . . . do you have a secret?' *AAAAGH!* Half the population of the world do it every month! What's so secret about *that*? I tell ya – there'd be a lot less of this po-faced reactionary,   this   keep-it-in-the-closet-let's-not-talk-about-it, let's-make-young-girls-embarrassed-when-it-first-happens-to-them . . . If it was *men* that had periods, ooh yes! Then it would be a subject for after-dinner conversation . . . (*Crusty posh male voice.*) 'It was a marvellous sunny day, I remember it well, a really terrific day, I'd just strolled out from the pavilion to bat, and, would you believe it, my period started. And I was wearing whites, and, as a young man, we did laugh!'

'Cause we love a laugh, don't we, us lads? We love laughing about our bodily functions, who'll piss highest against a wall, all farting, Gandhi's revenge, nobody smoke, nobody walk behind me, coo, I dumped one in the bog don't go in there for half an hour, coo, nuclear explosion! We love having a laugh about our bodily functions, don't we? We'd be having a laugh if we had our periods: 'Gawd, dear, we was down the pub, me an' Baz, flipping funny, we started menstruating! Well, we've always menstruated simultaneously ever since we were kids 'cause we're fucking good *mates*, all right?'

'Went in the toilet, never believe it, tampon machine's broken! Had to go home with a couple of beermats in our knickers, ah ha ha!' Yeah, we'd be having a laugh, we'd be boasting about it, us lads, we'd be boasting about the extent of our flow – 'Fuck me, I was bleeding last night, know what I mean?' 'You, bleedin? Bugger off – me, I nearly fainted!' 'Fainted? *I* needed a blood transfusion!' 'Piss off, you should see the size of my pads – it's like sitting on a fucking *brick*, piss off . . .'

That's what it would be like if men had periods. We'd have a week off, every month. The Pope'd make it a sacrament of the church, we'd be lighting candles to the blessed flow. Instead . . . (*Camp voice.*) It's a secret.

So, ladies and gentlemen, a real pleasure to be here, especially on this big night. I'm always remembering what Amnesty's about. But right now I'm going to say goodbye: my name's Ben Elton, thank you very much, goodbye!

'People will eat anything when they're pissed, anything! I mean, why do you think KFC stay open all night?'

Ben Elton

GOODBYE-EE

PETER COOK & DUDLEY MOORE WITH THE CAST

Cook and the rest of the cast stand behind Moore as he sits at the piano and plays.

MOORE: (*Sings.*) Now is the time to say goodbye.

COOK: (*Speaks.*) Goodbye.

MOORE: (*Sings.*) Now is the time to yield a sigh.

COOK: (*Speaks.*) Oh, *yield* it, *yield* it, baby doll!

MOORE: (*Sings.*)

Now is the time to wend our waaaayeeeeee . . .
(*Falsetto.*) Until we meet again, some sunny day.

MOORE: (*Sings.*)

Goodbye, goodbye,
We're leaving you, skiddly-dye,
Goodbye, we wish you fond goodbye.

COOK/MOORE: (*Singing.*) Fa-ta, fa-ta, ta-ta.

ALL: (*singing*)

Goodbye, goodbye,
We're leaving you, skiddly-dye,
Goodbye, we wish you fond goodbye.

Goodbye, goodbye,
We're leaving you, skiddly-dye,
Goodbye, we wish you fond goodbye-ee!

THE
FAMOUS
COMPÈRE'S
POLICE DOG

(*The* WORLD *Tour*)

**THE DUKE OF YORK'S THEATRE, LONDON
14, 21 & 28 JANUARY 1990**

INTERREGNUM
AN INTRODUCTION

The late 1980s saw Amnesty taking stock of the continuing proliferation of other benefit events, and careful not to dilute the very warm feeling that people still held towards earlier shows.

After a decade of staging bigger and bigger shows featuring more and more major stars, Amnesty decided to invest more wholeheartedly in the vibrant UK comedy circuit at the same time as continuing with big-scale filmed events (*The Secret Policeman's Biggest Ball* in 1989, *The Big 3-0* in 1991). In doing this, Amnesty was once more steering a distinct and bold route, freshening up its approach and still surprising a few people as it did so. The theatre director John Turner was thus given the brief of creating a series of shows whose major selling point would be that they did not seem 'anything like *The Secret Policeman's Balls*'. Informal and evanescent, in stark contrast to their increasingly grand and lovingly preserved predecessors, Turner's shows, with Amnesty's Alison Sanderson put together and grouped under the banner *The Famous Compère's Police Dog*, would have the character of a late-night modern cabaret, and feature mainly young up-and-coming talents rather than established big stars. At a time when stand-up comedy belonged mainly in strip clubs and bars, Amnesty was keen to provide a platform in the West End. 'The plan,' said John Turner, 'was to find a West End theatre and put on three nights that featured the cream of the New Talent on the [comedy] circuit.' In keeping with Amnesty tradition, these nights, he promised, 'would be unique'.

Running eventually for six years in total between 1988 and 1993, including *The Famous Compère's Police Dog: The Movie* (which was not a movie), *The Famous Compère's Police Dog: The World Tour* (not a world tour) and *The Famous Compère's Police Dog: Superbowl* (not a Superbowl), each one took place with three shows on consecutive Sunday nights at the Duke of York's Theatre in London. Among the performers were Eddie Izzard, Jack Dee, Jeremy Hardy, Julian Clary, Stephen Fry, Paul Merton, Jenny Eclair, Lee Evans, Harry Hill, Jo Brand, Mark Thomas and Arthur Smith – all still in the early stages of what would eventually become very successful careers and all still to appear on bigger Amnesty stages – as well as a strange and eclectic mix of jugglers, magicians, acrobats, character actors, singers, dancers, improv acts, poets, puppeteers and mime artists, who had somehow become connected, however briefly, to the alternative comedy circuit.

Staged quickly and often chaotically, the shows themselves received few reviews from the comedy critics and a mixed reaction from audiences, but they again demonstrated Amnesty's hunger for breaking new ground. Not only did they succeed in raising some much-needed funds but they also helped in publicising Amnesty's latest campaigns, including its support in 1991 for the young Burmese comedian Zarganar, who had recently been imprisoned (for the second time) merely for telling jokes about the government. Several articles in the British newspapers, designed to tie in with the latest cabaret event, brought his plight to the attention of a wider readership, and comedy once again helped highlight Amnesty's serious issues for a wider audience.

The sense, however, that Amnesty was still unsure of how best to collaborate with the comedy fraternity, now that it had stepped out from under the protective banner of *The Secret Policeman's Ball*, continued when Amnesty chose to celebrate its thirtieth anniversary in 1991 by staging a 'two-hour spectacular' called *The Big 3–0* not in a theatre, but, for the first time, in Central Television's Nottingham Studios. With, among others, Tom Jones, Morrissey, Rick Astley, Jason Donovan, Seal and Darryl Hall, and pre-recorded messages of support from the likes of Kylie Minogue, Brian Clough and Jeremy Beadle as well as the casts of *EastEnders*, *Brookside* and *Coronation Street*, the event was a glitter-sprayed curate's egg, never seeming quite sure of what kind of production it was supposed to be.

All three leaders of the main political parties combined to contribute their own tribute to Amnesty's activities. Labour's Neil Kinnock, the Liberal Democrat Paddy Ashdown and the then-Prime Minister John Major delivered the following joint statement:

> *Amnesty International has shown over the last thirty years that individual human rights can be easily and carelessly forgotten by government administrations all over the world. It is testimony to Amnesty International's persistence and independence that so many governments have had to concede time and time again that they can no longer abuse basic human freedoms.*
>
> *Together we toast Amnesty International's thirtieth anniversary celebrations and pay tribute to all its achievements over the years. It is vital that Amnesty continues to be a lifeline to all those individuals who need it.*

As a TV special the show might have lost some of the edginess of the live experience, but as a consciousness-raising exercise the occasion had served its purpose.

As time went on, however, the appetite for the old-but-bold *SPB* productions started to return. Realising that it had been a little perverse to ignore the power and prestige of the *Secret Policeman's Ball* tradition, but still eager to tune in to contemporary and youthful audiences, Amnesty went for a theme of evolution rather than revolution when, in 2001, it marked its fortieth anniversary by staging another big theatrical event (this time at the Wembley Arena), which it called *We Know Where You Live, Live!* – but in a conciliatory and canny nod to its own proud past they dubbed it 'The Son of the *Secret Policeman's Ball*'.

The idea that it was now resuming a living tradition was symbolised when its first comedy patron, John Cleese, agreed to be pictured handing over the baton to the new show's creative director and host, Eddie Izzard. Noting Amnesty's most recent Annual Report, which revealed that there were now prisoners of conscience in sixty-one countries and executions taking place in thirty-one countries, Cleese was keen to stress the continuing need for these popular benefit events, and Amnesty was equally eager to anoint Izzard as the man to lead the next generation of comic campaigners.

'It's quite an undertaking,' Izzard said. 'I have changed the title, which people will think is changing something sacrosanct. But I always thought the name *The Secret Policeman's Ball* was odd. Was it for secret policemen? No, we hate fucking secret policemen . . . *We know where you live* is what gangsters say, so I suppose it's still a bit double-headed, but the idea was to say to dictators or other people who violate basic human rights: "We do know who and where you are, and we will track you forever."'

The success of the occasion not only galvanised a new generation of politically active celebrities but also energised Amnesty's existing activists. 'That was my first year as [UK] director of Amnesty,' recalls Kate Allen, 'and seeing Eddie Izzard perform and reach out to a wide range of people on the issue of free speech inspired me . . . We need to continue working with such wonderful artists to help us to carry out our message of defending the basic rights of free speech and other basic rights.'

The right tone had been struck. 'Amnesty is a long-term thing,' explained Izzard as he contrasted it with the countless one-off campaigns. 'It's not like there's a southern-hemisphere-suddenly-everyone's-in-prison thing.' After more than a decade spent nurturing its relationships in 'alternative comedy', away from the big stage, Amnesty, with the help of Eddie Izzard and friends, was now one of the few comedy 'brands' able to sell out 11,000-seater arenas. The old drive was back.

Amnesty International presents

THE FAMOUS COMPERE'S POLICEDOG:
THE WORLD TOUR

· DUKE OF YORK'S THEATRE · ST MARTINS LANE ·
· LONDON WC2 ·

· JANUARY · 14TH · 21ST · 28TH · 1990 ·

THE FAMOUS COMPÈRE'S POLICE DOG, 1990

Amnesty had again changed direction, and by bringing up-and-coming circuit comedians to the West End, they were hoping to do something different. 1990's *World Tour*, for example, jumbled up a few stand-up comics (including Mark Thomas railing at the police, the army and the government, Gerry Sadowitz baiting the audience and Jenny Eclair mocking herself) with a cheesy magician, someone who sat down on stage and smoked a spliff, a self-styled 'angry young accordionist' and a very peculiar little character who contorted his facial expressions via a network of taut rubber bands. Very few of the shows from this period were recorded, and those that were ended up being edited quite brutally as packages for TV, so precious little remains on tape in terms of complete and effective comedy performances.

The *Police Dog* shows were a little uneven in terms of quality, but among the surviving fragments are some fascinating little insights into the evolution of certain comedians, such as the 28-year-old Eddie Izzard (only a couple of years into his professional stand-up career) still searching for the right balance (or imbalance) between satire and surrealism; Jo Brand – having only recently emerged from behind the disguise, and rigid rhythms, of her 'Sea Monster' persona – developing a mini-cab routine that would later become a memorably polished part of her stand-up act; and the lugubrious Michael Redmond (who would later come to the attention of a broader audience when he appeared as Father Stone in an episode of *Father Ted*) honing a deadpan delivery and delightfully bone-dry style of humour that would soon establish him as the kind of comic who is probably most admired and appreciated by other comics. The likes of Arthur Smith and Julian Clary, on the other hand, were captured seeming then more or less as they seem now: confident, self-assured and already settled into their respective styles.

DEATH SQUADS, HECKLERS AND LONDON
ARTHUR SMITH

Here we are at the end of another decade. There were some great things that happened in that decade, weren't there? There was the breaching of the Berlin Wall, the growing awareness of the need to protect our planet, and there was the fact that there was liberation in Eastern Europe – a lot of good things happened. But to me none of these really compensated for the fact that Wham! split up. Where's Andrew Ridgley now when we need him, eh?

Ten years. Ten years of Margaret Thatcher – which is three less than Hitler managed, at least. And it's a sad fact that there are probably a lot of people here tonight who have never had sex under a Labour government. It's tragic, isn't it? *I* can actually remember what it was like to have sex under a *Liberal* government! Gertrude Stein, she was a bit of a corker, I must say! So a lot of you have only ever done it under Thatcher? Well, it would have to be *under* her, wouldn't it – she'd never let you go on top, obviously!

Do we have any Iranian death squads in tonight? Well, they've got to have something else to do in the evening, haven't they? They can't spend *all* day killing people, can they? You'd want to go off for a few pints at night, wouldn't you? If there are any Iranian death squads in the audience tonight, I'd like to draw their attention to a book I've been reading. It's called *Muslims Are Crap* and it's written by Jeffrey Archer, and that's with a foreword by Margaret Thatcher, and published by Rupert Murdoch. And by the way, that's Jeffrey Archer of The Vicarage, Grantchester. You take the A40 out of town . . .

Not much heckling so far tonight. It makes me wonder if people ever used to heckle the Nuremburg rallies. 'Get off, Goering, ya fat bastard! You're not funny!' If they *did*, they only did it once, that's for certain. The hardest heckler I've ever had to deal with was in Denmark. And you don't really expect it in Denmark. I mean, in Denmark 'Chirpy-Chirpy-Cheep-Cheep' is still number three in the charts, isn't it? But this Danish guy, he gets up and says: 'Excuse me . . .' So I'm getting all my anti-Danish heckle lines together, like 'Sod off, you Danish git!' But he goes: 'Excuse me – I think you are very nice!' I thought, why waste a line, so I said, 'Sod off, you Danish git!' I don't play Denmark very often these days.

And here we are in London. London's really getting me down at the moment. London, you know, it's dirty, nothing works, there's dog turds everywhere – and that's just in my flat! I called in a builder the other day and asked him to give me a quote. He said, 'Do not forsake me, oh my darling.' I said, 'You're a bloody cowboy, mate!'

Of course, living in London, you do hear the most depressing phrase in the world, don't you? The most depressing phrase in the world is: 'This is the Northern Line Information Service.' I don't know why they don't just tell the truth: 'This is the Northern Line Information Service. Everything's buggered – go home, it's hopeless!'

I saw this guy up at King's Cross the other day. Oh, poor fella, he had a sign around his neck that said: 'I HAVE NO FRIENDS, I HAVE NO FAMILY, I HAVE NO HOME'. Oh, poor bloke. I thought I had to do something, so I walked up to him and said: 'Look, mate, have you thought about opening a high-interest investment account?' I think that cured his problem, all right.

DRINK, FIGHTS, FUNERALS AND DUBLIN

MICHAEL REDMOND

Good evening. Are you all right? Good. Because *I'm* not. Thank you for asking. The reason I'm not feeling well is because I got very drunk last night. I ate half a tin of dog food for a bet. I actually lost the bet. I bet that I *wouldn't* eat it.

(*A long, uncomfortable pause.*)

I wish I had more material . . .

I was in hospital over Christmas, by the way. A dislocated jaw. The trouble was, I didn't really mean any harm at the time but I was sitting in this pub on Christmas Eve. This big bloke came in and it was pretty obvious he was wearing a hairpiece. I merely suggested that he should take it off when he was indoors, otherwise he wouldn't feel the benefit of it when he went outside again.

What else has been happening? Why is it that people sitting opposite me on the Tube get so agitated when I train my binoculars on them? Nobody knows.

There's one thing I've noticed in life. It's almost impossible to get service in a vegetarian restaurant if you're wearing a soiled butcher's apron.

I went to a funeral on Tuesday. I was at the family home afterwards offering my condolences. Then after about five minutes or so the eldest son of the family came over to me and said: 'Would you mind leaving, please? We've had a family discussion and none of us has ever seen you before.' I mean, how do people expect to make new friends with that sort of bloody attitude?

People have a strange attitude to funerals. I mean, you hear religious leaders saying, 'Death is nothing to be frightened of, it's merely a peaceful passing from one life to another.' So how come religious people don't celebrate funerals, then? The last funeral I was at was my Auntie Emma's. Quite a lot of her family are quite religious but everyone started tut-tutting when I did a limbo dance under the coffin as it was being carried out.

I'm originally from Dublin. Is there anyone here from . . . Nairobi? You get a lot of American tourists in Dublin. I met one of the ones, he said, 'How you doin', I'm Rick, I'm from LA.' I said, 'Hi, I'm Michael, I'm from D.' Really screws them up.

One of the things that I've noticed about living over here is that a lot of people over here, particularly in London, seem to think that Dublin is just a small village. I was in a pub the other night ordering a drink, and there was this guy standing beside me, he must have heard my accent because he said, 'Excuse me, are you from Dublin?' I said, 'Yes, I am.' He said, 'Do you know Sean Cochrane, then?' There are over one million people living in Dublin, for Christ's sake! The annoying thing is, I fucking *do* know Sean Cochrane.

TRAINS, BUSES, CARS AND KNOBS
JO BRAND

Hello. Well, rather appropriately tonight I'd like to start off by talking about violence. Because I'm not averse to a good punch-up myself. Especially at the January sales. I don't actually buy anything; I just go around hitting people. Because I think it serves them bloody well right, really.

But, you know, I must say seriously that violence is becoming an increasing problem for women in London. I think, you know, having travelled on public transport over the years, I can say that I've become somewhat of an expert on modern weaponry. Mainly because I've seen such a motley collection of penises on the buses and Tubes. Well, is it a penis or is it a Swan Vesta, you just can't tell sometimes, can you? I think that most women will know what I'm talking about there – I'm getting pretty fed up of having to take my electron-microscope on the bus with me, just to see what those bastards are lobbing out.

And I have to say that I don't think that going by cab is any safer. I mean, I made the very serious mistake tonight of phoning my local cab firm, Camberwell Liars. And it's not really fair because I phone them up and I tell them the truth. I phoned them up tonight and I told them, 'Can you send round a big fat racist bastard, please, with a personal hygiene problem, sometime before I have my menopause?' But they haven't arrived yet so I assume that's what they're doing.

No, actually I have got a car and I was very pleased when I managed to afford a car because I assumed that all my problems in that direction with flashing, what-have-you, were going to be over and done with. But I was completely wrong there. Because I live in Camberwell.

And I was in my car in Camberwell just recently, about six o'clock in the evening, just about to pull away from the kerb, when some bloke tapped on the window. Now, rather naively maybe, thinking he was just going to ask me the time, I foolishly wound the window down. At which point he stuck his knob into my car. I was at a little bit of a loss as to what to do, really. Was this an over-zealous traffic warden, was it somebody dispensing with the formality of asking me out to the pictures first, or was it a novel form of hitchhiking I hadn't come across? Well, I don't think it was any of those, but of course, as women will know, you don't do anything sensible in that situation, like wind the window *up*, you just sit there like a bloody lemon, don't you?

And, of course, to make it a lot worse, the bloody car wouldn't start, so I was stuck there for a good five minutes with this thing waggling in my ear, and when I *did* eventually manage to get away it was not before this bloke had got very angry and kicked my car in. So I drove up the road a little way and saw a policeman, so I thought, 'Well, I might as well tell him about it for a laugh.' And when I'd got through explaining to him exactly what had happened, of course he stuck *his* knob in my car as well. You can always rely on them, really, can't you?

Now, actually, one of my other hobbies is that I'm a part-time agony aunt. I'm not terribly good at it, so at the moment I'm practising and I'm just going through newspapers and magazines finding problems and seeing if I can sort them out in a rather more practical way than *they* seem to.

And I'm going to start with one from the *News of the World*, so you'll all have to step down the old evolutionary ladder a bit to understand it but we'll give it a go. And this one says: 'Dear Unity, When I put on my daughter's slimline wellington boots I get very sexually excited. Is this wrong? I'm fifty-two and recently widowed.' Well, what Unity actually says is: 'No, it's not wrong, but it would be better to find yourself a new man because a man is much more fun than a wellington boot.' Well, Unity, I'm afraid I beg to differ there.

I actually went to Brunel University. Which is the Arthur Mullard of further education. And, coincidentally enough, my final year dissertation was entitled: 'Man: An Ethnomethodological Study – Is He More Fun than a Wellington Boot?' And I can tell you he isn't.

And the second problem – it's difficult to believe that someone sent this in but they did. And it says: 'Dear David, I was very upset by the answer you gave to a woman from Grimsby last week saying she had vaginal thrush. Grimsby is a respectable town and we most certainly do not have venereal diseases here.' Well, I was doing a gig in Grimsby last month, and I can reassure you now that they do. So that's all right, isn't it? No problem.

Now just before I go, I realise that I haven't said anything about periods yet, have I, and I'm afraid that, being a female comic, it's in my contract – I have to talk about them. For an hour, okay? No, I've got a short time, I'll keep it brief, but I'm not going to moan about them because I think they're great.

I do, I think they're brilliant. I managed to get out of netball at school by having a period for four and a half years. And periods allow me to indulge in my favourite hobby of lying on my bed and whining quite a lot. And they can be so useful, can't they? Particularly if you know someone you can't stand with a white sofa. (I only do that one to make the boys rush out and vomit.)

No, what I actually like most about periods is the way some people are so embarrassed about them. And a lot of people use these strange little euphemisms so they don't have to actually say the word 'period'. Among my favourite euphemisms are: 'I've got the painters and decorators in'; 'Arsenal are playing at home'. But actually my own particular favourite is: 'There's a vast amount of blood squirting out of my gusset, vicar!' Just my personal choice.

AN EMOTIONAL FLIGHT

JULIAN CLARY

Don't clap on your own, please. Someone will throw you a fish. Just getting my bearings. There's still nothing I like more than a warm hand upon my entrance.

I was sitting on a plane the other day, like you do. And the reason I was on the plane is quite interesting. My manager rang me up and he said: 'You've been offered a job in Reading at the Hexagon Theatre with Linda Lusardi.' And when I heard the news I was physically sick. Spontaneous projectile vomiting. I thought: 'That's not right, you need a holiday.'

So there I was, sitting on this plane. I was actually on my way to Thailand. I wanted to experience the Golden Mount. Turns out it was a Buddhist temple on a hill. I'd gone all that way on a terrible misapprehension.

I was sitting there on the plane looking forward to the baggage reclaim, because I like a baggage reclaim, it's very often the highlight of the holiday. I think that, being a homosexual, I haven't bred any children at all, but I imagine that waiting for your children to come out of school at half past three is really much the same sensation. Correct me if I'm wrong.

So there I was sitting on this plane and I suddenly felt something wet on my cheek. For one awful moment I thought that the air steward had gobbed at me. Then I realised that it wasn't gob on my cheek at all, it was a tear. A tear had forced itself out of my eye and was just pushing itself down my cheek.

The woman sitting next to me noticed this. She noticed most things. Perhaps there's a woman sitting next to you tonight who's very much the same. I sympathise. She was very interested in all my activities. I didn't mind chatting for the first few hours of the flight, 'cause you *don't* mind, but then you start to get a crick in your neck and are trying to think of an honourable way out. So I put my Walkman on. That meant I was officially incommunicado. But that didn't satisfy her at all. She picked it up (*Mimes someone lifting up one of his headphones.*) I went to the toilet and she came round the S bend.

Anyway, there I was, and she noticed this tear on my cheek, and she smiled sympathetically and offered me a sandwich. So I took the sandwich. And I wiped my face with it. Sat there with bits of tuna fish all round my cheek.

I had a look at her – a funny-looking woman; she looked like a Citroën 2CV Special. Which *I* drive – I *am* a homosexual and all homosexuals drive Citroën 2CV Specials. Now you know what's special about them. I've got a sticker on the back window that says, 'PULL BACK – GIVE MY BOYFRIEND A CHANCE!'

FIRST GULF WAR REFLECTIONS

PERFORMED DURING THE FIRST GULF WAR
EDDIE IZZARD

The forces have been out in the Gulf for months now – doing nothing and I was just thinking, 'I'll watch something crap tonight,' you know? 'Oh, *Newsnight*, okay, that first, then some crap. Oh, bugger, the War! It's on now . . .' And so the TV was on and then (*Mimes watching coverage of the Gulf War.*) I was watching! But, interestingly – before the war's start they were running War films like *The Winds of War.* They must have then just thought, 'Oh, enough of this – we'll get the *real* thing on.' We've seen the Second World . . . we've thought of the Third World War . . . Does anyone remember: 'The First World War: the war to end all wars'? The Second World War: 'Well . . . let's have another bash at it!' The Third World War: 'Oh, God – will we ever stop!'

Then suddenly the actual Gulf War. And whilst we were watching the missiles over Baghdad, I think we were all going – (*Watching the late-night coverage on TV.*) 'Whoa! Ooooh! Aaaah!' And making noises of great note. And the next morning we felt like we'd *done* something. We had actually been going around just making noises: 'Oh . . . whoa . . . oooh . . . phew . . .' The real forces were out there doing stuff. We weren't doing *anything*. I mean, in years to come, our kids are going to ask us, 'What did you *do* during the war?' and we're going to say, 'Er, I watched telly.'

But we're all just getting pissed off now, aren't we? We're saying, 'I just want to watch something else – anything! (*Mimes flicking through the channels.*) Gulf . . . Gulf . . . Gulf . . .' But then they all get these experts on, don't they, you know, a panel of these experts. 'Yes, I'm an expert, and my hair is specially styled to prove this. I know all about the special things they screw into the back of the wotsits. Yes, I do know that.' 'Well, what do you think?' 'Well, as long as they screw them in nice and tight, they should be all right. Otherwise, they'll drop off. And that's no way to run a war.'

CNN have got something strange going there, haven't they? They're still in Baghdad: 'This is CNN, we are reporting from inside Saddam Hussein's moustache.' On the first night they were saying, 'Hello, Harry, I'm hanging out the window – oooh, look, trees and stuff!'

And Iraq TV showed Saddam Hussein in Baghdad having a groovy time. 'Oooh, yeah, I love to go out on the streets on a day like this, yeah!' And he was greeted by the populace in Baghdad – eight people I counted, with moustaches sellotaped on. 'Thanks, yeah, thanks for getting us into *this* war, Saddam!' And the cameras panned round to show all the hordes and they were going: 'Shit – no one's here!' The eight people are going: 'Yeah, yeah, well done, Saddam, that was great! Nah, I didn't *need* my house, I didn't need it, mate. Yeah, we're such a small country, we *needed* that extra bit of bombing, well *done*, mush!'

It's just going to go and on, isn't it? The first day we thought, 'Oh, it'll be over by Christmas.' Because they're always over by Christmas, aren't they? Well, they *try* to be, don't they? This is why they waited until *after* Christmas to start the war – to get a big run-in.

Before it happened there was the hostage situation, right? And that was a bit weird because all these people who used to run countries were going up to Hussein and saying: 'Can I have some hostages, please?' And he was going: 'Ah . . . all right. You, Ted Heath, you can have thirty-three.' And Ted was going: 'Oooh . . . choices, choices . . .' It was like Hostages R Us, wasn't it? 'I'll have *him*, yes, he's quite nice, yes, those two smiling, yeah . . .' And they come back: 'Look, *my* hostages are much better than Willy Brandt's hostages!' And Tony Benn was going out there on a different mission, wasn't he? He looked as if he was taking some hostages *out* there! Saddam Hussein must have said: 'We're running out!' 'Ooh, okay.'

And then in the end Saddam Hussein, like some big kid, said: 'Oh, piss off! You can all fuck off now! Nah, you're not playing it properly! It's *my* game, *my* country! I'm going to play a new game. I'm going to play *Call My Bluff*. Okay, er, first word: "scud". Um, it's pronounced "scood", and it *could* be a Norwegian potato peeler . . .'

And the moustache thing! It's like the Moustache Wars, isn't it? It's like people go out into the desert and think: 'Ah, fuck it, I think I'll grow a moustache, too.' All dictators have moustaches – have you noticed that? Saddam Hussein: moustache. Adolf Hitler: moustache. Josef Stalin: moustache. Thatcher: moustache – but she wore it on her head.

Bush is going: 'Okay, send the troops in, right? Move them around, right? Send some more in, right?' He's doing all of that, and John Major's going: 'Oh, they've gone in, have they? Oh, good. Oh, they've come back, have they? Oh, that's nice. Yes, thanks for telling me, we didn't know. No, we'll be here, yes. Yes, you do have my phone number, don't you? Yes, we're in the book – Prime Minister of Great Britain, yes. No, we'll be here all night. Yes, we've got coffee and stuff. Not here at the weekend, though. Got a big house, need to do gardening and stuff. Yes, I'll say strong words. I'll say, "He's a bit of a bounder." Yes.'

And the Cruise missile. It's so accurate, isn't it? It rings people's door bells and they open the door and: *boom*! They just tap it into a computer: '43 The Mews, Baghdad – right? Go there, there's a window open on the third floor, right? Yeah, in there, and then go to the kitchen, right, and nick all their coffee and just run away, that'll be quite fun, that'll freak them out!'

And everyone says, if we get rid of Saddam Hussein then it should all be okay. Why can't they go to the Cruise missile and say: 'Er, he's got a moustache . . . often wears a beret, right? Um, just go and find him.' And the Cruise missile's got a little photo strapped to the front and it's going: 'Er, no . . . not *him* . . . no . . .' They could type in: 'If there's a problem, just catch a taxi.' 'Oh, right!' So it gets in. 'Where are you going, mate? Saddam Hussein's house? All right. Oh yeah, it's brisk this time of night, yeah. What, south of the river – nah, not at this time of night, mate!'

THE
BIG
3-0

CENTRAL INDEPENDENT STUDIOS, NOTTINGHAM 13 & 15 DECEMBER, 1991

Amnesty's thirtieth anniversary was celebrated in a television studio in Nottingham, with a busy little small screen-friendly event that featured a predominantly musical cast, although several comedians also took part, and many more recorded brief messages of support for the cause. John Cleese was one of the celebrities who appeared on video to introduce one of Amnesty's campaign reports.

Some of the best comedy performers were frustratingly under-employed. Alexei Sayle, for example, was making his first Amnesty appearance since 1981, but was restricted to a few brief on-screen moments, supporting Jonathan Ross (who, rather bizarrely, was given far more time to try to be funny). 'I'd just flown in from somewhere and was a bit jet-lagged,' Sayle remembers. 'I didn't do much more than a few links. I did try to tease a couple of the musical performers but they came up and said, "Don't do that," which I suppose was fair enough!'

Aside from the kind of routines that one had to be there to see and hear, rather than merely read – such as Steve Coogan and Phil Cornwell trading topical impersonations, and Mike McShane launching himself into an improvisation session – it was a night when a couple of TV double acts contributed the most crafted comedy routines. Mel Smith and Griff Rhys Jones, then in the middle of a very successful ten-series run with the BBC show *Alas Smith and Jones*, offered one of their regular nods to the spirit of Peter Cook and Dudley Moore in the form of a head-to-head conversation. Yet another Oxbridge generation was represented by Steve Punt and Hugh Dennis, who in those days were riding high with a strong teenage following as one half (alongside Rob Newman and David Baddiel) of the popular comedy sketch quartet *The Mary Whitehouse Experience*.

Spinal Tap appeared live in the studio minus Christopher Guest as guitarist Nigel Tufnel, who joined by 'satellite' and helped bring the proceedings to an end with a tribute that was cranked right up to eleven: 'Happy Birthday, Amnesty. Thirty years is a long time to be doing . . . what . . . you do.'

HEAD TO HEAD
MEL SMITH & GRIFF RHYS JONES

Smith and Jones are sitting opposite each other, both resting their elbows on the table and listening intently to each other.

SMITH: It's a terrible thing, isn't it?

JONES: Yes, it is. (*Pauses.*) What is that, then?

SMITH: To be in prison, just for your convictions.

JONES: Yeah. Well . . . that's why you were in prison, wasn't it? You were convicted for receiving stolen goods.

SMITH: Look, please, receiving stolen goods is a petty, insignificant matter of no importance whatsoever . . .

JONES: Yeah, well, that's what you told the judge, innit, but he still locked you up.

SMITH: I'm talking about Amnesty International!

JONES: Oh, I see. Amnesty. Yeah.

SMITH: Do you know, it is thirty years since they started their marvellous task?

JONES: Is it? Taking a while then, innit, really? I had some Portuguese kitchen fitters like that once –

SMITH: No, no, no, no, no, no, no, my friend. Amnesty are *not* like part-time labourers. No. Amnesty's work is unceasing.

JONES: Well. They're certainly not like part-time labourers, are they, 'cause *they'd* cease at any opportunity!

SMITH: Alas, and alack, their task is ever with us.

JONES: Verily.

SMITH: . . . so long as there is oppression and tyranny in the world, they must keep the light of hope burning . . .

JONES: Yeah.

SMITH: . . . tend the flame of compassion . . .

JONES: Right.

SMITH: . . . and stir the shit a bit from time to time.

JONES: You seem to know a lot about this Amnesty . . .

SMITH: (*Smugly.*) Well, I am a . . . I am a . . . supporter.

JONES: Are you? Do you go to *all* their matches then? Even the ones at –

SMITH: Look, *do* shut up!

JONES: No, but I wouldn't have put you down as a typical Amnesty International supporter, you know –

SMITH: 'Typical Amnesty . . .' – how would you describe the typical Amnesty International supporter?

JONES: I dunno, he'd be about six foot, he'd have his own psychiatrist and about seven million pounds in the bank.

SMITH: Well, apart from John Cleese, obviously!

JONES: I dunno. Well, he had a beard, didn't he?

SMITH: Well, what have beards got to do with it?

JONES: *I* don't know why they all have *beards*, you're the one who knows all about Amnesty! They just *do*, don't they?

SMITH: Look, beards – beards are *irrelevant*, mate!

JONES: Yeah . . .

SMITH: Beards have got nothing to do with it!

JONES: Oh, right, yeah.

SMITH: There are thousands of decent, ordinary, *beardless* folk – like me – who are committed to fighting injustice!

JONES: I didn't know you *were*. Are you committed to fighting injustice?

SMITH: (*Solemnly.*) If you looked beneath this breast, mate, you would see a heart *burning* with eternal vigilance . . .

JONES: Well, that's the cheese. Never eat it late at night, it gives you terrible heartburn.

SMITH: . . . for justice . . .

JONES: Yes, I see.

SMITH: . . . for freedom, for the individual rights of human beings to speak out against tyranny and oppression wherever they find it. I support that stand. I am part of that fight. I am at one with that struggle.

JONES: You mean you went to *The Secret Policeman's Other Ball* and laughed at some knob jokes?

SMITH: Basically, yeah. Very funny, though.

JONES: It *was*. I enjoyed it . . .

ON THE ENVIRONMENT

STEVE PUNT & HUGH DENNIS

PUNT: What are we *doing*, talking about *trivial* nonsense, when in 1991 we did *nothing*, next to *nothing*, to confront the *awful* problem, the awful, *terrible* things that we're doing to our environment! I mean, do you know that *every* year we *destroy* an area of rainforest the size of *Belgium*?

DENNIS: Why not just destroy *Belgium? So much easier*! And so much more environmentally sound!

PUNT: *Much* more environmentally sound! This is what they ought to have been talking about at the Maastricht Summit! I mean, we've got to make sure that our children don't repeat the same mistakes that *our* generation has made! I mean, *look* what we're doing! The ozone level's going, and there's acid rain, the ice caps are melting . . . We should be teaching our *children* about these things! Teaching them right from the *nursery*! Teaching them rhymes, like –

DENNIS: 'Dr Foster went to Gloucester in a shower of rain / He stepped in a puddle right up to his middle and said: '*Why has this water taken all the skin off my legs*?!?'

PUNT: 'Red sky at night, shepherd's delight / Sheep drowned in morning, global warming.'

DENNIS: 'Mary, Mary, Mary, quite contrary, how does your garden grow? / . . . It doesn't.'

PUNT: And what is probably *the* single worst thing for the environment? The motor car. And yet still we've made *no* attempt to give this up. We have a love affair with motor cars, and I don't know why this is. They're nothing but trouble. We drove up here today, went up the M1, and he was driving, I have to say, and while we were going along there, up the M1, he was doing something that really, really, irritates me whenever we're on the motorway. You're driving along, right, running a little bit low on petrol, and you see one of the signs that says –

DENNIS: 'Services ONE mile or thirty-two miles'.

PUNT: And then the driver says –

DENNIS: 'Oh, I think we can make it to the second one . . .'

PUNT: Why *is* that, eh? I'll tell you why. Because they think it's going to work out *cheaper* that way. Which is nonsense. When you finally get to the garage, there *might* be a bit of petrol there, there *might* be a bit of petrol if you're really lucky, but what there will *definitely* be, at the garage, is bags of fertiliser and charcoal briquettes.

DENNIS: They're so *useful* on the long journey, aren't they?

PUNT: Because all garages sell these but nobody has ever worked out why! It's like they expect every customer to be an arable farmer on his way to a barbeque! It's completely stupid! Of course, you don't get these types of problems if you drive for a living. If you drive professionally you can get even *worse* problems, if what happened to Nigel Mansel in 1991 was anything to go by. He had a bit of a bad season. Of course, he lost in the last Grand Prix of the season, and broke his ankle, and he really lost it a few weeks earlier – I don't know if you remember this, in October in the Portuguese Grand Prix, due to an appalling incident that happened to him in the pits. He went in for a pit stop. Now, for heaven's sake, right, those blokes who work in the pits, what do they have to do? They have to remember to change his tyres *once* in seventy-three laps. And it's not difficult. They've got walkie-talkies, they're in radio contact – 'Hello, Nigel? He says he wants to come in for his pit stop. He says he can come in on the next lap or on lap seventy-two . . .'

DENNIS: 'Oh, I think he can make it to lap seventy-two, yeah . . .'

PUNT: 'Oh, no, no, he says he wants to come in now!'

DENNIS: 'Oh, he's coming in *now*?!?'

(*They mime hurriedly changing the tyres and then waving him off again. Then Dennis holds something up.*)

DENNIS: What's this bit?

PUNT: Oh, *no*! Come *back*, Nigel!

DENNIS: Nigel, come *back*!

PUNT: *Nigel*!!

DENNIS: *NIGEL*!!

PUNT: *NIGEL*!!

DENNIS: *YOU'VE   FORGOTTEN   YOUR   CHARCOAL BRIQUETTES!!*

WE KNOW WHERE

You Live

LIVE!

★

WEMBLEY ARENA, LONDON
3 JUNE 2001

WE KNOW WHERE YOU LIVE, LIVE! 2001

The fortieth anniversary of Amnesty provided the occasion for another mixture of music and comedy, this time at Wembley Arena for one night only and a subsequent TV broadcast, after an unprecedented decade away. Hosted by an on-form Eddie Izzard, who had taken the baton from Cleese, the quality of the event struck most critics as vastly superior to other recent benefits, and prompted one to say that the evening 'resonated as Something Special'. Eddie Izzard and Amnesty had considered simply relaunching *The Secret Policeman's Ball* with the same name, but in the end they decided to pay homage while signalling change – Eddie Izzard wanted the name explicitly to 'turn the spotlight on the bad guys and say we know where you live!'

One new comedy trend that was taken on board was for character-based routines, as had been popularised in recent years by a succession of TV series (including, coincidentally, a Channel 5 show starring Simon Pegg, Sanjeev Bhaskar and Amanda Holden, called *We Know Where You Live*). Among those featured were Paul Whitehouse and Harry Enfield as the two cheesy but politically dubious radio disc jockeys Smashie and Nicey, Simon Day as the pub bore Billy Bleach and the team from the sketch show *Goodness Gracious Me* in their celebrated inverted-prejudice routine 'Going For an English'.

Among the stand-up acts, the manically effervescent Harry Hill dominated the first part of the show, although, inevitably for such a visually inventive performer, not much of his routine lent itself to transcription. Jeremy Hardy provided the most politically charged material of the night, sneering at his usual targets, while Sean Lock disarmed the audience with a droll monologue that reminded one of a comic tradition that was more cerebral than visceral.

The strangest aspect of the occasion was the revelation that, as
a result of an Independent Television Commission technicality so
ludicrous many assumed it was merely another joke, mention of
Amnesty was itself subject to censorship. Eddie Izzard thus observed
that, as a number of swear words were also due to be bleeped, 'If
anyone comes on and says "I'm a lifelong member of Amnesty," no
one on television's going to know whether he's a lifelong member of
Amnesty, cunt or motherfucker.'

SPORTS COACHES
EDDIE IZZARD

Skipping!

Huge fucking boxers, and very small girls are the only two social groups in the world that do skipping. Yes – little girls and huge fucking boxers.

(*Sings skipping song.*)

Little girls – 'Ran, tahn, turn about, turn about the . . . ah, I'm in, two, three, four, five, six, seven . . .'

But big boxers? I've never seen them do the bit where they get the other two big boxers holding the skipping rope going (*Deep voice.*) 'I'm *in*, two, three, four (*Mimes punching imaginary opponent.*) . . . and jump back, two, three, four . . . I don't know what . . . oh, (*Jumps back.*) now I'm in . . .'

What do those boxing trainers do? You know, when the bell goes and the trainers talk to their boxers? What can they *say*? They must be saying, 'Just *hit* him! *Hit* that bloke! Hit him in the *face!* Use the big red things on your hands! *Hit* him! See him? Just bloody *HIT* him! Don't *not* hit him – *hit* him – and then you'll win! (*Then he gives them a glass of water.*)

Now brush your teeth and get out there!!'

And football trainers are interesting as well . . . At half time, they must just go back, 'Kick the ball – in the net! Right?

'That ball? *Kick* it in the *net!* Don't fucking "four-four-two" me – just *kick it in the net!* Just take the bloody ball . . . If you kick it in the net a *lot* of times – we win!

Now brush your teeth and get out there!!'

FATHERHOOD
PHILL JUPITUS

I'm sorry, I'm in a bit of a shitty mood. Because I'm a dad, right. (*There is a yelp from the audience.*) Yes, someone has fucked *me*, sir!

I've got a bit of a situation at home. My eldest daughter brought a boy home for the first time, and I think it's quite safe to say that I reacted rather badly.

She went, 'All right, Dad, this is Billy.' And I went, 'Billy? . . . *Billy*, is it?' And I went up to this, ah . . . person . . . and I said, 'If you . . . so much as fucking *touch* her . . . I'll cut you!'

And this 'Billy', he started crying! Ha ha ha! Still, that's seven-year-olds for you.

———————•———————

MATHS AND MUSIC
HARRY HILL

Nice to see you. Nice to see one or two bald men in the audience. Welcome, hmm? Welcome, sir. The bald man. Er – tell me, was it the same for you? You just noticed it was taking longer and longer to wash your face? Hmm? Am I right?

My parents' marriage broke down, tragically. My dad became more and more deaf. He relied increasingly on lip-reading, and my mum – almost as if to spite him – became a Muslim Fundamentalist. (*He puts his hand over his mouth, like a niqab, and mimes talking.*) 'Your dinner's in the oven! Your dinner's in the oven!'

Now, it seems to me that, er, the vegetarians tend to be the same bunch that go on about the environment. Well, maybe there'd be a bit more environment about, if they wasn't eating all the plants . . .

Well, not just jockeys, I think all small people should have to wear a number! Er, hmm?

It's only really when you look at an ant through a magnifying glass on a hot sunny day, you realise just how often they just spontaneously burst into flames . . .

Oh, go on then . . . (*He pulls back the mic stand like a beer pump.*) Just a half, just a half, look . . .

Now . . . you remember . . . you remember when they allowed calculators in the maths exam? Hmm? Well, I asked for the Casio PF-100, hmm? Oh, yeah, a lovely calculator, yeah? The Casio PF-100. But unfortunately, my mum, she bought me the Casio PF-200, which, as you may know, is an electronic organ. (*Puts his head in his hands.*) Ohhh, Gawd, Mum . . . what did you have to go and get me *that* one for?

So, you can imagine me . . . there I am, in the maths exam, hmm, hmm, it's the multi-choice – it's a third of the marks, it's all-important . . . hmm? Hmm? 'Question 1 . . .'

(*He mimes playing the keyboard as the band's keyboardist plays 'Toccata and Fugue in D' by Bach.*)

'Question 2 . . .'

(*He mimes playing the keyboard as the band's keyboardist plays 'Green Onions' by Booker T & the MGs.*)

(*Singing along.*) A-hippy dippy doo dah, a-hippy dippy doo dah, a-hippy dippy doo dah . . .

I do think . . . that air fresheners must be very confusing for blind people. Don't you think? Eh? Air fresheners. Er, very confusing. For blind people. (*Mimes opening door and sniffing.*) 'Pine forest? (*More sniffing.*) I thought this was the *loo*!'

Now – ooh, one person clapping by himself! Always a bit embarrassing, I think . . . Particularly after sex, I find.

SMASHIE AND NICEY
HARRY ENFIELD & PAUL WHITEHOUSE

A blast of 'You Ain't Seen Nothing Yet' by Bachman Turner Overdrive is played. Whitehouse and Enfield – as, respectively, DJ Mike Smash and DJ Dave Nice – take the stage. Smashie is wearing a Mr Byrite-style 'fun' sweater and sensible cotton slacks. Nicey is wearing a shiny record company promo windbreaker and ill-fitting leather trousers. Enfield signals, and the music abruptly cuts.

ENFIELD: Rock a-doodle-doo, gherkins!

WHITEHOUSE: Pop a-doodle-doo, pilchards! I'm Mike Smash – quite literally, Britain's most pop-a-dap-a-dobulous DJ!

ENFIELD: And I'm Dave Nice – former DJ, and current chairman of 'Kent People Against Asylum Seekers'.

WHITEHOUSE: With all the money we've raised tonight, we're gonna spend it on little teddy bears, and send 'em to all those poor political prisoners who've been wrongly imprisoned. And that'll really cheer 'em up!

ENFIELD: Hang on a sec, Smash – you mean we're doing this gig here tonight for *prisoners?*

WHITEHOUSE: We certainly are!

ENFIELD: Well, call me old-fashioned, but I *hate* prisoners! Don't you?

WHITEHOUSE: (*Nervous laugh.*) You pilchard! Some of these poor people have been popped in prison for their political beliefs!

ENFIELD: What, you mean like *lefties*?

WHITEHOUSE: Indeed.

ENFIELD: Damn right! Lock 'em up! They're cunts!

WHITEHOUSE: (*Nervous laugh.*) Nicey, you un-PC pilchard! You know, there's a lot of electrode-testicle-trocious torture out there. Places where people are whipped, and stripped, and tied up.

ENFIELD: I *know* that club! It's off Great Portland Street. It's called 'Ouch'.

WHITEHOUSE: (*Fake laugh.*) What are we gonna *do* with him, ladies and gentlemen?

THE POLICE
JEREMY HARDY

Those of us on the left go on demonstrations and we get beaten to crap by the police. The police attack people and then people forgive the police. They say, 'Well, it is a difficult job.' Of course it's a difficult job! Jobs *are* difficult. People say, 'Oh, it's hard for the police. I mean, after all, the police are just *normal* people.' The police are not normal people. Who do you know who rides a horse around a shopping centre? The police are *shite* at their job. But they don't catch anyone who's guilty. Never. People say, 'Oh, that's ridiculous, why would the police bother to arrest innocent people?' Well, because they're easier to catch! Because they're not *expecting* anything. And they're generally more compliant. You know the police are never going to catch anybody who's guilty, are they? Because whenever there's some terrible murder they just come on the news and say, 'Now, this man knows who he is.' Madness, madness.

PRINCE WILLIAM

William is the great hope for the Royal Family because he's clever. Because he's gone to college. To study History of Art. Which is one of those courses they make up for people whose parents were cousins. History of Art is neither history nor art, is it? It's like geography of French, it's bollocks. 'Just put the paintings in chronological order.' Which, considering they have the dates underneath, is truly not that taxing.

BILLY BLEACH
SIMON DAY

To a blast of 'Lazy Sunday Afternoon' by the Small Faces, Simon Day enters, dressed as Billy Bleach, an interfering pub know-it-all from The Fast Show.

Awright? Nice to see you. Now, I've got a few tips, for all the boys, or men, in the audience, on how to pull the birds.

Now, if you *do* get involved with a bird now, chaps, it'll be what I call a 'modern woman', right? They might have a car . . . a Twingo, or Fiat Panda . . . (*Laughs.*) Isn't that a nice name for a car, eh, 'Panda', right? 'Cause girls see that and they go 'Oh, look, Panda,' and they think about all the Pandas in the zoo, with their funny faces and black and white eyes . . . and they go 'Aw, bless!' And then they crash.

Nah. *Some* do. So – she'd be a modern woman, right? And I've met this little bird round my flats – Kylie – and she invited me back to her place, right? So I've gone up there – you know what it's like, you're a bit nervous, when you go in someone else's flat. Don't be, guys! Have a dump on the toilet if you want. Don't matter. Just a way of showing her who's boss. But after you do, make sure you spray the old air freshener, and that'd give it that lovely smell of fruits of the forest. And shit. That's what the manufacturers are after. You know what I'm saying?

So we go into the bedroom. Er, I can't tell you what to do in there, you can buy films now, and pick up tips that way and all that . . . But I will say, guys, don't be frightened to let out a little cry as you ejaculate. Er, I don't know, maybe '*Yeees!*' Or '*Noooo!*' Or even, '*Whyyy?*' To express lost innocence. And she'd go, 'What a lovely bloke!' And you slap her on the arse, go, 'You *like* that, girl?' Pukka!

GOING FOR AN ENGLISH

THE CAST OF GOODNESS GRACIOUS ME:
SANJEEV BHASKAR, KULVINDER GHIR,
MEERA SYAL & NINA WADIA

Scene: Friday night, a Bernie Inn in downtown Bombay, just after the pubs have shut.

SYAL: Godammit, guys. I mean, Bombay is the restaurant capital of the world, right, so how come every Friday night we end up in *this* dump?

BHASKAR: 'Cause that's what you do, ain't it? You go out, get tanked up on luzzies and go for an English.

(A waiter arrives, dressed in a white shirt, black waistcoat, black trousers and a black bow tie.)

WAITER: Hello there, and welcome to this traditional English restaurant. My name is James, I shall be your waiter for this evening.

(All four diners start giggling.)

GHIR: *(Laughing.)* Can't understand a word you're saying! Speak *Hindustani*, boy!

BHASKAR: Look, leave it, leave it, I've been here before, I'll handle this. *(Turns to waiter.)* All wight, mate?

SYAL: *(Joining in.)* Ay say, Jahmes, yoire moi maite, ain't you, Jahmes?

WAITER: It . . . It's 'James'. James, madam.

SYAL: Yeah, yeah – 'Jahmes'. That's what I said, dammit.

WADIA: (*Looking at waiter.*) Hasn't he got lovely pale skin, yeah? So nice and pasty, no?

SYAL: But you know what they say about white men, don't you?

(*Wadia shakes her head. Syal glances at the waiter's crotch. Wadia gets the hint.*)

WADIA: Wow!

GHIR: (*Impatiently.*) Okay, okay, what we having, what we having, ah?

BHASKAR: (*Confidently.*) Right, Jamms. First up we'll have, eh what, ten, er, twelve, twelve *bread rolls.* Rolls . . . made of bread. And also bring some of that fancy stuff that comes with it, what is it, er . . .

GHIR: Butter!

SYAL: *That's* it – butter.

BHASKAR: Okay. Main course. What's everyone having?

GHIR: (*Cockily.*) What's the *blandest* thing on the menu?

ALL: *Ooooooh!*

WAITER: Well, er, the scampi is *pretty* bland.

GHIR: I'll have *that*! And bring a fucking *knife*!

ALL: *Ooooooh!*

SYAL: You crazy bastard!

BHASKAR: (*Boldly.*) Bring me a prawn cocktail!

(*The others are impressed.*)

SYAL: You're gonna regret that in the morning!

BHASKAR: (*Mimicking a Mancunian.*) I'm mad for it, I'm mad for it!

WADIA: (*To Syal.*) Okay, what are *you* having?

SYAL: Ah, I can't decide. What are your specials?

WAITER: Today's special, madam, is the Taste of England Platter. Which is a combination of the myriad tastes and textures of English cuisine.

(*Both women sound intrigued.*)

WADIA: Oh, what's in that?

WAITER: Chicken. Boiled until the skin turns just a little bit grey, and then drained of all its flavour and its mineral content.

SYAL: I don't think my rectum could take that. Come on, choose something, Nina.

WADIA: Okay, look, I can't decide between the pan of Hope and Glory and the Toad in my Hole.

SYAL: Ah. Tell you what – why don't you put your toad in my pan and we'll mix and match?

WADIA: Great!

SYAL: I think that's actually how you're supposed to eat this kind of food, you know, like *arrgghh* . . . (*Makes shovelling gesture.*)

BHASKAR: Okay, okay, now listen up, Jamms. First of all, we'll have a scampi, prawn cocktail, gammon steak – crab on the side – pan of Hope and Glory, and a Toad in her Hole. And make sure the toad is extra-large, grease just around the rim. Chips?

(*All four raise their hands enthusiastically.*)

BHASKAR: Twenty-four plates of chips.

WAITER: Sir, sir, I think you may have ordered too much food.

BHASKAR: What?

GHIR: (*Gets up drunkenly to his feet and grabs waiter by his waistcoat.*) Who asked *you*, eh, Clive of India? Ey?? Just bring the food or I'm going to punch your lights out!

BHASKAR: No, no, it's not worth it!

GHIR: (*Staggering.*) I'm going to do a mooney!

(*The others shriek with horror and rush to stop him.*)

‘ 'Cause that's what you do, ain't it? You go out, get tanked up on luzzies and go for an English.'

Sanjeev Bhaskar

CONFESSIONS
SEAN LOCK

I know a lot of comics say this, but, um, I *did* have terrible trouble getting here. It's dreadful, actually, quite traumatic. It started out with an unhappy childhood . . . Sixteen years, no lager – how did I do it? I don't know.

Because there are times during your childhood when you could really do with a drink, aren't there? There are some very stressful moments. And you think, 'If everyone would just stop running around, shouting, put their crayons down, had a pint, and just chilled out . . .' I'm only trying to draw a fucking elephant, you know what I mean?

And another little confession I've got to make. I'm also in therapy at the moment. I don't *need* it, obviously. I just got all these psychiatric gift vouchers for Christmas. The whole family clubbed together. I was very disappointed. I wanted a crossbow.

Did you know that sharks will only attack you if you're wet? That's a fact, that is, I found it out today. It's quite reassuring, isn't it?

I've had a busy week. On Monday, I invented a pill to cure obesity. Yeah, it's about that big (*Cups his hands to form the shape of a very large mouth.*) and made of cork. And on Wednesday I got a bit of a shock. My parents found out I was gay. Which was news to me. I was *very* shocked.

I just went round there for a cup of tea with my girlfriend. They said, 'Sit down, son, there's, er, something we've got to tell you . . . You're a homosexual.' I said, 'I'm not, I'm not!'

Apparently, I'd been outed by a local militant group, and they work on the 'one in eight' theory. We lived at number 8 – I was knackered!

I was watching *Top of the Pops* with my dad and Robbie Williams came on. He was going, 'Eh, son? Eh? *Phwoar*, eh? *Phwoar*!' He said, 'I bet you wouldn't mind getting rammed –' I said, *'LEAVE IT OUT, DAD*!!' Then my mum comes in, she says, 'Dinner's ready! It's your favourite – sausages! Yeah! Big fat juicy ones! A bit like COCKS!'

And then I was sitting at the table and they started flicking yoghurt at me, going, 'Do you like that? Do you like that? Do you like that?' *Yuck!*

MEN'S RIGHTS

On Thursday, in the spirit of this great event, I made some progress about the abuse of *my* human rights. Particularly my male rights. I made a protest outside the AA headquarters. Because I think that they really do abuse male rights and male privileges. Because their priority, the AA's number one priority, if you're a woman and you break down at night, you're number-one priority. If I break down, I could be waiting for four or five hours. If a woman breaks down a hundred yards down the road: *VOOF* – straight to her. That's a ridiculous way to treat men! What do you think we do? Do you think we just fend off attackers all night long? *BIFF!* Ha ha! 'Don't worry about me, I can hold them off for at least another four hours!' *BOOF!* 'More ammo!'

ON PAVLOV
EDDIE IZZARD

Pavlov – he was an experimentalist. He did experiments with dogs. Fantastic ones where he said: 'Day One: rang bell, dog ate food. Day Two: rang bell, dog ate more food. Day Three: rang bell, dog ate my leg.' But we know that with dogs: you're going to ring bells and dogs are going to eat food. But his cat experiments were never published. 'Day One: rang bell, cat fucked off. Day Two: rang bell, cat went and answered door. Day Three: rang bell, cat said, "There's a bell ringing." Day Four: went to ring bell but cat had stolen batteries. Day Five: rang bell but cat put his paw on bell so it only made a *thunk-thunk-thunk* noise. Day Six: cat rang bell, I ate food.'

THE POPE

Er, the Pope. There was a Pope John. Then a Pope John Paul. Okay. And we can see where they're going. The next one should be Pope John Paul George. And then Pope John Paul George and Ringo. It's the populist thing. That's where they're going with the Catholic faith. And he's got a Popemobile. And the only other person in the world who's got one of those is Batman. That's the only other person. There's Batman with the Batmobile and the Pope with the Popemobile. And the Pope's got a cave. And whenever they show a picture of a sinner on a cloud, then the Pope goes down to the cave and he's joined by . . . Altar Boy: *Na-Na-Na-Na-Na-Na, Altar Boy!* And the Pope's wearing his Pope Belt, with his Jesus discs (*Mimes throwing them at sinners.*) *Phitt-ooo! Phitt-ooo! Phitt-ooo!* 'Altar Boy, put out those candles!' *Phitt-ooo! Phitt-ooo! Phitt-ooo!*

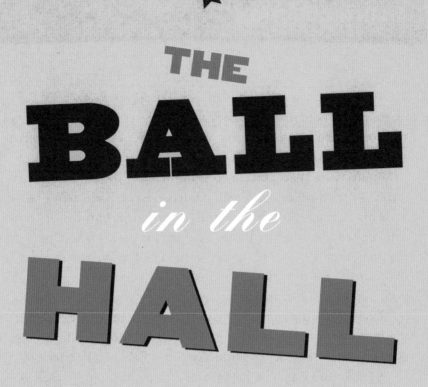

THE BALL in the HALL

THE ROYAL ALBERT HALL, LONDON
14 OCTOBER 2006

THE INTERNATIONAL ERA
AN INTRODUCTION

There had been tantalising signs of *The Secret Policeman's Ball's* international potential as far back as the early 1980s, when Amnesty first sought and found an international audience for the films, videos and albums of the shows.

Amnesty had particular success in the USA by partnering with a young American entrepreneur named Harvey Weinstein – who, with his brother Bob, had recently launched a film distribution company called Miramax Films. The plan originally was to put out the film of the 1979 show 'as was' in the US, but Weinstein judged that some of the material was probably too parochial for American tastes, so, when he heard that another show was about to be filmed, he also secured the rights to that. Miramax then decided to distil the best bits from both UK films and distribute them in the US as a single movie under the title *The Secret Policeman's Other Ball*.

A trailer of Graham Chapman in a tutu mocking the then all-powerful Moral Majority that had helped both the election of Ronald Reagan and the boycott of Monty Python's *Life of Brian* sold the film in the USA. Calling his version of these self-appointed moral guardians the 'Oral Majority', Chapman, in a sober jacket and frilly tutu, demanded that the movie be banned 'before it turns us all into weirdoes'.

The TV spot *was* banned by several fearful local stations – thus prompting media coverage culminating in an invaluable plug on the hugely popular network show *Saturday Night Live*, which had Chapman sit at a desk and make a solemn apology for causing any offence before rising to reveal that he was wearing stockings, suspenders and Stars and Stripes underpants.

Released in the US in the summer of 1982, the movie went on to be favourably reviewed by the critics – the influential Vincent

Canby wrote in the *New York Times* that the film contained 'some of the funniest sequences to be found in any first-run movie at the minute' – and to achieve considerable commercial success. This brought the concept of the *SPB*, and awareness of Amnesty, to a vast number of people in the USA.

As far as the brand of *The Secret Policeman's Ball* itself was concerned, however, the exposure (which had to be wide and sustained in a country as vast as the USA) soon faded, except among comedy fans and performers, and there would be a break of almost a quarter of a century before it once again started to build an international following. Long after the likes of *Live Aid* had caught the imagination of an international audience, Amnesty finally tried again to tap into what one newspaper called the 'talismanic power' of the *SPB* name and make its comedy events appeal far beyond the boundaries of Britain.

Now with well over two million members and with a mission to make the Universal Declaration of Human Rights a reality for all people in all countries Amnesty International recognised that sustained growth was essential.

Growth for Amnesty does not only mean financial growth; it also means more people understanding human rights and joining together in standing up for them. So, with a mission to reach out and engage with 'more and different people' – beyond the usual suspects – Amnesty again turned to its old friend in a shabby raincoat and trilby hat to help – albeit a 'rebooted' friend, now redrawn by artist James Jarvis to look 'like Alain Delon in *Le Samourai*, except with a beak'.

The re-launch of the *Secret Policeman's Ball* in 2006, *The Ball in the Hall*, was set in the context of a very different world to the one which saw John Cleese hand over the phone numbers of 'a few friends', and London theatres willing to stage four very long nights of entertainment after their regular shows ended. To get the desired impact, Amnesty had to embrace the new environment.

Amnesty signalled its willingness to compete in this new context by choosing the 5,000-plus capacity Royal Albert Hall as its base and by embracing new technology, and *The Secret Policeman's Ball* returned in 2006 'reinvented and rebooted for the twenty-first century'. In stark contrast to the brief printed press releases that used to announce the advent of the early productions, the imminent arrival of the next *SPB* was now trumpeted loudly via online animations, celebrity interviews, classic clips, podcasts and downloads, as well as plenty of well-placed features in more traditional media forms – and also the promise of a 'virtual tour' via a simultaneous cinecast in a series of screens spread around the UK.

The communications and messaging also began to make a more direct association with Amnesty's campaigning issues. Five animations were commissioned as part of the live event and associated marketing; voiced by prominent actors, they focused on Amnesty campaigns ranging from human rights in China around the Beijing Olympics, to arms control and stopping violence against women. An ad campaign of four short films featured a hapless comedy act (the Protect the Human Players) trying desperately to get booked for the show – even by kidnapping prominent Amnesty-supporter John Hurt. The broader appeal of the new show was highlighted by the inclusion of several US performers in the cast. Stars with strong fan bases in other countries were now helping to publicise Amnesty's cause.

It paid off. 'The Woodstock of Comedy roars back' exclaimed the media. The live show as well as cinecasts to screens across the UK sold out. The podcasts hit the number one spot in the charts, and the show won nominations for a BAFTA and the Golden Rose of Montreux. The rebooted *SPB* had begun to turn the heads of a new generation of artists and supporters.

As all *The Secret Policeman's Ball* titles have been filmed and recorded (and as all performers have donated their performances ever since the first shows) they have been kept alive and always attracted wide interest and exposure beyond the live arena, and far beyond the UK with video, TV and audio sales around the world. Amnesty was about to try to make the most of this.

After another show at the Royal Albert Hall in 2008, which extended its reach via cinecasts into the USA, Canada and Australia, the next step, as part of Amnesty's fiftieth anniversary, was to take a production physically beyond Britain. And so in 2012 the first *Secret Policeman's Ball* to be held on foreign soil was staged at New York City's famous Radio City Music Hall. 'We wanted to make it bigger and we wanted to make the event global,' explained Andy Hackman, the show's executive producer for Amnesty. 'We wanted to take all the nice things people have continually said about the early shows – "ground-breaking", "invented the charity benefit", etcetera – and use the anniversary celebrations to create a new *SPB* project worthy of its legacy and, more importantly, able to harness the invaluable support Amnesty has from all areas of the creative industries to introduce a new generation (both performers and audience) to Amnesty's work and encourage them to join and strengthen the movement.'

Amnesty gave the *SPB 2012* the strapline 'A Bad Night for Dictators, A Good Night for Free Speech'. The promotion featured online previews and competitions, podcasts, blogs, Twitter feeds and Facebook pages and YouTube trailers. Blessed by the man who helped start it all, John Cleese, as an event that 'reminds audiences how important free speech is, and highlights just how much vital work Amnesty International does to protect it', the grandest ball so far featured some of the best comic talent from either side of the Atlantic, as well as music stars Mumford & Sons and Coldplay. The most significant presence of all, however, was that of the Burmese comedian and former political prisoner Zarganar, who owed his own current freedom to one of Amnesty's tireless campaigns against oppression.

It was a timely reminder, to viewers in Britain, America and all over the world, why such events remain relevant. So long as there is injustice, there will be more of these balls –making people laugh, making them think, making them care and making a difference. Here's to many more tiny revolutions.

THE BALL IN THE HALL, 2006

Held in 2006 within London's cavernous Royal Albert Hall, the four-hour show – which had promised to be 'bigger, better and ballsier than ever before' – offered a more international outlook in terms both of themes and participants, with such topics as censorship, dictatorships, terror, torture and indefinite detention centres being satirised, and American stars mixing on stage with the British. The sheer size of the arena, combined with the massive video screens and disembodied announcements, discouraged many attempts to establish real intimacy with the audience, but a few did manage to strike up a surprisingly strong rapport (after all, at 5,500 seats, the Royal Albert Hall was surprisingly intimate compared to the 11,000-seater Wembley Arena, and it had a stage that projected into the standing audience).

Experienced stand-ups such as Frank Skinner coped with craft and charm, and one or two enthusiastic newcomers such as Andrew Maxwell won over the audience with their energy and eagerness. The American Sarah Silverman, making her debut in an Amnesty show, exploited the distance between the performer and audience by playing on the confusion caused by her combination of a sweet middle-class persona and some increasingly dark and solipsistic material.

The promise of 'ballsier' material was met to some extent by a number of overtly satirical routines, such as Omid Djalili's powerfully performed piece on a dictator dictating and Chevy Chase and Co's spoof on Guantanamo Bay. This aspect was also boosted by a number of short animated films with strong and sharp political messages, including a Jimmy Carr-narrated sequence about a door-to-door salesman offering a range of dolls for torture, a shopping channel parody flogging AK-47s and (with a deft little dig at how

recordings of past Amnesty shows had sometimes been re-edited so as to not to cause any offence) Robin Ince and Lisle Turner's anti-censorship 'Wise Monkeys'.

Jeremy Irons underlined the overall message of this most passionate of all *SPB*s when, during his 'stand-up without the jokes', he spoke of his pride in being 'one of nearly two million worldwide members' of Amnesty International – an organisation that 'stands up for humanity'.

WISE MONKEYS
WRITERS: ROBIN INCE & LISLE TURNER

In an animated short, a pair of bejewelled hands are holding a smoking cigar and, in Bond villain style, stroking a fluffy white cat. Hot ash falls on the cat and it yelps. Jo Brand supplies the voice of this intimidating figure.

MS MONEYPOWER: (*TV executive and owner of the hand.*) Send in the writers!

(*Three wise monks walk in, two are chanting a madrigal.*)

MS MONEYPOWER: Not the monks, the *other* ones!

(*Monks shuffle off.*)

(*Three more writers shuffle into shot – the three wise monkeys. See No Evil is bumping into the others. Hear No Evil is looking confused and scared. Once standing in front of Moneypower, See No Evil steps on Speak No Evil's paw, Speak No Evil makes the noise of a muffled expletive.*)

MS MONEYPOWER: Right. So you're my comedy writers. Good. Now, there's a reason I've asked especially for you. Do you know why?

(*See No Evil starts to speak, but Speak No Evil elbows him sharply. Hear No Evil still just looks confused.*)

MS MONEYPOWER: Exactly, you know not to mouth off. Now, the Secret Policeman's Ball is going to have a lot of fashionable communists – sorry, comedians – mouthing off with their bleeding-heart liberal nonsense. This won't do.

(*To make her point, the cigar is stubbed out on the cat's head. The monkeys look terrified.*)

MS MONEYPOWER: What they don't realise is that I've got to sell this all round the world. So I don't want to piss anyone off with this human rights abuse stuff. Nothing about Turkey, Zimbabwe, China and either of the Koreas. Oh, and just to be on the safe side, nothing that'll piss off North America, oh, or South America or Cuba. Don't mention kidnap, rape, torture, executions or any of that stuff. Nothing about people being persecuted for what they say, what they believe, who they worship or who they damn well are. And none of that freedom of expression, anti-censorship shit. This is showbiz – got it?

(*The three look perplexed.*)

MS MONEYPOWER: Oh, and if you're not sure what to do, for God's sake don't follow your conscience or you won't get a banana!

(*Moneypower throws three bananas. Hear No Evil manages to eat his banana. Speak No Evil keeps trying to jam it in his paw-covered mouth, while See No Evil can't find his. He scrabbles around, and eventually Hear No Evil surreptitiously sneaks the second banana in, leaving See No Evil with nothing.*)

MS MONEYPOWER: Now get to work!

(*They go behind typewriters, unable to use their paws. They just bang their heads on the keys and pages pour out.*)

'Day one, and God invented jam and helicopters and baked potatoes and Angola and Subbuteo players ...'

Eddie Izzard

EVOLUTIONISM, CREATIONISM AND GOD

EDDIE IZZARD

I want to talk about God. Because, well, Evolutionism, it's come back on the cards. Mr Charles Darwin – who looked a bit like God, which is interesting – wrote a book called *You're a Fucking Monkey, Mate*. He played around with the title for a while, and then he ended up calling it *The Origin of Species*. So that was that. And that, by the way, is a theory.

And then there are the Creationists, who now call it 'Intelligent Design'. Where the fuck did *that* come from?

Creationism. Do you remember Creationism? Now, if you look at Evolutionism, it *is* a theory, it has some holes. Evolution: things evolve, duh-duh-duh, we crawled out of the slime – I agree with that, 'cause who wants to be in slime? You know, at *some* point, *any* animal is going to say, 'I don't want to be in slime any more!' – and then there are a few holes. We humans laugh, hyenas laugh – no one else. And hyenas seem to laugh at *anything*. So you've got Evolution.

And the Creationist people say, you know, 'Ah, well, there's a few gaps there!' But I would argue that, if there *are* a few holes in your theory, you don't therefore turn to fucking *magic*!

Because that's what some people think religion is. It's fucking magic! 'Day one, and God invented jam and helicopters and baked potatoes and Angola and Subbuteo players and people called Jim and hair and hair nets and traction engines! Day two, he made gravy, and helicopters again, and large clouds and puffy things, and dogs that go "woof!" and the yapper dogs, which are bastards. On the third day he said, "Shit, I'd better get a list, I'm just making shit up here!"' That is not a *theory* – that's just fucking magic!

And it used to be Creationism and then the crazies changed it to 'Intelligent Design'. And if it's going to be Intelligent Design, I want to see two things: one, intelligence; two, fucking design!

Take bees. Who I really like and I think they do a lot of work because they make honey for bears and humans. That's it. They don't make honey for anyone else. There are no giraffes going, 'Mmmmm!' There are no dogs eating honey. Just bears and humans. And we don't eat it. We buy it, we take it home, we put it on a shelf and we close the cupboard, and we don't see it again until we come back looking for something else. And we see honey, and just stare at it and we wait until the *hon* has separated from the *ney*, but we don't eat it, because we did once when we were sixteen and what a fucking hour-long sandwich that was!

But bees make that. And in the hive – okay, follow this, 'intelligent design' people – bees are making honey for bears and humans, only those two. Bears don't make anything for bees – no hats, no banjos. And you've got worker bees – communist system; queen bee – monarchy system; drone bees – er, television presenters, I don't know. Worker bees going, 'Doo-doo-doo, we're making honey for bears . . .' (*Mimes bees happily labouring away.*) Drone bees going, 'Oh, I like what you're doin', very sixties, very nice style.' 'Fuck off, Brian! You don't do *any* work, do you?' 'I was talking to the Queen . . .' 'Ah, fuck off, *she* never does anything!' Suddenly a bear just goes shooom! (*Mimes a bear's paw crashing into the hive and scooping out some honey. The startled worker bees look up.*) 'Where's the fucking wall gone?' (*Mimes them resuming their duties.*) 'Doo-doo-doo . . .' Very short memories, bees.

Sharks. Sharks haven't evolved for two hundred million years! They've just stayed the same. If they were made by God – they've got no ears, you've noticed, because all nice animals have ears, we go, 'Ooooh, nice animal, ooohh . . . ', but sharks, nothing – God, if he was making them, was going, 'Jesus? Where's Jesus with the ears?' 'He's in the lav.' 'All right, fuck it, no ears for this one! Give me the box of teeth – ooh, I've emptied them all in!'

Sharks are just *evil* bastards. I'm quite happy if all the sharks just went, because they eat fish and us, and we need the fish.

Spiders. If spiders were made by a guy with a beard, then the face of a spider was obviously made with the sewing kit from some hotel. 'Ah, just bits of bobbins in there, some pipe cleaners in the back, come on . . .' How do spiders walk? They must go: 'Ooh, one, two, three, all right, come on, er, all right, now you two, yeah, er . . . Just give me *four* legs, four's fine, eight's *insane!*'

And they appear in bathrooms. And women and gay men come out of bathrooms and say: 'There's a *spider* in there!' And straight men and lesbian women have to go in there and deal with it. And straight men and lesbian women don't want to deal with it but they've read in books that they're supposed to deal with that shit. And they go in with *The Economist* and the spider's always in the bath, isn't he? Always just getting a bath going. 'How do they *get* in the bath? You're too big to get up the plug hole, where did you *come* from?' And then we kill the spider via a controlled method. (*Mimes stamping like crazy and then running away and checking the sole of his shoe.*)

They're just too fucking *scary*. They're supposed to catch flies, and I've seen spider's webs and they're quite intricate, yeah, but I've seen some with one fly in it. I haven't seen a mass of fucking flies in there.

Because if flies – if someone *invented* flies, then fuck 'em. If that's intelligent design, why are they completely – scary ugly? If you get a magnifying glass, they're *ugh*! There's no sweet spot. There's no 'Ahhh' bit.

And they're stupid. Do you know the number of flies in the world? There's over six hundred and twenty-seven flies in the world. Probably more, we got bored counting. But there's a *lot*! And they decide to leave a room by flying into the window. They go: *bzzzzz-doing*!

-bzzzzz-doing!-bzzzzz-doing! And you think, 'Oh you *stupid* fucking fly!' And you go and open the window right next to them and they go: *bzzzzz-doing!-bzzzzz-doing!-bzzzzz-doing!* And then you get a copy of *The Economist* and you flick 'em, and they go (*Mimes a fly going around in a circle and back to the closed window.*) and then they go: *bzzzzz-doing!-bzzzzz-doing!-bzzzzz-doing!* And you think, 'You stupid, dirty, evil fucking *thing!*' Invented by God! And you close the window and you pull the curtains and you leave them. And you come back seven hours later. And you hear: *bzzzzzzzzzzz!* . . . . . . *bzzzzzzzzzz!* . . . . . *bzzzzzzzzzz!*

And then they die.

And they go to fly heaven. Where St Peter the fly is at the Pearly Gates. *Bzzzzz-doing!-bzzzzz-doing!-bzzzzz-doing!* 'Bzzzzz . . . . window . . . bzzzzz . . . go round . . . bzzzzz . . . open window . . .'

HUMMING, MEN AND TERRORISM
ANDREW MAXWELL

Oh! Jesus, ladies and gentlemen, I know you don't know who the fuck I am, but I want . . . I want the *truth!* I'm gonna ask you some questions and I want the truth. And I know it's hard to get the truth from cheering. Who here likes cheering?

(*He holds the mic out as the audience cheer.*)

Who here *doesn't* like cheering?

(*Cheers and laughter.*)

From now on in, it's a humming show. I want you to hum. The hum is a baseline sound, and that means it's omnidirectional. So nobody'll be able to know how you feel about something, but

I'll get to fucking know. Now, I think we should have a practise hum. The sort of hum I'm looking for is a *dirty* hum. Sort of a 'Hmmmm'.

(*He holds the mic aloft. the audience mimic his hum.*)

It's quite a fun sound, isn't it? The sound of twenty pirates agreeing at once. 'I say we strike out for the island, and we steal their gold!'

(*He holds the mic aloft. The audience do the hum again.*)

Just the ladies –

(*The women in the audience hum.*)

It's a very different sort of sound, isn't it? That's if you've eaten something nice. 'Thank you very much, Deirdre, this cake is absolutely delicious. The mixture of the delicious cake and the malicious gossip you were telling me about my close circle of friends is making me feel . . .'

(*He holds the mic out again. The women in the audience all hum again – Mmmmmm – then laugh.*)

The world's fucked. And you know whose fault it is?

(*Audience member: 'It's yours!'*)

Men. *Me*, that's right! It's my fault. The only person on the bill you haven't fucking heard of! My fault! I heard the fuck-all round of applause I got! Ladies and gentlemen, blah-di-blah!! 'Ohhhhhh, yeah, fuck. Here comes blah-di-blah!' Ha ha ha ha!

It's men's fault! All the men who rule the world. Women should rule the world.

(*Women audience members shout out in agreement.*)

Hum it. *Hum* it, sisters, if you believe in it.

(*Women in the audience hum.*)

Women should rule the world! Us men, we've made a fucking mess of it! Yeah? It's true. It's true. It's true. It's true. It is true. It's true. It's true.

(*Shrugs.*) *You* clean it up.

We got any Muslims in? Any Muslims? Any Muslims? As-Salamu Alaykum, you're more than welcome. I want you to know something, Irish people love Muslims. We love Muslims. Irish people love Muslims. We *love* 'em.

(*He holds his arms aloft in celebration, then just sniffs and leans on the mic stand.*)

They've taken a lot of heat off us. Yeah. We're not the terrorists any more! We're the *Riverdance* people. 'How could anything so *cute* be so dangerous?'

We got any Americans here?

(*A few whoops and cheers.*)

As-Salamu Alaykum, you're more than welcome. Know the difference between us and Americans? The size of our fears. Our fears . . . American fears are huge. *Terrorism*! *Aliens*! (*Laughs.*) You imagine anyone in Britain or Ireland ever giving a shit about aliens? Even if there was an alien invasion. Mothership hovering over East London. *Bwwwwwww* – not the East End, that's got all trendy, I'm talking East London. Over Romford. *Bwwwww* . . . aliens kicking the locals about. (*Imperious alien voice.*) 'We rule! Puny Earthlings! We *rule*!' The most you'd get out of Londoners is 'Oi! *He* just pushed in! Silly *caahnt*!'

Size, man. It's the size. It's all the difference is. You know. In fear. I'd almost feel sorry for a fundamentalist hijacker taking over a plane-load of pissed swine from Britain or Ireland. Wouldn't it . . . oh, Ahmed, you picked the wrong flight. 187 EasyJet to Alicante . . . You've got a Stanley Knife. And a firm belief in your God. Have you any idea . . . just how many sovereign rings there are on this plane? You've clearly never been punched in the chip shop.

PELT THE RABBIT
THE MIGHTY BOOSH

Noel Fielding and Julian Barratt walk onto the stage. Fielding, as Vince Noir, is wearing a sparkling silver catsuit. Barratt, as Howard Moon, is dressed in a sober brown suit.

NOIR: I just thought – it's a bit of a party occasion, look, there's people standing up, she's got a face, it's all, you know, *crazy*, yeah – I thought, yeah, what we should do, yeah, is basically get them all juiced up, get them all warmed up, yeah, with like a *game* or something!

MOON: A game?

NOIR: Yeah! A game! Imagine that! I've invented a *game!*

MOON: For tonight?

NOIR: Yeah!

MOON: (*Sounding sceptical.*) Okay, talk me through it.

NOIR: Brilliant! Basically, right, it's called 'Pelt the Rabbit and his Big White Face'. Yeah, I know, the title alone is genius! Wait till you hear the rest, right? Basically, you're in here, or wherever, in a windmill, it doesn't matter, right, and this *massive* rabbit comes in and he's *huge*, right, and he's got a really big face, right? And he runs in and, like, you've got to leg it from him or like throw peanuts at him or take your boot off and just smash him round the head with it! 'Cause, basically, if he catches you, he just throws you on the floor and rapes you!

MOON: (*Unimpressed and discreetly alarmed.*) Yeah . . . that's not a *game*, is it, that? That's just a sequence of events. A sequence of terrifying events . . . culminating in a rape.

NOIR: Yeah, but it's not an *ordinary* rape. It's a rabbit rape. It's a terrific bunny bumming.

MOON: Yeah, but it's still not a game. Where's the strategy, eh?

NOIR: Yeah, but think about it – you never know when he's going to come!

(*The audience laughs.*)

NOIR: When he's going to *arrive*. (*To audience.*) Easy – it's not that kind of show! (*Back to Moon.*) He might come in ten minutes, he might come in a year, he might come in two weeks, he might come in fourteen minutes!

MOON: What if he's ill?

NOIR: He's got a brother who looks exactly like him!

MOON: Right.

NOIR: He's the worst of the two, really, he's smaller but more vigorous. If it's him, you might as well sit down and give up!

(*Moon sighs resignedly.*)

TOLERANCE
DYLAN MORAN

Hello! Hello, hello! Yes. All right then. Hello. (*Smiles groggily.*) So, this is a very big thing. People in a room to . . . to say 'Yes!' for freedom, and 'No!' to wearing a sack when you really don't want to.

But it is very, very important to be tolerant. Obviously. You know, people never, ever forget, if you're not tolerant. Even now, if you, as a liberal European, are talking to somebody from Germany, say, you're talking to them, and you know they're another liberal European, and they're saying, (*German accent.*) 'Well, you know, it's a critical time for Germany right now, er, we

. . . we . . . economically we're pretty good, we have been better, but we're very vibrant, in the theatre and arts and so on . . .' and all the time you're listening to this, you're thinking '*Mmm, mm, mm, mm* . . . Hitler Hitler Hitler Hitler Hitler Hitler Hitler, with the Hitler Hitler Hitler, we do the Hitler thing . . . HITLER!' (*German accent.*) 'And then the wall came down, and you know, it was very divisive between the East and the West . . .' And you're going, 'Yeah, yeah, you've got a little bit of cream on your lip there. You'd better wash that off . . .'

It never goes away! And this idea of preserving freedom is very important. Freedom to be wrong! As well. You know? Freedom to do the wrong thing, elect the wrong people.

Look at California – Arnold Schwarzenegger is the Governor of California. There's a perfectly ordinary English sentence. How the fuck did *that* happen? You know how that happened? You know how he got that job? By lifting things. Now, you and me, we *avoid* lifting things. It's unpleasant. A five-year-old child looks at a heavy thing and goes, 'I don't think so, I'd rather shove Lego up my arse, I'm not going to lift that.' He took a totally different approach. He lifted things. He didn't even *move* them anywhere! He put them back down in the same place! And then said to the people who had gathered, 'Look how good I am at lifting things! In my underpants!' And all the people who'd bothered to stop and watch, they're the really stupid ones, 'cause they said, 'You're the man! You're the one we want to control taxes and water rates and immigration and all that shit!'

But you've got to have the *opportunity* to be wrong. I don't know what all the fuss about lingerie is, anyway. Traditionally, there's never been a huge female requirement for male lingerie. That doesn't really exist in history. Traditionally, women have always been attracted to uniforms. That's what women want, really, there's no mystery to it. Fascists.

DIARY OF A DICTATOR

OMID DJALILI

Omid Djalili stands, dressed as a dictator, in a military uniform. David Armand is seated next to him, dressed in a much less grand military uniform, and taking dictation on a typewriter. Djalili speaks.

ANNOUNCER: Meanwhile, in some far-away country, a dictator is . . . dictating.

What are we doing? (*Composes his thoughts.*) Good. Okay, good! Wednesday, the 23rd: an exciting day! The election results were very slow to come out, so eventually, by 5 o'clock, I said, 'Fuck it – let's issue them anyway!' I always worry that 98 per cent approval is a *little* bit over the top . . . Eh, it sounds a bit phoney. So this year, we went for 87.8 per cent. Yes! I *like* that result. Yes . . . in fact, next year, we might have the same result *again*. Whoo-hah! (*To Armand.*) Write it!

Thursday, the 24th. More shit about me in the foreign press. I mean, where the hell do they get this stuff from? You know, *The Economist* was all, 'Oh, he's looking a bit thinner, the sanctions are beginning to bite!' Not thinking that, maybe, I'm on the Atkins? And due to a *hell* of a lot of willpower, *sticking* to it?

Friday the 25th. Shot a chicken. Ate it. Shot a pigeon. Ate it. Shot a horse. Lost two pounds.

Thursday the 26th. Long, long, chat with my wife. Oh my God. Thrashing it out, over and over again. Why don't I spend more time at home, you know? Should she start a computing course? Why did I have her brother shot, and buried in quicklime? Men are from Mars! Women . . . from Thailand!

Sunday the 27th. Had a meeting with all those tank and gun and aeroplane-selling guys. You know, it really pisses me off. Arms dealers, they get a very bad rap. They're a lovely bunch of guys! Fun, they're caring . . . very sweet. Except Mark Thatcher. What a *total* arsehole!

Monday the 29th. When, oh when, will all the people who oppose me be shot, or put in prison, at least? It's not as if I enjoy killing and torturing. *Well*, maybe some of it. Yeah, some of it can be fun. Like for example, how long a neck can stretch before it goes wobbly . . . mm? Oh, come on, you'll be trying that at home. Oh, and that thing we did with the newspaper editor. Ah, that was fun. You know, with the tins of paint and the donkey and the xylophones, ha ha! I pissed myself laughing!

(*Both he and the stenographer laugh.*)

Then, I went to the central labour camp. And, you know, I was very disappointed. Very disappointed. Hello, guys? Guys? The clue is in the name! I saw one guy, literally doing nothing, just sitting on the floor and bandaging his hands. I said, 'Hey, hey, hey, hey! This is a *labour* camp! Not a *leisure* camp!' And everyone started to laugh. So I said it again, 'Hey, hey, hey! It's a *labour* camp, not a *leisure* camp!' And everyone began to laugh again. And the guards, they began to prod people, to tell people they were allowed to laugh. The whole place was ringing out with the sound of people allowed to laugh. It was like *The Shawshank Redemption*! And you know, (*Starts to tear up.*) I felt so moved, because I thought I could actually see love, on their faces, looking at me . . . Although love and malnutrition *can* look similar.

But you know what was amazing? You know what was just *amazing*? When we left, I didn't even have that bandage guy shot. But, you know, that's so me.

Monday the 2nd. Actually, I *did* have the bandage guy shot. Just to be on the safe side.

ON THE SUN
RUSSELL BRAND

I wanted to talk to you about the *Sun* and that a bit, really. You know, 'cause I like . . . I like the *Sun* a *bit*, right? I've read it all my life and I sort of have an odd relationship with the *Sun* newspaper. I kind of think of it as a friend, but do any of you have a friend that you, like, fucking *hate*? One that's infiltrated your life and is trying to surreptitiously make you be a bit racist . . . with the offer of a £1 day trip to France?

'Come on, come on, it's all right, £1 day trip to France. It'll be well all right, it'll be pukka, it'll be pukka! There's too many asylum-seekers coming in the country!' What, what? *What?* 'Nah, just saying: £1 day trip to France. It'll be *pukka!*' You said something about asylum-seekers. '*I facking never!* Here you are, come on, do a sudoku! Be facking brilliant!'

Also, the *Sun* lives on its chief currency, which is, of course, the pun. From today's edition, I've seen: 'David Beckoned' – because his name is Beckham and he's been beckoned back into the international fold. My favourite pun *ever* from the *Sun*, right, you know George Takei? He plays Mr Sulu in *Star Trek*, he came out as being gay, right, and the article was really compassionate and sensitive – 'Oh, it's a brave decision for him to come out as being gay, oh, Mr Sulu and all that, let's all support him being gay, let's all get behind him and be nice to him and everything' – and the headline was: 'BEAM ME UP, BOTTY!' The compassion was undermined.

My favourite thing in the *Sun* ever is the *Sun*'s letters page, 'Dear Sun'. 'The page where *you* tell Britain what *you* think.' Not just any thought, though, like 'Move arm now' or 'Eat breakfast this morning.' But preferably some thought that might inspire some hatred and antipathy towards people that are slightly different.

(*Studies newspaper.*)

This one here, right, this is a story that concerns Ian Huntley practising witchcraft in his prison cell. And when I read that, I thought, what is the *point* of that story, right, because I, like most of us here, made my mind up about Ian Huntley when he killed those children. '*What*? Ian Huntley's practising *witchcraft*? Oh, you're *joking*! I liked 'im. You build 'em up and then knock 'em down, dontcha?' At the top of the page it does a little summary of the story so that we can all join in with the hatred together. Also, it's entitled 'The Big Issue', right? 'The Big Issue'. And they use the exact same typeface and name as the *Big Issue*, the magazine for the homeless. That's a bit out of order, innit? That's the only intellectual property that magazine's got. (*Impersonates someone at the Sun.*) 'That's a fucking nice font . . . we'll 'ave that! And we'll 'ave them fucking sleeping bags an' all! You shouldn't be so vulnerable then, should ya!'

(*Holds paper up.*)

Here *is* the summary. I'll read it out from my mouth: 'Soham killer Ian Huntley is carrying out voodoo rituals inside jail, an ex-con has revealed.' Oh, let's not query *that* source!

'Where did you get this information?'

'Oh, this desperate criminal told me it.'

'Did you give him any money?'

'Yeah, I gave him some money as an inducement to tell the story.'

'Yeah, that's all right, we'll print that, we'll print that, and we'll give 'em some fucking bingo, they'll *love* it!'

(*Reads again from paper.*)

'The 30-year-old uses clay dolls made in art class, paints their faces, gives them names and sticks pins in them. He *turned* to the black magic rituals . . .' – I like that: 'He turned to the black magic rituals . . .' (*Imagines Huntley browsing the prison library.*)

'Oh, er, Judeo-Christianity, Hinduism . . . *there's black magic rituals over here*! They're beguiling! I'm beguiled by them! Certainly worth *turning* to when you've lost your faith in conventional religion!'(*Starts reading again from paper.*) 'He turned to the black magic rituals after being befriended by 75-year-old paedophile father figure Fred Bull.' If you're going to have a *father* figure, in *prison*, probably best to have one who ain't also a paedophile! He may *abuse* that position!

(*Holds up paper again.*)

Here are just some of the letters elicited by that story. The first one is written by 'Dave Franklin, Swindon, Wiltshire', who I happen to know for a fact wrote about this story with this expression on his face: (*Bares teeth and squints in a strangely smug way.*) 'Ian Huntley whiles away his days playing video games, watching DVDs and making voodoo dolls in art classes.' That seems to be the situation, but this is the key phrase coming up: 'Most of us honest and *balanced* people . . .'

Right, what Dave has done here is created a sub-category of civilians, of which he is a member, that are 'honest and balanced' – it is by that which they are defined:

'Oi, you lot, what are you like?'

'Sort of . . . honest . . . and balanced . . . I suppose.'

'And what about Dave as an individual?'

'Yeah, yeah, I'd have to say he's quite . . . honest . . . and balanced. Hang on, I'll ask him: Dave, Dave, what are you like, mate?'

'I'm quite honest and balanced, I suppose!'

'Oh, that's good. Er, Dave, what do you think of my new hat, mate?'

'I don't *like* it, but it *will* keep the rain off – honest!'

Balanced: that's Dave Franklin!

(*Continues reading from paper.*)

'Most of us honest and balanced people find that much of our time is spent earning money so that we can pay our taxes to keep

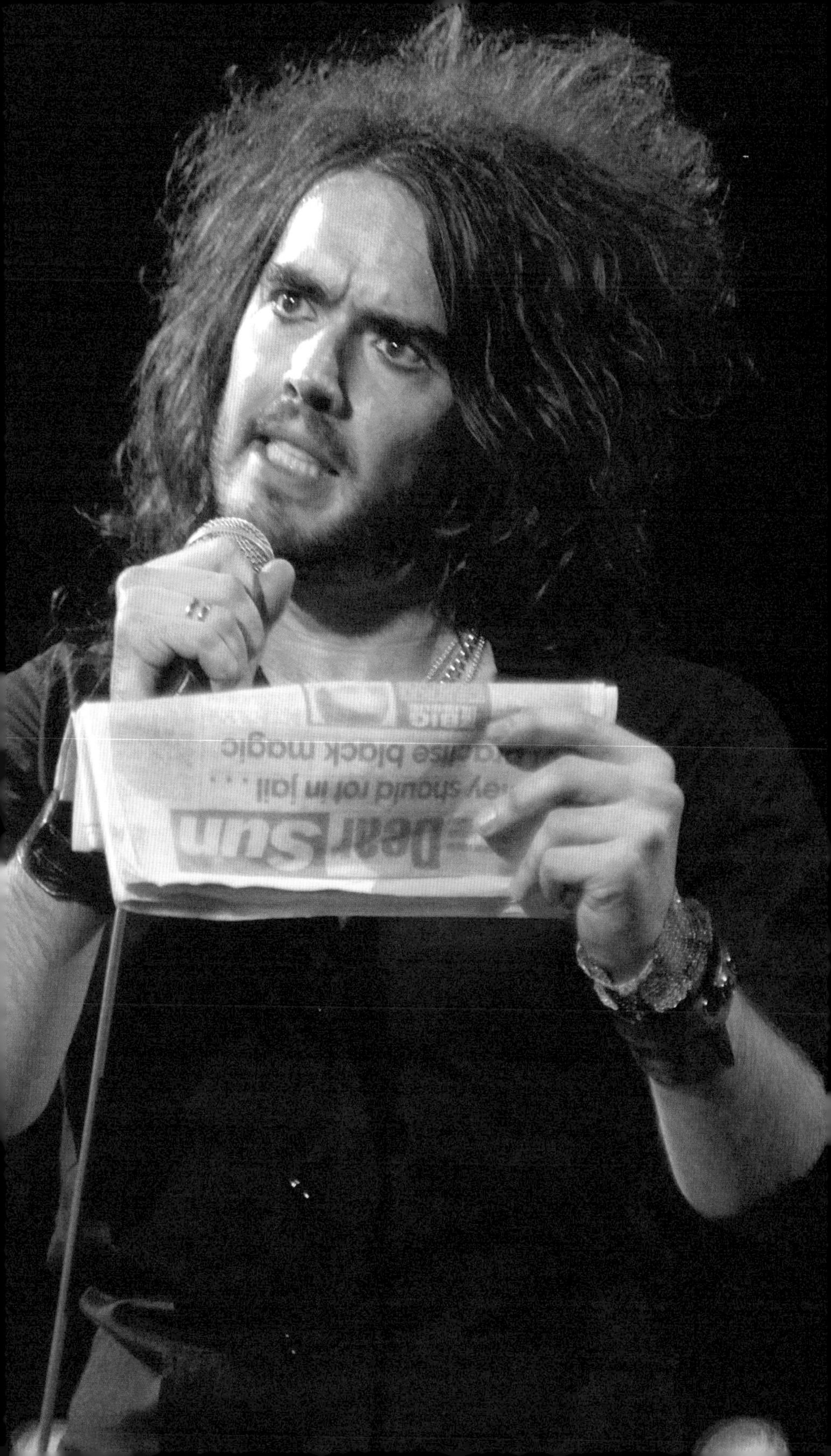
black magic
should rot in jail . . .
Dear Sun

people like him in a cushy environment' – honest and balanced, honest and balanced! – 'Would it not serve the country better if he was sent to Iraq to face the bombs and bullets our troops have been facing?' Yeah! That's what the situation in the Middle East needs – heavily armed paedophiles! We've not done enough damage in that troubled region. What we need to do is get Peter Sutcliffe in a tank and unleash him! Tell you what, let's get Rose West, take her to Basra, get her pissed, give her a jar of anthrax and just let her wander around like Ophelia! 'Have they still not taken to democracy?' 'No, they don't like it.' *'DIG UP JACK THE RIPPER!'*

I do not think that Dave Franklin should be dabbling in international diplomacy. He lacks the aptitude. His brand of knee-jerk reaction ain't what's required. 'Dave? Dave? You're not a bright man, are you, mate? Never . . . speak . . . again. You are essentially an oxygen thief.'

(*Holds up paper again.*)

Next letter: a very different tack, no less sublime. It begins thusly: (*Shouts in a strained voice.*) 'Voodoo is very real. And very dangerous. Often destroying those who practise it' – (*Breaks away from reading.*) 'Often'! He's not talking about *freak* occurrences, right? On my way here tonight, I saw . . . *five* people practising voodoo. Three of 'em were destroyed by it! *Look at the statistics*!

(*Resumes reading.*) 'With any luck, Huntley will destroy himself by opening up a doorway to a world beyond the knowledge of mere man.' (*Breaks off again.*) That's a heavy thing to sort of hope for, ain't it? And then to send it to the *Sun*? It is not a metaphysical newspaper! This is a proposition that if it came from Dante it would confuse you!

'Do you know what I 'ope 'appens to Ian 'Untley, right? I 'ope he destroys himself – '

'Oh, how?'

'This is the good bit! By opening a doorway . . . to a world . . . *beyond the knowledge of mere man*! A world so baffling and complex that whilst man and Huntley can perceive it – he has, after all, just opened a doorway *to* it – he can never *know* it! He can never integrate it into his understanding of what *is*, because he's a mere man! If he were a *meerkat* – better vantage points.'

(*Resumes reading.*)

But the 'star letter' is this one. It comes from Heidi Spiller, Coalville, Leicestershire, who writes: (*Adopts a shrill and angry voice.*) 'Why' – good start – 'Why is Huntley even allowed to have contact with other inmates? He should be locked up for twenty-three hours of every day and only allowed outside in a segregated area for the one hour' – fine – 'It's outrageous, too, that he is allowed pins . . .' (*Breaks off.*) It's not *outrageous*! I'm not outraged by him having *pins*! 'What? *What*? Has he got *pins* in there? The precious pin? The noble pin? The pin what we all do covet? I'll tell you what, I'll tell you what – *why don't you just give him a swatch of textiles, a Singer sewing machine and let him become the Coco Chanel of the fucking D Wing*?! (*Resumes reading.*) 'It's outrageous, too, that he is allowed pins to put into his voodoo dolls. His voodoo dolls should be taken away and burned.'

Now, I don't know *much* about voodoo . . . but I *do* think *that* is an improper solution!

'I sort of have an odd relationship with the *Sun* newspaper. I kind of think of it as a friend, but do any of you have a friend that you, like, fucking hate?'

Russell Brand

GUANTANAMO BAY
CHEVY CHASE, SETH GREEN, SHOBNA GULATI & NITIN GANATRA

Lights up. Green stands centre stage, in combat fatigues, holding a rifle. Behind him is a cluttered desk. Chase enters, dressed as a general, and opens the door.

CHASE: Private Parts?

GREEN: Sir, yes sir?

CHASE: Oh, there you are.

(*Saluting, Green drops his rifle butt onto Chase's foot.*)

CHASE: *Ow!* Jesus!

GREEN: Sorry, General Nuisance, sir!

(*He hoists his rifle back onto his shoulder.*)

CHASE: It is not 'General Nuisance,' it is General Nuissance.

GREEN: Sir, yes sir!

CHASE: What's the *matter* with you?

(*He walks over to his desk.*)

CHASE: What have we got lined up for today?

GREEN: Sir, the Chowdrays are here, sir.

CHASE: The what? The Char, cha? What?

GREEN: The Chowdrays, sir, they arrived from England yesterday.

CHASE: The Chowdrays?

GREEN: Sir, they arrived from the airport . . . in a *hire* car.

CHASE: A hire car?

GREEN: Sir, yes sir, they insisted. They said, (*Dick Van Dyke Cockney accent.*) 'It was awl part of the package deal from Thomas Cook's', sir.

CHASE: Is that the *way* they said it?!

GREEN: Precisely, sir.

CHASE: Well, bring 'em in.

GREEN: Sir, yes sir.

(*Green marches out. He returns a couple of seconds later, pointing his rifle at the Chowdrays – Gulati and Ganatra – who are both dressed in orange Guantanamo Bay-style jumpsuits. They are also pulling wheeled suitcases behind them.*)

GANATRA: No, just point it *away*, please!

GULATI: Just point it *down*!

GANATRA: Please, what are you doing?

GREEN: Move, move, move, move, move, move! *Move!*

(*They stand before Chase, looking baffled but defiant.*)

GULATI: Are you the manager?

CHASE: *Manager?* No, I am General Nuissance!

GULATI: We wish to make a *biiiiig* complaint!

CHASE: *Complaint?!*

GULATI: When we booked our chalet, we asked for a room with a sea view, a king-sized bed, *and* an en suite bathroom. But what do we get given? A room with no windows . . .

GANATRA: Ahhh!

GULATI: . . . a plank of wood to sleep on . . .

GANATRA: Mmmm!

GULATI: . . . and a bucket to pee in!

CHASE: They got a *bucket?!*

GANATRA: This is not what we were led to expect in the brochure.

CHASE: Do we have a *brochure?*

GULATI: *We* did! But this one (*Turning to Green.*) flushed it down the toilet!

GREEN: Discarded it in the latrine, sir!

CHASE: I know what a toilet is, Private Parts! Hoo-ra!

GREEN: Hoo-ra!

GULATI: And secondly, where is the *entertainment* we were promised? There's no knobbly knees competition. And no karaoke.

GANATRA: And, do you know, I had my gonads strapped to an electric toaster!

CHASE: My pleasure.

GULATI: And where is the Shane Ritchie concert we were promised?

CHASE: (*Gravely.*) There are some parts of the Geneva Convention that we will not break.

GULATI: Darling. Tell him.

GANATRA: Huh?

GULATI: Tell him!

GANATRA: Uh.

GULATI: Tell him about the flight!

GANATRA: Oh, yes, the *flight*! The *flight*. We were strapped to the chair . . . *chained* to the chair, with the gag in the mouth . . . and then we had no food or water for nine hours!

GULATI: That is the last time we fly EasyJet!

GANATRA: Aaaah.

CHASE: Listen –

GULATI: No, *you* listen!

(*She advances on Chase. Green covers her with the rifle.*)

GULATI: This is *not* what we expect from a holiday resort!

CHASE: This is *not* a holiday resort!

GANATRA: You're telling me, buddy! I mean, this morning, we had to share a shower with fifty men!

GULATI: Actually, I didn't mind that so much.

CHASE: Hoo-ra!

GREEN: Hoo-ra!

GANATRA: Hey, hey –

CHASE: Er, Guantanamo Bay is not a vacation resort. Although that's not a bad idea. Make a note of that, will you, Private?

GREEN: Note taken, sir!

GANATRA: Er . . . Guantananamo Bay?

GULATI: Huh?

GANATRA: *Guantananamo Bay?*

CHASE: No! Not Guantananamo Bay, it's –

GANATRA: Guantananamo Bay?!

CHASE: Guantanamo Bay!

GANATRA: Guantananamo . . . (*Turns to Gulati.*) I told you this wasn't Disneyland!

GULATI: Ari, I *saw* Mickey Mouse!

GREEN: No mice on the premises, ma'am. Only rats.

CHASE: Guantanamo Bay is *not* a holiday resort. It is a *detention* centre run by the United States.

GANATRA: What? But you . . . you . . . can't just bring people here on trumped-up charges with no evidence and no recourse to the law!

CHASE: (*Cheerily.*) Yes, we can!

GREEN: It's kind of our thing, sir!

CHASE: Yes, it's part of our thing.

GREEN: It's *really* our thing.

CHASE: Hoo-ra!

GREEN: Hoo-ra!

CHASE: *Hoo ra!*

GREEN: *Hoo-ra!*

GULATI: All right! You can. But you really, really, really *shouldn't.*

CHASE: Seems to have been quite a mix-up here, I'm really sorry to have ruined your holiday. Er . . . how about if Uncle Sam were to pay for first-class tickets back home?

GANATRA: Errr?

GULATI: Hmmm?

CHASE: And we were to give you, oh, a motel room for the night, while you're staying and waiting?

GULATI: Errr . . .

GANATRA: Errmm . . .

CHASE: And we could take a few snapshots of you, er, kind of a memento of your stay here? With you and Private Parts?

GANATRA/GULATI: (*Agreeably.*) Ahhhh!

CHASE: All right! Let's *do* that!

GREEN: Standard holiday photo pose, sir?

CHASE: Hoo-ra!

GREEN: Hoo-ra!

GANATRA/GULATI: Hey, hey!

(*Green drags Ganatra across the stage and makes him kneel on all-fours.*)

GANATRA: Er . . . Okay. All right. Okay . . . this is nice!

(*Green takes Gulati and makes her lie on top of Ganatra.*)

CHASE: All right. Smiles all around!

(*He produces a camera and bends to take a picture.*)

CHASE: Oh – wait a minute, wait a minute –

(*He rummages in his desk.*)

CHASE: Don't wanna forget the Mickey Mouse ears . . .

(*He produces some things from a desk and gives them to Green.*)

GREEN: Your Mickey Mouse ears, ma'am!

GULATI: Oh, delightful!

(*Green puts a black hood over her head.*)

GREEN: Your Mickey Mouse ears, sir!

GANATRA: Thank you very much!

GREEN: Helps you get into the festive spirit!

CHASE: Smile!

(*Green grins and points at the prisoners.*)

CHASE: How do you say 'cheese' in terrorist?

THE PUB LANDLORD
AL MURRAY

Murray, dressed as the Pub Landlord, rides onto stage via a motorised bar, using the beer pumps to steer it. When he arrives he steps off and pulls himself a pint.

Let's hear it for the beer, ladies and gentlemen! All hail to the ale! And welcome the wine – for the ladies! Good evening!

(*He serves some drinks to people the audience: 'Those are the rules: a pint for the fella, a glass of white wine, fruit-based drink, for the lady! Those are the rules. And if we didn't have rules, where would we be? That's right – FRANCE!'*)

I'm sure you'll agree with me when I say this, that the current state of political debate in Great Britain – the most sensible, normal, down-to-earth country in the world – is fucking woeful at the moment, innit? Yeah? It's shocking, innit? Yeah? *Shocking!* Even a serious issue, such as, for instance . . . (*Bends down and groans.*) the Euro – on which I hold certain views, involving its passage over my dead body – even a serious issue, like the Euro, is not going to get debated properly in this country any more. It's going to degenerate into some sort of bad fucking pantomime. And I'm worried – and this is my message to you tonight – I'm worried that if we're not careful, 'cause of this pantomime fucking politics, we're going to end up with that Euro creeping up on us, creeping up behind us, and we're not even going to fucking *notice*. That is something that worries me.

(*A large cardboard Euro coin is slowly rolled onto the stage. The audience shout: 'It's behind you!'*)

What do you mean it's *behind* me? What the fuck are you on about? There's nothing behind me except for my bar! What do you *mean*, it's behind me? This is *not* a fucking pantomime! Oh, no, it isn't! (*The audience shouts back: 'Oh, yes, it is!'*) Oh, no, it isn't! (*The audience shouts back: 'Oh, yes, it is!'*) OH, NO, IT FUCKING *AIN'T*!! (*The audience shouts back: 'OH, YES, IT FUCKING IS*!!') Fucking hell, for a right-on crowd you ain't half turned!

All right, if you're going to act like children, I'm going to treat you like fucking children. What I'm going to do is, I'm going to count to three, and when I get to three, I'll turn round, and if there's anything there apart from my bar – fair play, I'll have to give it to you. Right? Here we go: One . . . two . . . (*The coin rolls back off stage.*) . . . three! (*He looks back and sees nothing but his bar.*) Yep, you're a bunch of fucking timewasters! (*He heads over to the bar and pulls himself another pint while muttering to himself. Then he spots the coin rolling slowly back on stage.*) What the fucking hell is THAT? (*To the audience.*) Why didn't you say anything? Right, okay, I'll deal with this!

(*He gestures to the audience to 'shush,' then he tiptoes up to the Euro and tries to push it away. He finds seven dwarves, Snow White and a pantomime horse trying to push it back. They fight and he wins. 'Piss off,' he shouts as they all run away.*)

It's all right – I can fix this with me currency converter. Here we go! (*He turns the coin around to reveal the head of the Queen.*) There you go, Your Majesty! My work is done 'ere!

(*He walks back to address the audience.*)

I have to go, ladies and gentlemen. I'd like to leave you with a thought. It's a simple thought. What is the driving force of human nature? Any idea? *Necessity* is the driving force of human nature, because it's the mother of invention. I can prove that to you with an example now: on July 25th 1909, Louis Bleriot was the first man to fly from France (*Winces.*) to England in a monoplane aircraft of his own manufacture. And on July 26th 1909, work on the anti-aircraft gun began. Because necessity is the mother of invention!

ON SEX, RACE AND GRANDMOTHERS

SARAH SILVERMAN

I'm so honoured to be doing something for Amnesty International tonight. I'm an amazingly charitable person myself. I'm very thin-skinned, I'm very sensitive.

Like when I see these documentaries with starving children in Africa and their big bellies and their flies . . . These are one-or-two-year old *babies*, you know, nine months' *pregnant*, and it's heart-breaking. And I don't give money because I don't want them to spend it on drugs.

I'm going to adopt. If I have kids at all, I'll adopt. Probably from China, um, probably a boy, because, er, I don't know, somebody told me that the girls there are, like, useless or something.

My niece, er, came out recently as a lesbian. She's seven – did I mention that? She announced to the family that she's a lesbian. I don't even know if she knows what it means, but I am behind her a hundred per cent. I support her. And do you know what's heart-breaking? My sister punished her for it. Can you believe that? 'No pussy for a week!'

I'll be honest. I woke up and I really just had the *blaaghs*. I woke up with the *blaaghs*. I really needed some good news, so I got an AIDS test. Because *I* don't have fucking *AIDS*! And they go through a questionnaire, and they ask you a whole bunch of questions – that's what a questionnaire is – and about halfway through I realised, 'Oh my God – I have fucking *AIDS*! I have AIDS!' At first I'm all cocky. She's like: 'Have you ever had unprotected sex?' I said, 'Is there any other kind?' So she said, 'Well, how many times have you had unprotected sex?' And for that I felt that I should write it down and slide it to her. She said: 'There are *two* numbers

here.' And that's when I told her: 'Well, this one's for the front . . .' She pointed out they were the same number, and I explained to her I'm totally obsessive-compulsive that way.

The worst part . . . and kind of the best part . . . um . . . was when she said, 'Have you ever had a blood transfusion in the eighties?' And I said, 'Oh my God – yes.' And she said, 'You did? You *did* have a blood transfusion in the Eighties?' And I was like, (*Smiling with relief.*) 'Oh my God – *no*! I misheard you! I thought you said, "In Haiti"!' So that was a relief.

I'm an optimist, but I really think that, if anything goes wrong, I'll become a fatalist. You know? I always think that if I were ever stuck in an elevator, I would just say, 'We're going die here. Um, we're going to be here for a really long time, and why don't we designate this corner as the bathroom and I'm going to take a shit right now.' And then we'd probably be saved immediately and who would have egg on her face? Big S.

I finally saw the DVD of *Brokeback Mountain*. I watched it with my boyfriend. And it was beautiful. He had to close his eyes during all of the, like, gay sex scenes. He's not homophobic, it's just, you know . . . the only way he can come.

Do they have Gay Pride here? I went to the Gay Pride march this past summer. And, er . . . (*Someone in the audience whoops. Silverman points mockingly at them.*) Gay! (*She screws up her face in disgust.*) *I'm not gay* – I just wanted to support! And I had a blast. But I don't want people to *label* me as 'straight' or as 'gay', you know? I just want people to look at *me*, you know, and . . . and . . . see *me*. As white.

I can say that! I totally used to go out with a guy who was half black. Who broke up with me, 'cause I'm a fucking loser. And, um . . . (*Pauses to think for a moment.*) I just heard myself say that – that is the most pessimistic thing! I have the worst attitude! He's half *WHITE*! And he broke up with me.

The point is that whether you are black or white or Asian, deep down – but just those three – deep down we're the same. And I don't care if you think I'm racist. Honestly, I'd rather just you think I'm thin. A thin racist. That's more important to me.

(*She suddenly seems emotional.*)

This is probably the worst time to do this, but before I leave I wanted to take a second, you know, and, ah, dedicate – this is so queer – dedicate this to my, ah, grandmother who passed away a year ago tonight, so . . . (*Looks up at the heavens.*) This is for you, Nana! Ha, um . . . sorry . . . (*She looks on the verge of tears and has to pause. The audience start applauding sympathetically.*) Thank you . . . oh, this is hard. She was ninety-seven so, obviously, I suspect foul play. (*Looking emotional but very determined.*) And I am spending my own money, and I am getting her body exhumed, and I am going to get a full rape exam performed. And I am going to get to the bottom of this. (*Bitterly.*) And my parents are not behind me – what *else* is new? They never are. They don't believe in me. So . . . (*She looks like she's going to cry again.*) They are *wrong* this time, so . . . sucks for them. (*She suddenly looks up at the heavens anxiously.*) Oh God, *please* find semen in my dead grandmother's vagina!

★

THE
SECRET
POLICEMAN'S
BALL
(2008)

★

THE ROYAL ALBERT HALL, LONDON
4 OCTOBER 2008

Secret, Policeman's Ball '08

AAA

178

Another grand affair staged at the Royal Albert Hall, the 2008 *SPB* moved along, compared to its own past standards, with near-military precision, with most performers diligently limiting themselves to tight five-minute slots. The big-screen projections and wireless microphones were back as each tiny figure moved about in the distance, but, with a number of comics who were now fairly used to working such enormous halls, the atmosphere seemed a marked improvement on the previous production.

The recent tendency to feature more topical themes in a more overt manner continued with several routines that dealt directly with current affairs. Frank Skinner achieved the surprising feat of marrying a George Formby tribute with some gags about Abu Hamza and Osama Bin Laden; the Indo-Canadian comic Russell Peters contributed a monologue on the war in Iraq; and the Iranian-born Shappi Khorsandi supplied both comical and serious spots about intolerance.

The production as a whole, however, was a little more balanced than in 2006, with Mitchell and Webb reviving the tradition of the *SPB* double act, which had dropped out of fashion for a while after Fry and Laurie went their separate ways; Tim Minchin bringing back the comedy song, which had been pioneered for such shows by Neil Innes; and Sean Lock providing the kind of conventional stand-up routine that had always been a staple ingredient of such an event.

Eddie Izzard, by now firmly established as the current driving spirit of the *SPB*, was as distinctive as ever, but it was arguably Shappi Khorsandi – self-deprecatingly explaining her presence as an administrative error ('I think they thought I was Shami Chakrabarti') – who was the breakthrough star of the night. Given the relative paucity of female performers in the *SPB*'s (and the rest of British comedy's) past, her success was especially encouraging.

COMEDY WAR SONGS

FRANK SKINNER

It's great to be at the Albert Hall. It's lovely, isn't it? I notice outside it's got one of those double pelican crossings . . . do you know the things I mean? Where you get a green man and you have to get to the central reservation then get *another* green – are you with me? You know the ones? The *double* pelican? They've plagued me for years those, because I thought, why not just have *one* green man that stays on twice as long? Why have the one on the central reservation? It's a waste of money.

And then I was doing a gig in a little club one night and I was talking to this bloke in the audience and I said, 'What do you do for a living?' He said, 'I work for the roads department.' And I said, 'You're *just* the bloke I've been looking for.' I said, 'Why do they have the second green man on the central reservation in the middle?' And this was what he said, right – and he wasn't joking, he was serious, and he said it with an air of some authority, right – he said, 'Oh,' he said, 'er, that's in case people change their minds.'

So, some people, apparently, they get to the central reservation, look across at the other side of the road, and think, 'Hmm, actually, now I see it close up . . . not sure. Luckily, I have a get-out clause . . . (*Mimes pressing a button.*)

I was in a club, and I was talking about Heather Mills – Heather Mills McCartney, as was. And I was talking about how people hate her, right? And I said to this bloke, you know I was talking, and he said, 'Oh, I really hate her.' And I said, 'Have you ever met her?' He said 'No.' I said, 'Well, that's crazy, isn't it, to hate someone you've never met?' Not that *I've* ever met Heather Mills. Something I'm sure will be remedied in a couple of years' time when we both arrive to disappointingly lukewarm applause at the *Big Brother* house . . . But I was, you know, I was trying to stick up for her. He said, 'I love Paul McCartney,' he said. 'I can't understand . . .' He said, 'He could have had anybody,' he said. 'I dunno why he married a one-legged woman.' And then his mate said, 'Well, people will do anything for a parking space.' No, that . . . I was horrified. Because what I don't get is, usually if people are disabled, they get the benefit of the doubt a bit, you know? You admire them for battling against the odds, don't you? You'd agree with me there, yeah? I mean, take, for example . . . er . . . Abu Hamza.

You know him, the Muslim cleric with the two hooks, right? Now, you might think he's a bad person, who spreads, you know, hatred, or whatever, but – be fair to him – he lost both his hands in an accident, right? Terrible. Imagine having to go through life with two hooks for hands. Luckily, he likes corn on the cob.

He lives by me, actually. Well, actually, he used to. He's moved now, to, er . . . to prison. I used to see him on the Tube in the morning. 'You all right?' 'Yeah, I'm fine thanks.'

(*He mimes Abu Hamza sliding up and down the handrail on the Tube with one of his hooks, a leg of lamb on the other one.*)

I'm fifty-one now. No, when I got to fifty I thought, I'd better start looking after myself a bit. I thought, I'll join a gymnasium. Then I thought, no, no – I'll just get some multi-vits. That'll do it. So I got some of these multi-vitamin tablets called 50 Plus, right. And I've been taking them, and there's a very odd side-effect that I didn't anticipate. They – and this is absolutely true – they have made my urine completely luminous. Right? To the point where it *glows in the dark*. It *glows* in the dark! If I wake up in the middle of the night, it's like there's a little runway between my bed and the en suite, formed by dozens of slightly dribbly return journeys.

And you know the toilet rug, round the front of the toilet? Ah, man, you should see my toilet rug. At night. It's fantastic. It's like flying over Vegas.

And the other thing, right – now, how *sad* is this? As in 'old man things to do . . .' I've started using my satnav for *walking*. Right? So I actually walk like this . . . (*He mimes walking slowly whilst consulting a satnav.*) Well, not quite like this because that would be ridiculous, but I use the satnav . . . and, you know the satnavs where you get a map and you get like an arrow where you can see where you're going? Yeah, you can still get the little arrow even though you're walking, so . . . Obviously, it moves a lot slower. But you can watch yourself moving along the map. It's quite exciting. I got to a main road, and I could see the main road on the map and I could see me as the little arrow and I ran just into the main road just a few inches, and then out again. And then in again, just at a slightly different angle . . . and I managed to recreate the opening titles to *Dad's Army*. (*Sings.*) 'Who do you think you are kidding . . .'

That song, incidentally, you know, that 'Who Do You Think You Are Kidding, Mr Hitler', I've always thought that was an *odd* song, to have a light-hearted comedy song about the Nazis. Struck me as a bit strange. It turns out that, during the Second World War, it was a very popular thing. People like George Formby, British comedians, would bring out lots of comedy songs about Hitler, and stuff like that, right? And it was a kind of a way of coping with the stress of the war.

And I thought, it's a shame we've lost that tradition. I think it's a brilliant idea. But, can you imagine it now if a British comedian brought out a song about, say a light-hearted comedy song about the Iraq war? You don't feel it would sell that well, do you? If you was watching the lottery show on Saturday night and they said, 'And now, with his new single, ladies and gentlemen, Frank Skinner.' And I come on . . . (*Capers cheerfully across the stage and sings.*)

My mate Ali was a dentist
Now he's a Muslim fundamentalist
Oh bang bang Bagdhad
He's gone bomb mad
Bang bang Baghdad boy!

Drove a car bomb through the cordon
Watch out, Mister Traffic Warden!
Bang bang Baghdad
He's gone bomb mad
Bang bang Baghdad boy!

Who would buy that?!
(*Audience applause.*)
Oh, that bloke! . . . Oh, quite a few people!

The other thing that's changed as I've got to fifty, I've got to be honest with you now, I feel I know you well enough to be, er, to be straightforward . . . is that my sexual attitudes have changed quite a bit. When I was starting out in this job, I used to have quite a lot of one-night stands, right? I've, er, I've stopped now. I think for a fifty-year-old man it's sordid, would you agree? But I do I miss the *adventure* of it, because I used to get into some scrapes, and I miss that, you know?

I remember on one occasion, I – this is a completely true story – I met this woman, she's a very lovely woman, and I went back to her flat, right? We got back, and, erm . . . now, I'm going to have to be slightly graphic here, 'cause the geography of this story is quite important. We were having sex from behind, 'doggy-style', they call it, don't they? Yeah. So we were having, er, we were having the 'sexuals' from behind, right? Now, we hadn't . . . I hadn't . . . there'd been preliminaries. I hadn't just crept up on her, you know? She might have had hot tea! In those days, this is going back a bit, I used to be very keen on the orals. I used to give the orals with great gusto, right? I was fearless . . . And, erm, nowadays, I . . . I . . . (*Pulls a face.*) I'm not . . . I've grown out of it. I don't ever . . . You know, the occasional peck on the majora, but I rarely visit the inner folds.

I've got nothing against it, you know what I mean, I'm not squeamish about it. Some men . . . in fact, I read in *Marie Claire*, right, that some men suffer with this thing called clitoraphobia . . . which is not an irrational fear of the Lancashire town of Clitheroe. It's . . . some men are actually scared of the female . . . I don't like the word . . . the . . . the (*Deliberately mispronouncing.*) *cly-tor-is*. They're scared of the cly-tor-is, right? Now, that is not my problem. In fact, I'd say nowadays that's one of the few things in a hood I'm *not* scared of.

So it was going well, we were having the doggy-style sex, and I was holding on for grim life, right, because I find . . . What it was . . . she wasn't standing, she was kneeling on the bed. And I find when a woman kneels, I find after a bit they tend to draw away from me. I don't know if I over-thrust . . . but I . . . they get, er . . . You know when you're in a conga and it gets a bit stretched?

(*Mimes someone trying desperately to hang on in a conga.*)

So I was holding on, and I dunno, I had something on my mind, something was plaguing me, and I was having sex in that position. And you know when you've got something on your mind sometimes you need two hands to think, and I was having sex like this –

(*He holds his head with one hand whilst stroking his chin with the other, all the while miming pelvic thrusts.*)

I looked down. I realised for the previous three minutes I'd been what I can only describe as 'air-fucking'. She was *eighteen inches* away! Well out of my range!

Now, I'm going to leave you with a song. It's a comic tradition in this country and I'm happy to keep it going. Here you go:

(*He strums the ukulele.*)

Can you hear my instrument?

(*He strums some more and then sings, in a cheerful George Formby voice.*)

What happened to that nasty man,
So pally with the Taliban?
Oh, oh, oh, oh – Osama Bin Laden!

I believe you promised to buy this . . .

He had one big hit, then he went away,
Like a terrorism Macy Gray,
Oh, oh, oh, oh – Osama Bin Laden!

Every now and then he sends out a videotape,
To say he's doing great and he's full of hate,
Well, if he's doing so great, then please tell me
Why a videotape not a DVD?
Oh, oh, oh, oh – Osama Bin Laden!

You might think that he's wicked and depraved,
But think of him stuck in that fucking cave.
He takes girls back there now and then,
But the clerics just throw stones at them,
Oh, oh, oh, oh – Osama Bin Laden!

All music's banned by the Taliban,
So he always misses the ice cream van,
Oh, oh, oh, oh – Osama Bin Laden!

Taliban TV ain't got a lot of laughs in,
Their biggest show is called 'Strictly No Dancing'.
No one comes to his parties any more,
It's like being Michael Barrymore,

Oh, oh, oh, oh – Osama Bin Laden!

NAZIS
DAVID MITCHELL
& ROBERT WEBB

David Mitchell and Robert Webb are dressed as SS officers. Webb is standing up, looking through field glasses. Mitchell is sitting with his cap in his hands. He looks troubled.

WEBB: They're coming . . . Now we'll see how these Russians deal with a crack SS division.

MITCHELL: Erm, Hans . . . ?

WEBB: Take heart, my friend!

MITCHELL: Er, yeah, er, Hans, I've . . . I've just noticed something.

WEBB: (*Not really listening.*) . . . These communists are all cowards.

MITCHELL: Yeah, um, have you . . . have you looked at our caps recently?

WEBB: Our *caps*?

MITCHELL: Yeah, the badges on our caps. Have you looked at them?

WEBB: Er, no, a bit . . . what?

MITCHELL: They've got *skulls* on them.

WEBB: Hmm?

MITCHELL: Have you noticed that the little badges on our caps have actually got pictures of skulls on them?

WEBB: I don't, er . . .

MITCHELL: Hans, are we the *baddies*?

WEBB: Of course we're not the baddies! What we're doing is entirely just! We're fighting for the future of Germany, against the communists and the decadent Western powers who betrayed us at Versailles!

MITCHELL: Uh, yeah, yeah, that does sound just . . .

WEBB: Of course.

MITCHELL: . . . But on the other hand – and sorry to go back to it – but we *have* got little pictures of *skulls* on our SS caps. And that just seems very much the sort of motif you'd associate with a *baddie*.

WEBB: I'm not with you.

MITCHELL: Well, I mean, what do skulls make you think of? Er, death, beheading, cannibals. Er . . . pirates.

WEBB: Pirates are *fun*!

MITCHELL: I didn't say we weren't *fun*, but . . . fun or not, pirates are still the baddies. I just can't think of anything good about a skull.

WEBB: What about . . . pure Aryan skull shape?

MITCHELL: Even that is more usually depicted with the skin still on. Whereas the Allies –

WEBB: Oh, you haven't been listening to Allied propaganda? Of course *they're* going to say *we're* the baddies.

MITCHELL: Yeah, but they didn't get to design our uniforms. And their symbols are all, you know, quite nice. Stars, stripes, lions, sickles . . .

WEBB: What's so great about *sickles*?

MITCHELL: Well, nothing. And if there's one thing we've learnt in the last thousand miles of retreat, it's that Russian agriculture is in dire need of mechanisation.

WEBB: Yeah, tell me about it.

MITCHELL: But still, you've got to say, it's still better than a skull. I mean, I can't think of anything worse as a symbol than a skull.

WEBB: A rat's anus?

MITCHELL: Yeah, and if we were fighting an army marching under the banner of a rat's anus, I'd probably be a lot less worried, Hans.

WEBB: Eric, why are you worrying about badges and symbols? They're not *important*.

MITCHELL: Well, you know how they say that history is written by the victors, so that their symbols will be remembered in a positive way, and their defeated enemies in a bad way? Well, I'm just a bit worried that, if the Allies win, we've kind of done quite a lot of that work for them already, with the skulls.

WEBB: Yeah, and the rat's-anus people are *really* screwed!

MITCHELL: As we've discussed, they don't exist.

WEBB: Oh. Yeah. So . . . where's all this leading?

MITCHELL: Well, you know how at the beginning of the war we did really well, and the Allies nearly lost, but now things seem to be going a lot better for them?

WEBB: Yeah?

MITCHELL: Well, have you ever seen a film?

WEBB: What's your point?

MITCHELL: Well, I have never seen a film where the goodies start off really successfully, really nearly achieve their goals, but then the baddies come back very strongly, but the goodies still eventually win. Whereas I have seen a *lot* of films where the baddies start off really successfully but then the goodies come back and eventually win . . . I'm just increasingly uncomfortable about our place in the narrative structure of this war . . .

(*Lights down.*)

THE LONELY PLANET GUIDE TO IRAN

SHAPPI KHORSANDI

Hello! Well this is great. Now, er, I caught sight of myself in the mirror as I came out to the stage and I had never seen me before either, so you're not on your own. And I am a female Iranian stand-up comedian. The other acts backstage, they're all calling me 'the Box-Ticker' . . .

So I've brought for you tonight a copy of the *Lonely Planet Guide to Iran* and I thought I'd share some of it with you, in case you were planning to go there, skiing. Very useful advice.

(*She reads from the book.*)

'Pubs and night life . . . dream on', it says. This is useful – 'Gay and Lesbian Travellers' . . . 'Homosexuality is illegal in Iran and punishable by hundreds of lashes, or even worse, death. But this should not deter gay or lesbian travellers.'

Oh, I wish Iran had more moderate leaders, you know, like a Mullah Lite . . . take the edge off.

I tell you what, if you ever want to have a real laugh, travel to America with an Iranian passport. If you haven't got one I'll give you one of mine, I've got loads. And a lot of Americans still don't know the difference between Iran and Iraq. And I always have to explain to them, we're the ones *with* weapons of mass destruction. I mean pistachio nuts, you can take someone's eye out with those.

I've always been Iranian. And it's, it's . . . I actually moved to Britain in 1979 because my father's a writer and as you know the Iranian regime strongly advocates free speech, but there's no freedom *after* you've spoken. So we became refugees in Britain long before it became fashionable.

And I worry because they keep saying they're going to bomb Iran next, and if there are any Americans in the audience tonight . . . (*Sings 'Let My People Go . . .'*) I rang up my granny in Iran and she's very worried because she's building an extension to her house and she's worried that she'll end up with an extension but no house. Possibly not the most powerful anti-war argument you've ever heard, but builders in Tehran are pricey. There are no Polish people. If you're wondering if that joke is politically correct, it's fine – I checked with my cleaner . . .

What I love about Eastern European immigrants is that they've confused proper old-fashioned racists. Have you seen them now, they're like, 'What do we do, what do we say? They're *immigrants*, but they're *white*. *Shit!*' I heard a bloke saying the other day, 'Bloody Poles, coming over here, with their work ethic.' See, I get *too* politically correct. I was at a party recently and I said to my friend, 'Have you met Steve, who's a really nice guy?' And my friend goes, 'Which one's Steve?' Steve was the *only* black guy in the room. I found myself going, 'Steve, yeah, he's over there, he's got blue jeans on, a grey T-shirt, sort of curly hair . . . and a Nigerian accent.' My friend goes, 'Shappi, do you mean the black guy?' I was like, 'Oh, is he *black*? I didn't notice!'

Then, I met this Chinese bloke. I nearly said 'Chinaman' then, you can't say 'Chinaman', it sounds too colonial. 'I met a "Chinaman", jolly good, then I shot him in the eye . . .' I said, 'So, what's your name?' And he said, 'Koh Me Tahm.' And I did that very politically correct thing of, I repeated his name and added a little accent to it, to show that I cared very much that I was pronouncing it correctly. I said, oh I see, 'Kommetaahm' . . . and he went, 'No, no, no. *Call . . . me . . . Tom.*'

I have a little sister. Very different generation, her and her twin brother are ten years younger than me, and my little sister said to

me recently. (*Does London teenage accent.*) 'Shappi, it's like really weird? 'Cause like we're sisters? And we both live in London? But I never see yoo-oo?' And I think, 'That's 'cause of the way you talk . . .' And she likes all those bands. She doesn't like the Spice Girls, she thinks they're like 'old time'. But she likes Girls Aloud because they do this with their microphones (*Fans her fingers on the mic.*) and that means they're proper musicians and not just corporate fuck-puppets, yeah? And she likes those girl bands that don't really sing, they talk. Do you know the ones I mean?

'I'm not really singing, I'm just talking, and I dunno why I'm talking in this accent, 'cause I'm originally from Surrey, and you shouldn't have fucked my sister, that was a bit disrespectful, but I possibly shouldn't have gone down on your dad . . . Alfresco.'

'I wish Iran had more moderate leaders, you ,know, like a Mullah Lite . . . take the edge off.'

Shappi Khorsandi

ANNOYANCES
SEAN LOCK

Good evening. It's lovely to be here tonight. Really lovely to be here. I *mean* that as well. I know it doesn't sound like it. I've got one of those voices, you know? Doesn't matter how positive, upbeat, I try to be, it always sounds like I'm taking the piss.

Anyway, a friend of mine the other day said he was going on holiday in Wales. I said, (*Deadpan.*) 'Oh, that'll be nice.' He said, '*Yes*, it bloody *will*!' I don't get birthday presents any more because I can't do a convincing 'Thank you'. I stopped altogether. I thought it would be much better if I just said, 'Wow.' In my mouth, the words 'I love you' sound more like 'Happy now? Can I go? Will that do?'

I never do any adverts. You'll never ever see me do an advert or hear me do a voiceover. Not out of any high-minded, lofty principle. It's just that, if you do an advert, you've got to sound like you *mean* it. Don't you? And if I was to do, like, the Morrisons ad, yeah . . . (*Flat and non-commitally.*) 'Get yourself down to Morrisons . . .' It sounds like I'm being held hostage. 'Get yourself down to Morrisons or they'll cut my ears off.'

I don't think I'm the ideal sort of person for this show. I'm actually a very narrow-minded sort of person. Very intolerant person, you know. Very bad tempered. In fact, d'you know the people I'm *most* intolerant of? People who are intolerant of wheat. They really fuck me off. I'm not just intolerant with them, I fucking *hate* them! I really *hate* them! 'Cause you offer them a sandwich, which you've made, you offer them a sandwich, and they don't say, 'Oh, no thanks.' They go, 'Oh, I *can't*, I'm intolerant of wheat!' (*Makes exasperated noise.*)

And do you know what that *means*, if they're intolerant of wheat?

What it means is, if they have some wheat, nothing happens. And if they have a bit more wheat, nothing happens. If they keep eating wheat for about two weeks, they feel a bit *ooohhh*. But they carry on like they've got fucking spina bifida or something!

Yeah. I pick my targets! I do!

All sorts of people. People annoy me. You know the people who really annoy me? People who advertise for their lost pet, right, with a reward! *Eurgh*! I think, what do you *think* of me? You – what do you *think*, I haven't got the common decency, the common humanity, to reunite you with your lost pet? Do you think I want *money* for that? Is *that* what you think? I'm some kind of lowlife scumbag? I will keep your pet until you have handed over the money to me and I have given you your pet? Is *that* what you think of me? What am I going to *do* with it anyway? Dress it up in an orange jumpsuit and send videos to Al Jazeera? What is the *matter* with you people? And they always say: (*Mimes talking into a phone.*) 'Have you got him?' 'No – I'm just pissed off!'

I've just been banned from my local pub, actually. Not my fault. I went in the wrong toilets, not my fault at all. You know a lot of pubs they try and be a bit light-hearted with the toilets, have a bit of a *laugh* with the toilets, you know? The pub's called The Stag. So instead of calling them, you know, normal Ladies and Gents, they've got two pictures of deer up and underneath it says 'Hinds' and 'Bucks'. And when I went up there, I wasn't sure. I thought, 'Am I a hind, or a buck?' And you don't really need that when you're busting for a piss, do you? A quiz. I just want to go to the toilet . . . I thought, 'Well, I feel like a buck . . . (*He thrusts his pelvis.*) like a buck . . . like a buck . . .' But it could be . . . (*He bends over.*) 'Buck me,' couldn't it? Buck me. That's not an image you want stuck in your head, is it? Maybe I'm a hind, bit of a bastard. 'Oooh, he's a *hind* ' . . . I notice they don't do it in the disabled toilets, do they? *They* get off scot-free. *They* haven't got a picture of a deer with an antler like that (*Mimes a broken antler.*) 'Straight in. Straight out. Nae bother!'

TABOO
TIM MINCHIN

This is a song about the language of prejudice. It's called 'Taboo'.

In this modern free-spoken society
There is a word that we still hold taboo
A word with a terrible history
Of being used to abuse, oppress and subdue

Just six seemingly harmless letters
Arranged in this way will form a word
With more power than the pieces of metal
That are forged to make swords

A couple of Gs
An R and an E
An I and an N

The six little letters, all jumbled together
Have caused damage that we may never mend

And it's important that we all respect
That if these people should happen to choose
To reclaim the word as their own
It doesn't mean the rest of you have a right to its use

So never underestimate
The power that language imparts
Sticks and stones may break your bones
But words can break hearts

A couple of Gs
(Geez unless you've had to live it)
An R and an E
(Even I am careful with it)
An I and an N
In the end it will only offend
Don't want to have to spell it out again . . .

Only a ginger can call another ginger ginger.
Only a ginger can call another ginger ginger . . .
So listen to me if you care for your health
You don't call me ginger 'less you're ginger yourself, yeah
Only a ginger can call another ginger ginger, yep

When you are a ginger, life is pretty hard
Years of ritual bullying in the school yard
Kids calling you ranga and Fanta pants
No invitations to the high-school dance

But you get up and learn to hold your head up
You try to keep your cool and not get het up
But until the feeling of ill has truly let up
Then the word is ours and ours alone

Don't you know that . . .

Only a ginger can call another ginger ginger.
So if you call me ginge, I just might come unhinged
If you don't have a fringe with at least a tinge of the ginge in it
Only a ginger can call another ginger ginger, yeah yeah

Now listen to me, we're not looking for sympathy
Just because we're sensitive to UV
Just 'cause we're pathetically pale
We do all right with the females

Yeah, I like to ask the ladies round for ginger beer
And soon they're running their fingers through my ginger
    beard
And dunking my ginger nuts into their ginger tea, yeah
And asking, can they call me Ginge

(and I say I don't think that's appropriate – 'cause . . .)

Only a ginger can call another ginger ginger, yeah
And all the ladies, they agree, it's a fact:
Once you gone ginge, you can't go back to . . . .
Only a ginger can call another ginger ginger

Yeah, go ginge, go motherfucker, go!

Yeah, you can call us Bozo or fire truck
You can even call us carrot-top or bloodnut
Yeah, you can call me matchstick or tampon
But fucking with the G-word is just not on

If you're a gingerphobe and you don't like us
We'll stand up to the fight if you wanna fight us
But if you cut yourself you might catch gingervitis
So maybe you should shut your fucking mouth

Yeah, only a ginger can call another ginger ginger, yeah yeah
So if you call us ginge, you can't whinge if you're injured
If you don't have a tinge of the ginge in your minge
Only a ginger can call another ginger ginger, yeah

And I know my kids will always be clothed and fed
'Cause papa's gonna be bringing home the gingerbread
And they'll be pretty smart because they will be well-red
And by red I mean red and the other kind of read, wooo!

Only a ginger can call another ginger ginger
Just like only a ninja can sneak up on another ninja, yeah

Only a ginger, Only a ginger, Only a ginger . . .

Are you listening-a
I'm not pointing the finger
I'm just having a sing-a
I am just re-min-ding ya
That only a ginger can call another ginger ginger!

ANCIENT HISTORY
EDDIE IZZARD

So, errrrrrrrrrrm, yes. Er, the world was made four thousand five hundred million years ago, as you may know. Human beings, we turn up five million years ago. We're supposed to look like God. So he made it four thousand five hundred million years ago and then waited . . . a-fucking forever before we turn up. *Why*?

I mean, he must have made it, and then gone, 'Errr . . . err . . .' And his kids are going, 'Dad, dad, fucking *do* something!' 'All right, all right, all right, Besus!' I think God had many children, and Jesus was the seventh son of God. Asus, Besus, Cesus, Desus, Esus, Efsus, Jesus . . . It seems a logical progression. He's alphabetical . . . He was just working his way through the . . . even though I don't believe in him . . . because it's quite funny. It's really weird. Five million years ago we turn up and then the Stone Age kicks in about two million years ago. Before the Stone Age, how did they do hunting? We were hunter-gatherers, but there's no stones. And they were just going, 'Look, bison! Bison! Come on. Bison!!'

(*He mimes punching at bison.*)

'Help me, help me – fucking bison!' 'Buffalo! Buffalo!! I think there's a buffalo!!!' 'It's bison.' 'Buffalo . . . same thing!'

(*He mimes more punching.*)

'Fucking hell!'

(*He mimes grabbing a rock and hitting the buffalo with it, and then watching it collapse.*)

'Well, *that* worked . . .' And the others come running up. 'Sorry we're late, sorry we're late. Traffic was . . . tricky . . .' But there were no excuses for being late in the Stone Age, were there? 'Traffic was . . . I had to write a report . . . I was backing out the cave . . . and . . . uh . . . sorry I'm late. What the *fuck* happened?' 'I hit the bison with a . . . with this, and he *fell over*! He's *dead*!' 'That's fucking brilliant! This could be the beginning of an *age*, Geoff!' 'That's what I thought! The Big Things Falling Over When Hit By Things Age! Yes!' 'Or Stone Age.' 'Stone Age, yes!'

And so it began, the Stone Age. And you think of the Stone Age now, you think, the Stone Age. Oh, it's the oldest, the crampiest kind of Stone Age, but in fact at the time it was the most advanced that any creature on this planet had ever been. The Stone Age! It was like right now when you're on your iPhone waiting for the new update. People going, 'Come on, Jim, it's the Stone Age! You got to get with the programme, man. It's the Stone Age! Forget about your clay. The Clay Age is dead! Hunting with clay is . . . was always stupid. How the fuck did you *do* that, anyway?' 'I would make a mould of their face and then I would ask them to die – you young people with your stones! I can't get with it, man. I'm a purist. I'm a clay fighter.'

Stone Age. And there's an Old Stone Age and a New Stone Age. People got bored of the stones. They were going, 'God, these stones are pretty shit. They're really crumbly.' 'Oh, Steve's got new stones.' '*New* stones? Can we upgrade?' 'No, no, it's a whole new thing. You have to sign on with him for two years and you have to give him moss every month, and it's really weird, man.' 'Ah, fuck, I'm not doing that.' 'But they're brilliant, they're *flints*, man. You can use them as stones and you can make *arrowheads* out of them, whatever they are, and uh . . . and you can light a *fire!*'

The Stone Age. It was the most amazing time. We were hunter-gatherers. I would have been a hunter. I don't know about you gatherers. I thought hunters used to hunt and then gather the stuff and bring it home. I thought that's what it was. Apparently not. Gatherers gather berries, and I wouldn't have done that because it just . . . seems . . . boring. And I know, boring in those days . . . Life was just fear and starvation.

But everyone looked brilliant. That was the upside to the Stone Age. We looked fantastic. 'Let's go hunting. Jemima, Steve, Kenny, Rogers, come on! Let's go out! Just wear underpants, we look fantastic. You look brilliant. Actually, hold me over a pond, hold me over a pond, I want to see what I look like.' – there were no mirrors. 'Hold me over a pond.' 'How do you look, sir?' 'A little bit hangy-downy but pretty good.' 'Let's go hunting!' And they would go out. And I would have been with the hunters. Even if they didn't want me to be. I'd have been there, 'Let me be a hunter!' 'Fuck off, kid.' 'I've killed a load of rats. Got them in a bag.' 'How many?' 'Twenty-seven in a bag. Use them as starters.'

Yeah, because the gatherers, that's just kind of, you know . . .

(*He mimes picking berries individually.*)

'Twelve, thirteen . . .'

(*He mimes eating them individually.*)

'Twelve. Eleven. Fuck, man, these are good! How many you got?' 'I got seven. I lost the will to live.' 'Fuck, they're going to kill us when they come back! Fucking seventeen berries. It's ridiculous.' The hunters return. 'We have killed bison and buffalo and badgers and beavers and balloons and – mainly 'b' animals today. Tomorrow we will kill cats and chinchillas and crocodiles. Then dogs and Daktari. Then elephants. Then foxgloves . . . that'll be a long day . . . Then helicopters and, er, . . . God. How many berries do you have?' 'We have a total of seventeen.' 'Seventeen? That's a bit shit.

It's been three hours! *Seventeen* berries?' 'It was windy.' '*What?*' 'I don't mean windy . . . what's the . . . uh . . . crackly . . . it was noisy.' 'That's even worse!' 'It was windy. It's . . . seventeen.' 'Well, make me a smoothie.' 'We cannot make smoothies. The Vikings have not yet attacked and brought the miracle of yoghurt!'

So the hunter-gatherers . . . we were the hunter-gatherers. And then we became farmers. That's the step up in civilisation. It's a step up in civilisation and a massive step down in sexiness. Farming is not sexy. And that's why farmers keep animals. They keep animals, noisy animals, not the quiet ones. You can farm quiet animals . . . Llamas make no noise. Snails, very little noise. Giraffes. Giraffes make no noise. If a giraffe sees a tiger, it would . . . it makes no noise. It has no noise to make. We've seen it on the screen. And if a giraffe sees a tiger, it would experience two emotions. One, fear and, two, surprise. Fear because it is a . . . *tiger*! And surprise because it is a . . . *tiger*! And there are no tigers in Africa.

It would normally be a lion but this bit of material doesn't work with lions, so fuck off. So, they see a tiger and they turn to other giraffes and . . . nothing. There's no . . . (*Trumpeting sound.*) . . . There's nothing. No fucking horn. Apparently they can cough. I looked on Wikipedia. They cough. So they must just be going . . .

(*He clears his throat and mumbles.*)

Other giraffe's just going . . .

(*He mimes a giraffe eating leaves off a tree while the first giraffe tries to convey the word 'tiger' to him through the medium of charades.*)

. . . And then they run. And you've seen this. They fucking run. They shift it, those giraffes.

I want to finish off by talking about Noah. Because Noah was in the Bible. Noah was real, I think, Noah was real. I think Moses was real. I think Jesus was a real guy. His real name is Joshua, so why he's called Jesus I don't know. But Noah was there. He built an ark. He built a boat and he . . . built a boat, put his family on the boat. Well, that's good and logical. And then he put his barnyard animals on the boat. Did he put two of every animal in the world on the boat?

No.

How can I be so sure?

Try it. Just fucking *try* it. It would be im-fucking-possible. You'd be there going, 'All right, Margaret, here we go. Two by two. Two tigers, two mice, two squirrels, two rats, two dogs, two, er . . . leopards, two, er . . . horses, two iguanas. How many we got so far?' 'So far . . . just two tigers – er, one leopard made it, as well.' 'Oh, for fuck's sake, this is ridiculous! How's this supposed to work?' The tigers would eat everything. The big cats would munch them up like crazy. We know this. Have you ever been *near* a tiger? I have. I've been near a tiger, in a cage, and it almost tried to eat me, and it was eighty. In human years it was eighty years old. That's how hungry they are. So at the end of the ark, after forty days and forty nights of rain, which – if you work it out – is forty days, isn't it? Forty days and forty nights. The nights are implicit, for fuck's sake. That's just padding out the Bible, isn't it? 'And forty nights, and forty lunchtimes it rained, and forty afternoon teas.' That's just what we did in our English essays, '. . . and on and on and on and on, a lot of rain, never seen rain like this, oh, it's unusual rain, wet . . . wetter than normal . . .'

At the end of that, they'd be there and they'd be coming off the ark and the people from the Bible would be there: (*Does starchy Pathé newsreel-type voice.*) 'We're here from the Bible and the ark is making landfall, and here they come, two elephants there, and two tigers. Two leopards and a squirrel, a hedgehog, and a rat . . . uh . . . where is everyone here? Just talk to this squirrel. Mr Squirrel, how's it going?' (*Disturbed Vietnam vet voice.*) 'It was a nightmare, man. Fucking nightmare on there. Fucking stripey bastards, they ate everyone, man . . .' 'Ha ha ha haaa. That's very good. And so did God's plan work?' 'It's a fucking nightmare, man, you write that down in the Bible. Fucking nightmare. Mr Squirrel says so. Fucking not going back on there. They killed *everyone*, man. It's murder, man, fucking *murder*. Fucking Amnesty should get on to those fuckers.' 'Ha ha ha. Where's your wife?' 'She got away, man, she got away on a boat with an owl and a cat . . .'

THE SECRET POLICEMAN'S BALL

(2012)

RADIO CITY MUSIC HALL, NEW YORK CITY
4 MARCH 2012

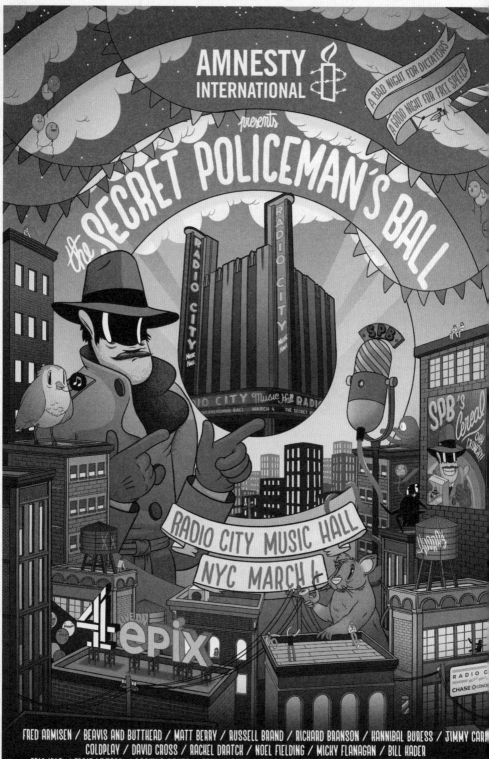

The long-awaited return of the *SPB*, this time on American soil, began with a recorded message: 'I'm Archbishop Desmond Tutu. And I'm a funny guy. No, that's *true*! I'm *very* funny. People always say, "Archbishop, you are so *funny*, why didn't you go into comedy, instead of devoting your life to fighting injustice?" I say: "Comedy is too hard."'

The action then began. There were Pythons and Muppets. There was satire and smut. There were routines about presidents and propagandists, WikiLeaks and censorship, interrogations and obscurantism, and the different contextual meanings of words that sound like 'ass'. It was the cream of UK talent merging with the cream of US talent. The media coverage was enormous, and there were many comments along lines such as this: 'As we celebrated the fiftieth anniversary of Amnesty International, we were treated to LITERALLY one of the best line-ups ever to converge on the stage of Radio City Music Hall' (*People's Choice*). It was a case of the *Saturday Night Live* troupe taking the reins – with the venerable Pythons now appearing via satellite link.

There were some obvious contrasts with the first Amnesty venture into comedy thirty-six years before: reflecting broader cultural changes, most of the comic material was constructed quite differently, with the old structural rigour, literateness and range of recondite references replaced by something more fluid, prosaic and populist, while many of the performances were slicker, more straightforward and far more self-aware. Whereas some of the biggest laughs in 1976 had been prompted by allusions to Proust, philosophy and iambic pentameter, many of the loudest whoops in 2012 came in response to references to reality TV, Twitter and texting.

Another difference was the ability and willingness of the 2012 performers to engage so directly with many topical themes and

controversies, which, by comparison, made the performers of 1976 seem quaintly amateurish and escapist. Russell Brand and Noel Fielding's comic *cri de coeur* for Amnesty, for example, was strikingly brash and aggressive, while Jon Stewart's interview with Rex Lee as North Korean leader Kim Jong-un was one of the night's most cleverly choreographed exchanges.

A nostalgic note was sounded when Michael Palin, who was first on stage back in 1976, returned via video to make his implausible excuses, and the sight of an overrunning Russell Brand being urged to 'wrap it up' provided a nice reminder that, even in a production as polished as this one, comedy will still bring a degree of disorder. Throughout all of the performances, the audience heeded Archbishop Tutu's sage advice 'to find them all funny – even the one or two who inevitably are going to blow it'.

AN APOLOGY
MONTY PYTHON

Michael Palin appears on a TV screen from his home in London. He is looking rather sheepish.

Hello, I'm Michael Palin. The legendary 'Sixth Python'. And I'm so excited to be with you live on tape at the *legendary* Radio City Music Hall in *legendary* New York for the *legendary Secret Policeman's* legendary *Ball*! What a great, great occasion! Of course, I would have given *anything* – given my *all* – to be there with you tonight to celebrate fifty years of my work, er, of *Amnesty's* work. Um, unfortunately, I . . . I just am not able to make it.

I've . . . I've broken both my legs, actually. Funnily enough. Just the other day. I was writing away and, er, off they went: *snap*! *snap*! You know how they do? Probably putting a little bit more pressure on the chair or something like that. So both legs gone. Very difficult. Unfortunately, er, not able, um, um, to be there.

Ah, well, of course, it *is* possible to travel with broken legs. I mean, that's absolutely possible. But, unfortunately . . . one of the legs has gone. Um, gone missing. Er, probably . . . You know, they *do* go. Ha, it's just one of those things. I'm not going to *brag*, but if you *are* reasonably well known, bits of your limbs will fetch quite a bit for charity auctions and that sort of thing.

And so, um, that's probably what's happened. So, obviously, with . . . with . . . with one bit of the leg missing, um – well, actually, an *entire* leg missing – I couldn't make it.

But anyway, I just hope you have the most wonderful evening at the Radio City Music Hall. I just wish I could have been there to celebrate my, er, Amnesty's fiftieth anniversary at *The Secret Policeman's Ball*. But, er, obviously not. Um, because of the legs.

Thank you for being so understanding.

WORDS IN ENGLISH AND AMERICAN
BEN STILLER & DAVID WALLIAMS

WALLIAMS: Good evening, my name is David Walliams and I am British.

STILLER: Hi, I'm Ben Stiller and I'm an American. (*He encourages the audience to join him chanting.*) USA! USA! USA! USA!

(*Walliams winces and gestures to Stiller to stop.*)

WALLIAMS: Amnesty International have invited us here this evening to explain the different meanings of words in Britain and America, to help strengthen the union between our two nations.

STILLER: The first word is: 'Jugs'.

WALLIAMS: In Britain, this is a container with a spout and handles for pouring liquids.

STILLER: Tits.

WALLIAMS: Next is: 'Hooters'. For the British, these are steam whistles in a factory that signal the cessation of work.

STILLER: Tits again.

WALLIAMS: 'Alu*mini*um': a silvery-white metal.

STILLER: 'A*lum*inum': a silvery-white metal.

WALLIAMS: It's 'alu*mini*um'.

STILLER: It's 'a*lum*inum'.

WALLIAMS: 'Alu*mini*um'!

STILLER: 'A*lum*inum'!

WALLIAMS: 'ium'!

STILLER: 'um'!

(*Walliams rolls his eyes and continues.*)

WALLIAMS: 'À la mode': from the French – 'of the fashion'.

STILLER: With ice cream.

WALLIAMS: 'Passport': an official government document that permits a citizen to travel abroad.

STILLER: We don't have that word in America. 'Dentist': a person trained to look after the health and appearance of your teeth.

WALLIAMS: We don't have that word in Britain. 'Obese': anyone over 200 pounds.

STILLER: Anyone over 2,000 pounds.

WALLIAMS: 'Blue Steel': a British air force missile.

(*There is silence. Walliams looks at Stiller expectantly, but Stiller appears to be lost in his own private world.*)

WALLIAMS: In America . . . ?

(*Stiller smiles smugly, then, recalling his* Zoolander *character, looks back and looks forward again like a super-cool model.*)

WALLIAMS: 'Piers Morgan': an annoying man who used to be on TV in Britain.

STILLER: An annoying man who's now on TV in America.

WALLIAMS: 'Bush': a private part that is too embarrassing to mention.

STILLER: Same meaning here, then. 'Sudden-Death Penalty Shoot-Out'.

WALLIAMS: A way of settling scores in soccer.

STILLER: A way of settling scores in Texas.

WALLIAMS: 'Voicemail' . . .

STILLER: A place where friends and family members leave messages for you to listen to later.

WALLIAMS: A place where friends or family members leave messages for journalists to listen to later. 'Harry Potter': a fictional boy wizard who goes to Hogwarts School.

(*Stiller does a double take.*)

STILLER: 'Fictional'?

WALLIAMS: Y-Yeah, of course . . . Harry Potter is fictional.

(*Stiller continues to seem confused.*)

STILLER: Okay . . . Okay. But . . . but . . . the, er, Quidditch thing . . . that's real, right?

WALLIAMS: No, no, you know, it . . . it's all made up, it's fantasy, like, er, *A Night at the Museum*.

(*Stiller bridles upon hearing this title.*)

STILLER: *A Night at the Museum* isn't *real*?

(*There is a brief embarrassed silence between the two men.*)

WALLIAMS: Now our final word tonight is: 'Ass'. A donkey.

STILLER: Buttocks. Booty. Junk in the trunk. Bubble butt. Dookie maker –

WALLIAMS: (*Embarrassed.*) Yes, thank you, we get the picture!

STILLER: Well, I think you will agree, my British friend, that we Americans and you Brits really do speak the same language.

WALLIAMS: (*Offended.*) No, we fucking don't!

STILLER: It's '*alum*inum'!

WALLIAMS: Oh, shut up!

(*They walk off in opposite directions.*)

AN AUDIENCE WITH KIM JONG-UN
JON STEWART & REX LEE

Stewart walks on stage as himself. Lee, dressed as the North Korean dictator Kim Jong-un, arrives on stage standing on a podium that is being pushed by four soldiers.

STEWART: Good evening, I'm Jon Stewart.

KIM JONG-UN: And I am the Supreme Leader of the Democratic People's Republic of North Korea.

STEWART: (*Looking confused.*) We are here tonight –

KIM JONG-UN: Supreme Commander of the Korean People's Army.

STEWART: We are here tonight –

KIM JONG-UN: General Secretary of the Korean Workers' Party. Lord and Protector of the Great Peninsula. Great Chancellor of the Great Korean People's Pipe Fiddlers Local 1/17. And two-time Grammy nominee. Kim Jong-un.

STEWART: (*Baffled.*) Ah . . .

KIM JONG-UN: Your line.

STEWART: Ah, right. (*Addressing the audience.*) Ah, we have a great show, and . . . (*Turns to Kim Jong-un.*) You know what, actually, I was told that I was doing this with a different Kim, so, ah, the copy, the presenter copy doesn't –

KIM JONG-UN: We can make this work! (*Nods and puts his thumb up.*)

STEWART: (*Looking uneasily at his autocue, he addresses the audience again.*) Well, thanks, Kim, I know 'keeping up with you . . .' (*He breaks off and shakes his head, then tries to rewrite his script as he speaks.*) . . . keeping up with . . . the number of political prisoners . . . (*He turns again to Kim Jong-un.*) Look, I . . . I really don't think actually . . . You see, I thought this was going to be Kim *Kardashian* and –

KIM JONG-UN: *Who*? Who that?

STEWART: Kim Kardashian, er, she has, er, a television show.

KIM JONG-UN: Oh. She is actress?

STEWART: (*Awkwardly.*) Well, no, actually, um, er . . . cameras follow her . . . she . . . she has sisters, and, ah . . . she has a clothing store and, er, a very zaftig figure. She got married but it didn't take and, ah . . .

KIM JONG-UN: Ha! I'm just fucking with you!

STEWART: What?

KIM JONG-UN: I know who she is. But I wanted to hear from *you* – how you would describe her.

STEWART: (*Resentfully.*) That's very clever, Kim.

KIM JONG-UN: (*Cackles.*) Ha ha ha, you should have seen your face! 'Ooh, ooh, very *zaftig*, ooh, *camera* . . . *sister* . . .' (*Shakes head contemptuously.*) Classic!

STEWART: (*Now looking rattled but still trying to seem pleasant.*) Either way, I . . . I don't think this event is for you, quite frankly, so –

KIM JONG-UN: Oh? Because I'm *Asian*?

STEWART: (*Chuckling with embarrassment.*) No, not because you're Asian.

KIM JONG-UN: Asian people don't like shows?

STEWART: No, I don't . . . I'm not saying –

KIM JONG-UN: And we can't play basketball, either, right?

STEWART: No, believe me, I'm not saying that –

KIM JONG-UN: Except – we *can*! A little thing called Linsanity!

STEWART: (*Reluctantly.*) Yes, Linsanity.

KIM JONG-UN: (*To the audience.*) Am I right?

(*The audience – recognising the topical phrase inspired by the Asian-American basketball player Jeremy Shu-How Lin, whose recent appearances for the New York Knicks had coincided with a winning run that had thus been dubbed 'Linsanity' – start whooping and applauding.*)

KIM JONG-UN: Yes! In this day and age, Jon Stewart!

STEWART: Yes.

KIM JONG-UN: Lincredible!

STEWART: (*Half-heartedly.*) Yes, it's Lincredible. (*Trying to change the subject.*) Look – it's not because you're *Asian*. You're . . . You're a vicious *dictator*! You arrest people and you send them to internment camps!

KIM JONG-UN: Don't you mean . . . *Lin*ternment?

STEWART: No. I don't, no. That's . . . that's . . . (*Thinks for a second.*) Fine – 'Linternment camps'! Yes, very nice.

KIM JONG-UN: It is fun to do, right?

STEWART: (*Tetchily.*) Yes, it's very nice. Look – this show stands for everything you're *not*! We're here to support Amnesty International – a group that has worked to protect free speech around the world for fifty years. You're a *dictator*! You *hurt* people! You don't *deserve* this night of laughs, music and entertaining presenter banter!

KIM JONG-UN: (*Sarcastically.*) Wow. Your words have really *moved* me!

STEWART: Thank you.

KIM JONG-UN: No one has ever spoken to me this way before.

STEWART: Thank you.

KIM JONG-UN: (*Dismissively.*) It was nice knowing you.

STEWART: What's that?

KIM JONG-UN: (*To his soldiers, while pointing at Stewart.*) To my travelling acid bog!

STEWART: (*Startled.*) No, no, no, no! No acid bog! We . . . we don't do that here!

KIM JONG-UN: All right, fine, I won't have you dissolved.

STEWART: Thank you. Very kind of you.

KIM JONG-UN: *If* you put me in a sketch.

STEWART: I'm not putting you in a sketch.

KIM JONG-UN: (*Turns to his soldiers again.*) Fellas . . .

STEWART: No, no, no, no! You're not *funny*! You're not funny!

KIM JONG-UN: (*Incredulous.*) 'Not funny'?

STEWART: Yes.

KIM JONG-UN: 'Not *FUNNY*'?

STEWART: That's right.

KIM JONG-UN: (*Clears his throat.*) Knock, knock!

STEWART: Who . . . Who's there?

KIM JONG-UN: Kim Jong-un!

STEWART: Kim Jong-un who?

KIM JONG-UN: 'WHO'? How *dare* you! (*Points.*) To the acid bog!

STEWART: No, no, no! That's fine. You're not funny.

KIM JONG-UN: Okay, okay, okay . . . Who on first?

STEWART: Who?

KIM JONG-UN: (*Triumphantly.*) Correct! Gim-Ri Hu! The Great People's Democratic Republic of Korea champion of the baseball diamond will man the first-base area!

STEWART: If I put you in a sketch, will you –

KIM JONG-UN: . . . not force the imperialist scum of America to bow before my greatness?

STEWART: I was going to say 'leave'. Will you leave if I . . . I wanna work with you here.

KIM JONG-UN: Good! Negotiating with North Korea *always* leads to positive results.

STEWART: All right. Look, if we promise to put you in a sketch, one sketch, will you leave?

KIM JONG-UN: (*He ponders this for a moment.*) Yes.

STEWART: All right, good, you're in a sketch. We'll put you in a sketch later in the show and that'll be fine.

KIM JONG-UN: Ideally with Seth Meyers.

STEWART: (*Looking eager to move on.*) Yes, I'll see what I can do. (*He gestures to the soldiers to push the podium off stage.*) Now, would you please just, just go –

KIM JONG-UN: (*Addressing the audience as he is pushed off the stage.*) Radio Citizenry, soon you will quake with viscosity for the radiant comedy stylings of the Supreme Commander Kim Jong-un! Radiant, I tell you! I will dance and be funny because I am the Supreme Commander . . .

(*Much to Stewart's relief, Kim Jong-un disappears into the wings.*)

A TWEETED HECKLE
STATLER & WALDORF

STATLER: That was terrible!

WALDORF: Horrendous!

STATLER: I'm offended!

WALDORF: I'm appalled!

STATLER: Yes, and I'm *tweeting* about it!

WALDORF: Mmm, me too!

STATLER: You know, this tweeting thing is really great! Much better than heckling out loud – it saves your voice!

WALDORF: Yeah, yeah, and you can avoid the risk of genuine human interaction!

STATLER: Oh, anything but that, yes!

WALDORF: Ha-ha! There! We've tweeted our heckle! Now what do we do?

STATLER: Well, I guess we just wait for our followers to laugh.

WALDORF: Er, how many followers do we have, anyway?

STATLER: Er, just two – me and you.

'When I'm away from home, I sometimes get lovesick. Well, they call it chlamydia.'

Jimmy Carr

RECRUITMENT DRIVE
NOEL FIELDING & RUSSELL BRAND

BRAND: We are here to give you information about Amnesty International.

FIELDING: Exactly. Not enough of you are Amnesty members. I mean, (*Asking a man in the audience.*) are you a member, sir?

(*The man in the audience replies: 'Yes.'*)

FIELDING: Oh, fuck!

BRAND: Put your hand up if you are not a member of Amnesty International.

FIELDING: That's a better way of doing it.

BRAND: Right. (*Pointing.*) There's a woman, there, she is not a member of Amnesty International.

FIELDING: Right: everyone else – kill that woman!

BRAND: So what we're going to do now is convey to you some important facts because we're going to design a pamphlet to make Amnesty International more attractive to people.

FIELDING: Because the pamphlet at the moment is a bit boring. It's a bit dull.

BRAND: (*Pointing again.*) The pamphlet has driven away this selfish cow of a woman! (*Consults piece of paper.*) Here are some genuine facts about Amnesty International. There are 250,000 political prisoners in Burma, and *no* Amnesty members. In England – we're from that country – there are 250,000 Amnesty

members and no political prisoners. *There's a relationship between those two facts*!

FIELDING: It's like a mirror!

BRAND: If you pass through the Amnesty mirror, a political prisoner will be freed. It is our objective (*Pointing again.*) to make that selfish woman join Amnesty and go to Burma and free all 250,000!

FIELDING: You've got to go through the mirror!

BRAND: Noel, I've got another Amnesty fact. Listen to this thing. (*Reads.*) 'Trade in both bananas and dinosaur bones have international treaties to regulate them. But not guns. Anyone can sell guns and bullets to dictators' (*Points.*) – like *that* selfish cow – 'who regularly use these arms to kill their own people.'

FIELDING: (*To woman in audience.*) How many guns have you got on you? *Forty-three?*

BRAND: And how many bananas? Two!

FIELDING: Because that's regulated! You come up for four dinosaur bones and we'd go, 'You can only have one. Come back next week for another one.' We'd have to stagger it. Even if you were making a xylophone kit out of a dinosaur's ribcage.

BRAND: (*Pointing again.*) Which is the sort of thing this selfish woman would do to a stegosaurus!

FIELDING: I can *see* the dinosaur ribcage poking out of your handbag!

BRAND: I'm going to grab her!

(*Brand goes off and drags the woman onto the stage and the two men attempt to cajole her into joining Amnesty International.*)

FIELDING: One more fact, stay there, we're going to give you one more fact!

BRAND: (*Reads from paper.*) 'In Iran you can be stoned to death for having an affair. Ten women are at risk from execution in Iran by stoning now.' (*Points at woman.*) You should be joining them!

FIELDING: Ten women? That doesn't sound that much. What are you talking about?

BRAND: That isn't that many, that fact is not as bad.

FIELDING: You slept with ten women last night – that's nothing!

BRAND: I *am* responsible for most of the Iranian stonings. But we are also responsible for this woman. (*Points at her.*) Don't you *dare* fucking try and leave! This is our political prisoner now. We're keeping her until she joins Amnesty International!

FIELDING: Yeah, we're keeping her until the next *Secret Policeman's Ball*, and that could be forty years away!

BRAND: It's going to be forty years because of the lack of freedom of speech! This woman will now be punished! The next time you see her she will be a raggedy corpse! Ta-ta!

FIELDING: Thank you!

ANOTHER APOLOGY
MONTY PYTHON

Eric Idle appears on a TV screen from his home in Los Angeles. He is looking rather sheepish.

Hello, Eric Idle here, and I am the Sixth Python. Er, well, the Sixth Nicest Python. Look, the thing is, I would really give anything at all to be with you tonight in New York City to celebrate the five-hundredth anniversary of *Monty Python*, er, of Amnesty International. But sadly I *do* have a problem. Er, with my legs.

Er, you see, I recently got *new* legs, um, *two* new legs, ah, secondhand, and . . . and they don't seem to fit very well. Um, they don't seem to be my size at all. Ah, mine, obviously, were long and elegant as befits a model and philosopher, and these are short and fat and hairy. Er, in fact, somebody suggested they might well be Michael Palin's legs, er, because his were notoriously short and fat and hairy. Um, and indeed they *could* be Michael Palin's legs because they do seem very, very, very tired. As if they've spent the last seventeen years walking around the world talking to cameras all over the darn place.

Anyway. So, you see, that's my problem. I- I- I can't walk with these legs. Er, the best I can do is hop. And sadly I can't hop all the way to New York City, er, because most airlines now do have a no-hopping rule on . . . on planes. Especially into New York City.

So there it is. Er, do have a jolly *wonderful* evening, er, without me. Um, most people seem to. Ah, and thanks very much indeed for listening!

THE SEX

JACK WHITEHALL

Good evening, New York City!

Oh, yes, what an honour it is to be here this evening. I'm Jack, I'm from London, but it's amazing to be here in your fine city. I love New York. You have stuff here that we don't have back in England. I found this out the other day: you have this thing called, umm, Customer Service! That shit is amazing! We don't do that back in England. It throws me every time I go shopping in New York. I went to the Apple Store – oh my God, I didn't know what to do! Before I even had my foot in the threshold of the door there was some douchebag in my face – 'Hey, Buddy, my name's Drew, how's your day going, hombre? What brings you to the Apple Store today?' 'Umm, I'm here to buy a phone, not make a friend. Fuck off!'

And I never wanted that as well, I never wanted to be someone that went to the Apple Store, because I never wanted an iPhone. Give me a cheer if you're an iPhone user? (*Huge cheers.*) Yeeeah, a lot of you. It's your fault! It's your fault that I'm an iPhone user as well, because I gave in like we all give in at some point to the iPhone Nazis. You know these people that say, 'You need to get the *iPhooone*, it's the most *amaaazing* phone ever, it's a *smaaart* phone, you'll need a *smaaart* phone.' I don't need a smart phone. Do you know what I miss? I miss a dumb phone. I miss a phone where I knew where I stood. You know the phone I miss? I miss the Nokia 3310. Oooh, yeah. Yeah. There was a *phone*. Screw the iPhone with all of its apps and its maps and its GPS shit. The 3310 gave a man all he needed – stopwatch, calculator and Snake. Fuck anything else. And there was no pretention as well, there was no pretention with the 3310. The most pretentious the 3310 got is when it upgraded itself to the 3330. The only thing they added to that model was a currency converter on a phone that didn't even work abroad.

Text messaging – that was a joy as well with the old phones. Predictive text – there was no pretentiousness. You'd try to type in a word and if it was more than, like, four letters long it would give up! It was like it was saying, 'Yeah, you wanna use fancy language like that – you're on your own, mate!' Not with the iPhone, the iPhone is constantly jumping to conclusions. And where does it get this vocabulary from? No one talks like that! It doesn't matter what you put into the fucking thing: A . . . N . . . 'Did you mean androgynous?' No! AND! *AND!* I meant AND!

I like simplicity in my life. I need everything to be simple, and that goes for everything in my life as well – sex, for example. When I'm doing The Sex, I like it to be kept very simple. I'm quite British when it comes to The Sex . . . I want three minutes, in the dark, then we both roll over, assume the foetal position and cry for a bit. That's how it's done . . . And that all harks back from when I started doing it, 'cause when I started having The Sex I was still living at home with my mother. And if you're living at home with your mother, that is not a good place ever to bring back a girl. 'Cause my mum would do anything she could to deter me from having sex in the family home. Like the first thing she did, as soon as I turned eighteen, she bought me a new bed. The loudest bed I've ever had sex in in my entire life. This thing would creak in space. And it wasn't like I was having *loud* sex in it as well, *(Motions 'quiet sex' thrusting.)* I was trying to have the quietest sex – *(To a man in the front row.)* I'm sorry, I don't know why I'm looking at you there, sir – the quietest sex I could possibly have, because I was very conscious that my mum could . . . Like proper stealth sex, I'd be doing it so quietly that me and my girlfriend were having sex like we were Anne Frank's parents, it was that quiet . . . Shhh!

Yeah, she didn't put *that* in the diary! Sex for me became a bit like arriving late at the theatre and trying to find your seat, just a lot of shuffling and a bit of shushing, a pause, and then from somewhere in the darkness just the whispered, 'I'm sorry.'

But, no, it's a joy, it's a joy to be here in America, and on American TV as well. I just love American TV, your shows are brilliant. Even the ones that should be boring are exciting, like the news – I love watching American news. It's amazing. My favourite ever story I saw on American news was on Californian forest fires. This guy – really intense – was there, on the screen, he was like 'During the Californian forest fires, 300 mobile homes have been destroyed in the blaze.' Only in America can that happen. I'm not an expert on the mobile home, but I would imagine that one of the benefits of the mobile home is that you're not really tied down to an area. Especially if the said area is on fire! MOVE!!

My favourite show, though, is a show that I'm not even allowed to watch at home. I love *America's Next Top Model.* That show is brilliant and I'm banned from watching it, because my dad, he's worried that I'm too effeminate, and he's always trying to butch me up – I know. I think you'll agree that he's done a pretty fabulous job. (*Pirouettes.*) But I'm not allowed to watch it, and I love watching *America's Next Top Model* because of one person, and one person alone: Tyra Banks. Oh my God, the shit that comes out of her mouth! It's incredible! For those of you that haven't seen it, right, ten aspiring young models compete to become America's next top model, and each week, at the end of their task, Tyra judges them, and each week these young, aspiring models are subjected to a face-full of the most nonsensical, pseudo-philosophical bullshit I have ever seen – it's glorious! They walk up in front of Tyra like lepers coming towards Jesus. And Tyra stands there holding her photographs and then she just unleashes hell!

'Ten beautiful girls stand before me, only one can become America's next top model. Shaniqua, this week your shots were fantastic, but unfortunately as a human being you have to face up

to your issues, and the best way to do this is to take a step back, turn around and run away, because, you see, life is like a swing: you go forwards and backwards, forwards and backwards, often using your leg in a kicking motion to propel you to an optimum velocity, but you see this swing doesn't just go forwards and backwards, it goes left and right, in and out, up and down, it's not like a swing at all, in fact in many ways it's more like a roundabout that see-saws up and down and swings from left to right, and you have to clasp at each opportunity like it were a monkey bar on a trellising, but don't you ever think that life is like a playground, because it is not! It's like a playground that the play or the ground is just swinging nothingness, and only then can you truly understand that if you wanna become an individual you have to strive for individuality in a group, in unison, on your own, together, momentarily, forever . . . Shaniqua, you're still in the running to become America's next top model, let me see you smile!'

New York – you've been wonderful, thank you very much. I've been Jack Whitehall, goodnight.

'I think you know you're getting old, I feel like I'm getting old. I was watching porn last week. I found myself thinking, "That bed looks comfy".'

Jimmy Carr

AN INTERVIEW WITH JULIAN ASSANGE
JOHN OLIVER & BILL HADER

Oliver is preparing to address the camera. Hader, impersonating Julian Assange, is seated among the audience.

OLIVER: Good evening, I am John Oliver, and I'm standing here in the aisle of Radio City Music Hall – because the producers were too cheap to reserve me a comp seat. Tonight, Amnesty International has invited several renowned figures who live at the intersection of technology and freedom of expression to share their thoughts. First up this evening is a man who has become virtually synonymous with anonymous, whose work as the founder of WikiLeaks has helped expose classified information regarding both systemic human rights abuses and also what Tony Blair looks like naked. Please welcome: Julian Assange!

(Assange gets up from his seat and acknowledges the audience's applause. He is holding a glass of red wine and smiling smugly.)

OLIVER: First off, Julian, you're currently under house arrest in England, I believe, so how is it exactly that you are here with us tonight?

ASSANGE: Well, you see, I'm not actually here. What you see before you is just a holographic projection.

OLIVER: Right, I mean, you *say* that, but *(Puts his hand on the side of Assange's head.)* I'm physically touching you now, so . . . ?

ASSANGE: It's a really *good* hologram. *(Boastfully.)* That's the level Julian Assange operates on, eh?

OLIVER: Dear me! Er, Julian, you've done a lot to expose government excesses in a variety of circumstances, yet for some reason you're not embraced as a hero. Now, why do you think that is?

ASSANGE: Simply put: er, I'm kind of a dick. Ah, I do the right thing but I look and act like a Bond villain. A case in point, this is my laugh: *MWAHAHAHA!*

OLIVER: Right. Um . . . do you have anything else for us, Julian?

ASSANGE: Yes. (*He suddenly looks very serious and menacing.*) A warning to all Americans: if you continue to persecute me, things will get *very* bad for you. I won't just get into your email. I'll get into your Facebook! You know that friend request from the weird kid from middle school you've been ignoring? You just accepted it! (*Smiles mischievously.*) You sent the message: 'OMG, we should hang out!!!' Have fun with Gerald, America! He's still into dinosaurs! *MWAHAHAHAHAHA!!*

A GRAVE INJUSTICE

SARAH SILVERMAN

I'd like to tell you a story about a woman who was walking down the street of her home town with her boyfriend. She said something that she believed to be true and was immediately punished for it. Brutally punished for speaking her mind. One woman's voice, silenced. And this horrifying injustice happened in a country you may have heard of. It's called the United States of America.

You see, apparently it's illegal in the United States of America to tell Keith Dunnigan you love him six weeks into dating him. And this woman, this hero, had sacrificed *everything* for this man. Including being captured by evil dictators, which he conveniently called Christmas in Connecticut with his parents. To her credit, this beautiful, stylish, easily-could-play-32-year-old woman refused to play the victim. She *refused* to be told what to think. She *refused* to be told what to feel. And she *refused* not to call Keith ten to several times a day on his home, work and cell numbers, to tell him, 'Hey, Keith – I love you, Keith!'

She *chose* to utter those forbidden words. She *dared* to speak her mind despite any and all consequences.

Eventually the police were brought in. That's right: the American police. It's pretty scary stuff. Deeming her expressions 'stalking' and in violation of California Criminal Code 18/F.

And that is a true story of one of the worst violations of human rights that has ever happened. I get my news from celebrity Twitter feeds but I'm pretty positive that's an accurate statement.

I dream of living in a world where a woman can say, 'I love you, Keith', and move in with him, and buy him this new pill I hear they have that makes you not allergic to cats any more, or less allergic. Or the cat takes the pill, maybe? I'm not sure.

But one thing I am sure of is that oppression is real and it must be stopped. And that's what Amnesty is all about.

Amnesty International works to reverse injustices to all humans around the globe. It's a great reminder that we are all one. We're just lumps of molecules – nothing more, nothing less.

And we are miracles. We are. Think of this: every single person in this room tonight at one point was small enough to fit on the head of a pin. Millions of you on the head of a pin.

There was a time when I was a microscopic speck. A nothing. Drowning in my dad's cum.

My dad – Donny 'Schleppy' Silverman – who does my taxes and who I Skype with every Saturday. There was a time – not long ago in terms of history. A *blip* . . . when I was literally living in his balls, choking on his jizzum, and in a moment I don't wanna conjure, but I will for *you*, that probably went like, 'Oh-oh-*uuhhh*!', I shot out of his penis hole!

It's amazing. It's amazing to think I was ever that thin.

What I'm trying to say, and in conclusion, is: wherever you live, whatever your culture, whatever you believe – we all came out of penis holes. So let's love each other. Thank you!

'People claim to be into recycling, but you should see their faces when you rinse out a condom.'

Jimmy Carr

YET ANOTHER APOLOGY

MONTY PYTHON

Terry Jones appears on a TV screen from his home in London. He is looking rather sheepish.

I'm Terry Jones, the *real* Sixth Python. And I have something rather *serious* to communicate with you all.

I'm not quite sure how to put this, but, um, the other Pythons have been *lying* to you. *None* of them has broken his legs, nor lost them. Nor undergone leg-implant surgery, if such a thing exists. These are barefaced *lies*, told in order to exculpate the Pythons from failing to attend this evening's celebrations of Amnesty International's fiftieth anniversary here at legendary New York's legendary Radio City Music Hall.

I cannot conceive how they could bear to tell such enormous *whoppers*. Which are the exact *reverse* of the truth.

The *truth* is that *I* am the only Python to have lost his legs. As you can observe for yourselves. (*The camera pulls back to reveal Jones resembling a modern-day Toulouse-Lautrec, with his kneecaps resting inside a pair of soft beige slippers.*) I simply wore them down to these *stumps* that you see, running after my fellow Pythons. Believe me, I would have loved to have been able to attend this evening's celebrations, er, here in, er, legendary New York's legendary Radio City Music Hall. But you see to what I am reduced by my devoted service to my fellow Pythons. And *this* is how they repay me.

(*Close to tears.*) I feel betrayed and saddened. But I don't want to spoil the show . . . er . . . so go ahead. Enjoy yourselves. And, er, I hope you have a wonderful evening. And, er, as little Bob Cratchit used to say, 'God bless us all.'

ON LATIN
EDDIE IZZARD

The history of the world has been something I've been very interested in, and the Classical Period, well, that's when it all happened. Back in the old days.

And the Romans: we love the Romans, we love what they did. They murdered a lot of people but we don't know their names so it's okay now. And they did amazing things. They built aqueducts, viaducts, they moved ducks around faster than anyone's ever done. They conquered the known world. And it was brilliant. But they did all of this with a language that we all know from school is *shit*.

It's called Latin, it's impossible, and it has a nominative, vocative, accusative, dative, genitive and ablative. Why not have nine *more* declensions? It's bloody impossible!

If, back in Roman times, you go, 'Steve – do you wanna beer?' You have to go, (*Thinking carefully.*) 'Er, beer . . . the beer's coming towards me . . . motion towards . . . er . . . berrari . . . berraro? . . . rarrari? . . . I, er . . . Steve, do you wanna beer? Just do this . . .' (*Gestures thumbs-up or thumbs-down.*) They invented this (*Gestures up and down with his thumb once again.*) because their language was so fucking *hard*.

Hannibal was a famous Carthaginian general. When he attacked from Carthage he went, of course, across the Mediterranean into Spain and through France, if you know your geography. If you're American: through France down past Russia on through China back up to Istanbul, Westanbul, and into Italy.

And he went over the Alps on elephants. Which we know now – 'Yeah, he went on elephants' – but it's fucking *insane*! It's like coming on *pandas*!

But he did, and he was winning battles. He was winning battles left, right and centre. I think the Romans, for the first time, they were *scared*.

And messengers were running around with messages, and the Romans were losing battles, and the messages were coming in, and they were having to explain the messages in Latin, which was fucking impossible. It was like: 'Hannibal, er, arriveramus? . . . arriverandus? . . . arriverderci? Er, veni, vidi, vici?' 'Veni, vidi, vici? Er, maintenant, immediamente?' 'Absolument.' 'Mit soldatus?' 'Well, of course mit soldatus. He's not on bloody holiday.' 'Eh bien – quel numerati di soldati?' 'Okey dokum – the numerati of soldati ist – MMMCMLM . . . MM . . . CLM . . . XXXIV.' 'Forty-seven soldiers?' 'No – *A MILLION AND NINE*!' 'Oh, right, right . . .' '*Multo soldiers . . . Maximo soldiers . . . Infinitatus soldi*!' 'Hang on: infinitatus, soldatus . . . mathemataculus – impossibilatus! If you don't believe us, ask Pythagoratus!'

'Pythagoratus?'

'*Yeah?*'

'Infinitatus?'

'*Impossibilatus, mate, I just tried it on the abacus – all me fingers fell off!*'

'Pi?'

'*Oh, Pie – yeah, ta, thanks! (Eats.) Also: Hannibal – he'll be coming round the mountains when he comes.*'

'He'll be coming round the mountains when he comes?'

'*He'll be coming round the mountains, coming round the mountains, coming round the mountains when he comes! Und er kommt mit elefanten mein Herr.*'

'Mit ELEFANTEN?!'

'*Mit Elefanten.*'

'Quod . . . the *fuck*?!? Let's run motha fuckus!'

And that is why Latin is a dead language.

AIR TRAVEL
HANNIBAL BURESS

I travel a lot. My main nemesis in travel is airport security.

I don't like them at all. They seem so dedicated to keeping bottled water out of the sky. That's their main thing.

It's probably easier to get cocaine on a plane than a bottle of water. The only way that you could get cocaine on a plane is if they looked and said, 'What is this? *Powdered water*?' 'Nah, it's cocaine.' 'All right, enjoy your flight.'

You can't bring liquids on a plane because a few years ago a terrorist did a weird liquid bomb thing and now nobody can bring liquids because one person messed it up for everybody. But I feel that's being reactive instead of proactive.

Because terrorists are always trying new stuff. So next time there's gonna be some kind of Snickers bomb, and after that happens you can't bring full-sized Snickers on a plane any more. You can only bring miniature Snickers just because one person messed it up for everybody.

Now you're talking to security trying to negotiate your Snickers situation. 'Hey, is it all right if I bring four miniature Snickers? That's about the same size as a full-size Snicker?' Security snaps: 'Don't *play* with me! This is not a *game*! We are saving the *world*! One Snickers bar at a time for America and your freedom!' 'Hey, relax, man, I'm just *hungry*, stop yelling at me!'

I hate it when they try to make conversation with me. 'Are you going to New York for business or pleasure?' 'I'm going to talk about *you* in front of strangers. So I guess it's both.'

I don't wear my glasses in my driver's licence photos, so when they go, 'Can you take your glasses off?' I go, 'Yeah, yeah, sure,

Captain America – it's still me!' Who you catching? Are you seriously thinking that terrorists are gonna use *glasses* as a disguise? You want me to put the same shirt on I had when I had my licence outfit on also? It was eight years ago – I don't have that shirt any more! I don't wear FUBU jerseys any more, man – nobody does!

The darkest moment of my life was when I had to take a shit on a plane. That had never happened to me. Sixteen years of flying, I never shit on a plane. It was horrible. I went through so many emotions. The first was anger. '*Dammit, I gotta shit on a plane!*' Then there was denial: '*I'm not shittin' on this plane!*' Then there was sadness: '*I gotta shit on a plane!*' Then there was acceptance: '*Aw, I guess I gotta shit on this plane!*' Then there was happiness: '*Y'all, I'm shittin' in the sky!*'

CENSORSHIP
BEAVIS & BUTT-HEAD

BEAVIS: You know, Butt-Head, that does kinda suck, you know what I'm sayin'?

BUTT-HEAD: Er, what?

BEAVIS: You know, that thing they were sayin' about? How there's like countries where you can't say what you want? That would suck.

BUTT-HEAD: Er, oh, yeah. There's places where, like, you're not even allowed to say, like, 'poop'!

BEAVIS: Yeah, or 'wiener'!

BUTT-HEAD: Or 'boobs'!

BEAVIS: I don't know what I would do if I wasn't allowed to say 'boobs'!

BUTT-HEAD: Er, yeah, but I think it's like, more like, you can *say* those words but you're not allowed to call certain *people* those words, or something . . .

BEAVIS: Oh, yeah, so it's like, you can say 'bum-hole', but you can't say, 'That guy's a bum-hole!'

BUTT-HEAD: Yeah. It's like, you can say, 'I have a bum-hole', but you can't say, 'Shut up, bum-hole!'

BEAVIS: Yeah, that's just way too many rules!

BUTT-HEAD: It sure is, Beavis. (*Turns to audience.*) And that's where you come in. By becoming involved in . . . Amnesty International, you'll be helping millions of people who aren't allowed to call other people 'bum-holes'.

BEAVIS: That's right, Butt-Head. And not just 'bum-hole', but 'turd-burgler', and 'ass-monkey', and 'butt-munch', and so many other freedoms that *we* take for granted.

BUTT-HEAD: So please make a tax-deductible, er, and like, give some money to the number on the screen, and join this wonderful group today. Thank you.

BEAVIS: I don't think there's a number on the screen, Butt-Head.

BUTT-HEAD: Shut up, bum-hole!

BEAVIS: Cut it out, butt-hole!

BUTT-HEAD: Heh heh, freedom of expression kicks ass!

A MESSAGE OF THANKS
ZARGANAR

Zarganar, one of Burma's most popular comedians, takes to the stage. In 2008, he had spoken out against the Burmese government's handling of the Cyclone Nargis tragedy that left 140,000 people dead and millions homeless, and he led a movement that saw money and supplies delivered to the victims. The government's response was to sentence Zarganar to fifty-nine years in prison – simply because he had publicly criticised the government. Due to Amnesty's support, he was released in October 2011. He now addresses the audience inside New York's Radio City Music Hall.

Good evening, ladies and gentlemen. My name is Zarganar. Although I am a comedian, tonight I am not here to make jokes. I am here to honour the fiftieth anniversary of Amnesty International. I would like to take this opportunity to express my appreciation to Amnesty International for the release of the political prisoners – and not only in Burma but also around the world.

During my life I have spent more than eleven years in prison. Largely just for making jokes. And nights like the one you are enjoying would be impossible in my home country. And that's why I am calling on all of you to support this incredible organisation.

For half a century, Amnesty International has championed the basic freedoms that allow human intellect, spirit and soul to flourish. And as much as they have accomplished, there is still much work to be done.

In my country, we now have a new parliament, a new government and a new constitution. But our struggle for democracy and human rights is far from over. The military still controls the powers, and has given themselves twenty-five per cent of the seats in the parliament. That's why I am going to suggest they should give the Burmese comedians twenty-five per cent of the seats. That way, half the parliament will be crazy!

Thank you, Amnesty, for helping me mock the powerful.

INTERROGATION SKETCH

SETH MEYERS, JASON SUDEIKIS, FRED ARMISEN, RASHIDA JONES & REX LEE

The scene is set inside an interrogation room. Two officials, played by Seth Meyers and Jason Sudeikis, enter, dragging their prisoner, played by Fred Armisen, until they have positioned him on a chair. They stand either side of him and prepare to commence the interrogation.

ARMISEN: There's been a huge mistake!

SUDEIKIS: Yeah? No kidding, eh? That's what they all say!

ARMISEN: I didn't *do* anything!

MEYERS: You didn't do *anything*? You didn't speak out against the Supreme Leader in public?

ARMISEN: I would *never* do that. I *love* the Supreme Leader. Of all the leaders in the history of the world, he is like my *favourite* leader!

SUDEIKIS: Oh, yeah? Well, that's not what our witnesses say.

ARMISEN: They're *lying*! Please – I'm innocent!

(*Meyers moves to strike him, but Sudeikis intervenes.*)

SUDEIKIS: No, no, I'll handle this. (*Turns to Armisen and adopts a friendly tone of voice.*) Now, look: this would be so much easier if you just admitted it, okay? So what, right? You said the Supreme Leader was crazy – it's not a big deal!

ARMISEN: It's not?

SUDEIKIS: No! And, hey, can I tell you a secret? There are times, you know, when even I thought the Supreme Leader is, like, *crazy!*

(*Upon hearing this, Armisen suddenly shouts into his sleeve: 'We got him!' and he and Meyers manhandle a startled Sudeikis onto the chair.*)

ARMISEN: We got you!

SUDEIKIS: What *is* this?

MEYERS: You're under arrest, buddy, under the orders of the Supreme Leader! We *got* you!

SUDEIKIS: W-Wait, okay – hold on! So this whole interrogation was just a set-up to get me to speak ill of the Supreme Leader?

MEYERS: Yeah!

SUDEIKIS: Wow! Okay. Wow! All right, well, first off: (*Points at Armisen.*) you were great!

ARMISEN: Oh, thank you, thank you very much!

SUDEIKIS: That was incredible, seriously. The crying, and the acting like a little bitch the whole time – just excellent work! Have you ever considered acting as a profession?

ARMISEN: (*Awkwardly.*) Er, the Supreme Leader considers acting a waste of time, everybody knows that.

SUDEIKIS: No, I know that, but *surely* you'd rather be an actor than doing this shit, right? I mean, that was incredible!

ARMISEN: (*Softening.*) Well . . . yeah, of course.

SUDEIKIS: Yeah?

(*Suddenly, Sudeikis shouts into his sleeve: 'All right, we got him!' and he and Meyers manhandle a startled Armisen back onto the chair.*)

ARMISEN: Come ON! This whole thing was a *double* set-up?

MEYERS: Yeah – been in the works for months!

ARMISEN: Well, I gotta say: (*Points at Sudeikis.*) you were great!

SUDEIKIS: No, don't even try it. I just *did* that!

ARMISEN: H-Have you ever thought about acting?

SUDEIKIS: Will you *stop* it? You're *embarrassing* yourself!

ARMISEN: Sorry. It was worth a shot, right?

SUDEIKIS: Yeah, well, you gotta try, yeah, you gotta try.

ARMISEN: (*Now gesturing at Meyers.*) And you, you're just the strong and silent type.

MEYERS: (*Blushing slightly.*) Oh, I don't know about that.

ARMISEN: No, to be honest, you remind me of the, erm, the Supreme Leader.

SUDEIKIS: It's true.

MEYERS: Well, ah, maybe, but, er, I don't have his tiny dick, right?

(*Suddenly, both Armisen and Sudeikis shout into their sleeves: 'We got him!' and they manhandle a startled but strangely impressed Meyers onto the chair.*)

MEYERS: You guys teed me up and I bit on it!

SUDEIKIS: Amen, amen!

MEYERS: I imagine I'm going to get executed now?

SUDEIKIS/ARMISEN: Oh, yeah, yeah, big-time execution!

MEYERS: Well, it was a good run.

SUDEIKIS: Yeah.

ARMISEN: Let's get you fitted for a blindfold.

MEYERS: All right.

SUDEIKIS: Let's go, here we go.

(*Sudeikis and Armisen help Meyers up and start to lead Meyers off, but he turns back and says to Armisen.*)

MEYERS: You know, for the record – he *does* have a tiny dick.

ARMISEN: Yeah, I know.

(*Meyers shouts in triumph and he and Sudeikis turn and manhandle the startled Armisen back to the chair.*)

SUDEIKIS: Take a seat! Take a SEAT!

MEYERS: We got you! Boom!

SUDEIKIS: Margaret's going to measure your head for *your* blindfold.

(*They start to lead Armisen off. While Meyers accompanies him off stage, Sudeikis is called back by a mousy little bespectacled woman played by Rashida Jones. She is carrying a small plastic pot.*)

JONES: Honey – hi!

SUDEIKIS: Oh my God. Honey, what are you doing here? What are you doing at work?

JONES: I came and brought my husband lunch.

SUDEIKIS: Oh my gosh, I'm a lucky guy!

JONES: It's your favourite – it's veggie lasagne.

SUDEIKIS: Oh, that's great – I love your veggie lasagne! (*Sotto voce.*) I love it more than the Supreme Leader!

(*Suddenly, Jones shouts into her sleeve: 'We got him!' and she gestures to Meyers and Armisen to return and manhandle the startled Sudeikis onto the chair.*)

SUDEIKIS: This is bullshit – we've been married fifteen years!

JONES: Um, it's called 'undercover work'?

SUDEIKIS: But we have kids!

JONES: Yeah – both in on it.

SUDEIKIS: What? They're four and seven!

JONES: Both in on it!

MEYERS/ARMISEN: Gotcha!

SUDEIKIS: Incredible! All right, okay . . .

(*Rex Lee, as the Supreme Leader Kim Jong-un, enters holding a large flat box and looking very stern-faced. He speaks loudly but very stiffly.*)

JONG-UN: Hello! . . . Pizza . . . delivery!

(*All of the other baffled-looking actors step out of their characters and look at each other in confusion.*)

JONES: I . . . I don't remember this from rehearsal.

SUDEIKIS: What . . . What *is* this?

MEYERS: Oh, you know what? Er, Kim Jong-un – Jon Stewart told me he wanted to be in a sketch. Er, I think he just decided to walk into ours.

SUDEIKIS: Okay, all right, let me riff on this shit. (*Calls out to Kim Jong-un.*) Hey! Thank you, you can drop the pizza . . . and then go.

(*Kim Jong-un says nothing and stares impassively ahead.*)

SUDEIKIS: Oh, ha-ha-ha, look at him! Oh, he completely froze up, the little guy!

JONES: Why does he want to be in a *sketch*? Did he think he was going to be good at *comedy*?

MEYERS: Well, he's a dictator, Rashida, they think they're good at everything!

SUDEIKIS: That is true, yeah.

ARMISEN: Well, ah, some dictators *are* good at everything.

SUDEIKIS: Who? Name one.

ARMISEN: Um . . . Gaddafi.

SUDEIKIS: What?

ARMISEN: He was a great singer.

MEYERS: Fred, what did Gaddafi sing?

ARMISEN: Oh, you know . . . 'Whee-hee, shamone, whoo-ooh . . .'

JONES: No, no, Fred, that was Michael Jackson.

ARMISEN: Oh my God! You are totally right, how did I get them confused?

MEYERS: Jesus, Fred!

SUDEIKIS: Yeah, also, side note – awful Michael Jackson impression.

JONES: Terrible.

SUDEIKIS: Awful.

MEYERS: Oh my God, look at Kim Jong-un, he just turned around.

(*Kim Jong-un is now standing with his back to the audience.*)

MEYERS: He's *so* bad at sketches!

JONES: (*Shouting.*) Just drop the pizza and go!

ARMISEN: Thank you!

SUDEIKIS: Just drop the pizza and go!

ALL: DROP THE PIZZA AND GO!!!

(*Kim Jong-un turns to face them. He seems unsure of what to do. Then he nervously puts the pizza box down in front of the actors and then tries to walk past them and off the stage. The actors stop him and point in the opposite direction.*)

ALL: No, no, leave the way you came!

(*He bows to them and turns and walks off.*)

SUDEIKIS: You dumb dick dictator!

(*Disoriented, the actors look at each other.*)

JONES: Okay, let's just get back to the sketch. What were we doing?

SUDEIKIS: It doesn't even matter – he's ruined it!

MEYERS: Dictators ruin everything!

SUDEIKIS: They do!

ARMISEN: Ah, I don't know about that. Did Gaddafi ruin 'We Are the World'?

SUDEIKIS: Oh my God, Fred, what are you talking about?

MEYERS: Are you thinking about Gaddafi or are you thinking about Michael Jackson again?

ARMISEN: Michael Jackson – sorry, sorry!

MEYERS: Stop *doing* that!

SUDEIKIS: Why do you *do* that?

MEYERS: What is *wrong* with you?

JONES: Hey, just do your last line, Jason.

SUDEIKIS: Oh, the last line of the sketch, okay: (*Adopts a cheesy tone.*) 'Well, I guess that's just life in a dictatorship!'

(*They all laugh in a bad-sitcom style, freezing as the lights fade.*)

MEDIA REPORTS
RUSSELL BRAND

I want to talk to you about some important things. Like, I'm trying to understand your country, America, that I've been living in for a little while.

Because you know we have different media institutions that are trying to encourage us to be more bigoted, in case we're not bigoted enough? For example, you have Fox News. Say you're not bigoted enough, Fox will help you with your bigotry. You might naturally not have enough bigotry, they'll say, 'Do some bigotry!'

Like I was initially disappointed because the first time I watched it, right, it was for six hours, and I didn't see one story about foxes. I thought, 'That's already misleading.'

It was just some stories about immigrants. They're very worried about the immigrants. And gays. They're very worried about gays. And paedophiles.

I think that immigrants – don't worry *too* much about immigrants because that's just a person who used to be somewhere else. That's just a person who's moved from one place to another place. That's not that frightening. 'Aaagh, have you always been here?' 'No, I used to be there.' '*Aaaghhh!! Where will you go next? You're not static, you're an unstable object moving around on a rock in infinite space!!! Where will you go next – and how will we tax it correctly?*'

Also gays. They don't like there to be a gay marriage. I asked someone why and they said, 'Because it's *gay*!' There's no rational reason for it.

Also Fox News are very scared of paedophiles. That is a little bit more legitimate, but why are they trying to make *me* scared of paedophiles? I'm thirty-six years old. I haven't got to be scared of paedophiles. If a paedophile comes near me, I'll just fuck it. 'I don't think you'll find the snow-white innocence you were searching for here! This is going to go in *another* direction!' *Phkteoww*! 'Fuck 'em back to purity!' Just one of the services I offer.

In our country, England, we enhance our bigotry with a newspaper called the *Daily Mail*. Say you don't have enough hatred of someone because they're a bit different, it'll help you to find ways to hate those people. They're the same as Fox News – they want you to be scared of *everything*.

Like, listen to some of the things you're supposed to be scared of: 'Gays! Immigrants! Paedophiles!' We're meant to be scared of all those things. Once in the *Daily Mail* they were trying to make us scared of snow! 'Snow!!! There will be *SNOW*!!! Immigrant snow – it's not even our snow!!! Immigrant gay gypsy paedophile *SNOW*!!!! Down from the heavens with a terrible mission! Do *NOT* build a snowman in your garden – it will come into your house and fuck your children!' *Grrrrrhhh*! *Grrrrrhhh*! 'I hope you like carrots . . . !'

I've been here before, I had to do something for MTV. I've noticed, from my participation in popular culture, that it functions to prevent synaptic connections occurring in our minds so we can't think properly. Like you'll be formulating a thought – because we're sentient human beings on our way to enlightenment – a thought will be formulating, then popular culture functions like a pink pony trotting through our brains shitting glitter.

I remember while I was doing MTV, I was hosting it, and I was trying to encourage people to do a cohesive thought. 'Do a cohesive thought,' I was trying to suggest. But it was impossible, because in the synaptic gap the pink pony would come in and obliterate that thought with shit. With glitter shit. It would *oglitterate* it!

They're preventing us from thinking properly, I think.

Here is some media analysis from some American print media. (*Unfolds a piece of paper and prepares to read from it.*) Here is a story

from American media which I think has something to do with
freedom of speech. This is an American newspaper – I don't know
the name of it because it wasn't relevant to me: 'Seattle!' I notice
at the beginning of American news stories they shout the place
where it's happening. 'Seattle!!!' Like you have to be transported
to Seattle. '*SEATTLE*!!!'

'A Seattle woman is complaining that she –' Right, that's just
bad grammar, because she's not still complaining *now*, is she? Is
she in a *vortex* of complaint? That's the continuous form. A Seattle
woman *has* complained. 'A Seattle woman is complaining that she
was at the Lake City Library with her kids recently when she saw
a man watching hard-core porn on a computer with the screen
facing the room.'

Right. These are the things that are important to me already
in this story. The phrase 'hard-core porn' has survived – that's
nice. It's kind of antiquated: 'Ah, hard-core porn! How I lament its
passing! Its whimsy, its soft focus, its bushy mounds!' The other
thing is, if you're watching pornography in a library, you probably
haven't got a house – 'cause pornography, that's already one down
from *sex*, right, and then to take that from there (*Points to a very low
level.*) to in a library (*Points even lower.*) . . . Why has the protagonist
of this story not been given the correct character details? Because
he's obviously (a) homeless and (b) mentally ill! Right? Because of
the people here, us human beings who are basically the same as
that man, *I've* done some unusual things in my time, but I have
never masturbated over pornography in a library. Though I *do* like
the quietness, as there is an erotic charge to it.

'Oh my God, you're all so QUIET! Quiet with your SEX
ORGANS!!' Whereas in a lap-dancing club I feel the vibrant crash
of God in my mind as the decadence spills out before me. I think,
'Er, no . . . go to the library.'

(*Returns to reading from the newspaper.*)

'She' – the woman in the story who was complaining, remember
she's perpetually complaining – 'She asked the librarian to move
the man to a more discreet location.' I like that. 'Would you mind

masturbating over there behind that plant?' At least then there'll be a botanical subtext. You could be like a sloth or some creature. Like a bonobo chimp with their liberal sexualities freed from our conscious minds.

'The librarian refused.' She refused to do that. '"She could see the screen from where we were standing and was sympathetic."' Nice attitude from a librarian. (*Adopts sympathetic expression.*) 'It *is* bad that the man is masturbating. I *identify.*'

'"She said though that the library doesn't censor content."' Nice. Nice, because freedom of speech don't just mean freedom to say good things like, 'Ah, we're all equal', and 'Death is an illusion'. Oh, no, no, it also means, 'That man's going to be masturbating in your library!' Freely!

This is what the librarian said: '"We can't be in the business of monitoring what our patrons are doing at any given computer."' That's what the librarian's job is! 'I can't be expected to put these books back on the shelves! Learn the intricacies of the Dewey decimal system!'

'Hal, who was in the DVD section when she saw the man scream, then asked him to move to another computer. He also refused.' I like that. I *like* the idea of a man masturbating in a library, being asked to move and saying, 'No, I shan't! I *won't* do that! Now, if you'll excuse me while I kiss the sky . . .'

'Hal said one of her daughters, who are aged seven and ten, had seen what the man was watching.' In a way, though, you know, it *is* bad that the children had to see what the man was watching, but, in another way, that man could have been distracted from his masturbatory fantasy by seeing, like, fucking *Harry Potter* or something. 'Ooh, I was just on the precipice of a glorious orgasm when I saw, like, *Twilight* on a bookshelf – it made me realise there was nothing to live for! The orgasm went back inside itself and exploded!'

A CRITIQUE
STATLER & WALDORF

WALDORF: So: what did you think?

STATLER: Well, I'd *tweet* you about it but my tweetin' thumb's gone all arthritic.

WALDORF: I know what you mean, Statler. Maybe the world has passed us by.

STATLER: Aw, I was just thinking that, Waldorf. It's a *young* curmudgeon's game out there now. Twitter. Viruses. Mashed potatoes . . . The world's just passed us by.

WALDORF: Yes. There's no place in this world for old men to insult people.

STATLER: Yeah. Except Washington.

WALDORF: Yep.

'Well, I'd *tweet* you about it but my tweetin' thumb's gone all arthritic.'

CITY
MUSIC
HALL
ITY
MUSIC
HALL
RADIO CITY Music Hall RA
L PRESENTS THE SECRET POLICEMAN'S BALL MARCH 4 THE SECRET

ACKNOWLEDGEMENTS

AMNESTY THANKS THE ARTISTS . . .

A Poke in the Eye With a Sharp Stick (1976)
Alan Bennett, John Bird, Eleanor Bron, Tim Brooke-Taylor, Graham Chapman, John Cleese, Carol Cleveland, Peter Cook, John Fortune, Graeme Garden, Terry Gilliam, Barry Humphries, Neil Innes, Des Jones, Terry Jones, Jonathan Lynn, Jonathan Miller, Dudley Moore (Narrator), Bill Oddie, Michael Palin.

The Mermaid Frolics (1977)
Peter Atkin, Connie Booth, Brian Bowles (The Bowles Brothers Band), John Cleese, Peter Cook, Julie Covington, Des Jones, Sue Jones, Terry Jones, Jonathan Miller, Julian Smedley, Peter Ustinov, John Williams.

The Secret Policeman's Ball (1979)
Rowan Atkinson, Eleanor Bron, Mike Brearley, Buckman and Beetles (Chris Beetles, Rob Buckman), John Cleese, Billy Connolly, Peter Cook, Suzanne Church, Anna Ford, Clive James, Clive Jenkins, The Ken Campbell Road Show (Paul Abrahams, David Rappaport, Sylvester McCoy, Marcel Steiner), Michael Palin, Tom Robinson, Pete Townshend, John Williams.

The Secret Policeman's Other Ball (1981)
Rowan Atkinson, Jeff Beck, Alan Bennett, John Bird, Tim Brooke-Taylor, Jasper Carrott, Graham Chapman, Eric Clapton, John Cleese, Phil Collins, Peter Cook (voice of Secret Policeman), Sheena Easton, Donovan, Johnny Fingers, John Fortune, Bob Geldof, Barry Humphries, Neil Innes, Chas Jankel, Chris Langham, Michael Palin, Tom Robinson, Griff Rhys Jones, Alexei Sayle, Sting, Midge Ure, John Wells, Victoria Wood.

The Secret Policeman's Third Ball (1987)
Joan Armatrading, Aswad, Chet Atkins, Joe Berhart, Richard Branson, Jackson Browne, Paul Brady, Rory Bremner, Kate Bush, John Cleese, Robbie Coltrane, Phil Cool, Paul Gambaccini, Andy De La Tour, Duran

Duran, Ben Elton, Stephen Fry, Craig Fergusson (as Bing Hitler), Peter Gabriel, Bob Geldof, David Gilmour, Lenny Henry, Bob Hoskins (voice of Secret Policeman), Mike Hurley, Nigel Kennedy, Nik Kershaw, Mark Knopfler, Hugh Laurie, Nick Mason, Warren Mitchell, Youssou N'dour, Bill Oddie, Emo Philips, Courtney Pine, Lou Reed, Tony Robinson, Jonathan Ross, Andrew Sachs, Spitting Image, Ruby Wax, Loudon Wainwright III, Who Dares Wins (Jimmy Mulville, Rory McGrath, Philip Pope, Tony Robinson, Julia Hills), Working Week, World Party, Paula Yates.

The Secret Policeman's Biggest Ball (1989)

John Bird, Rory Bremner, Simon Brint, Kathy Burke, John Cleese, Robbie Coltrane, Peter Cook, Adrian Edmondson, Ben Elton, French & Saunders (Dawn French, Jennifer Saunders), Stephen Fry, Lenny Henry, Jools Holland, Chris Langham, Hugh Laurie, Helen Lederer, Dudley Moore, Jimmy Mulville, Steve Nallon, National Theatre of Brent (Jim Broadbent, Patrick Barlow), Michael Palin, Rowland Rivron, William Rushton, John Williams.

The Famous Compere's Police Dog (1990)

Les Bubb, Jo Brand, Otis Cannelloni, Julian Clary, Lee Cornes, Jenny Eclair, Simon Fanshawe, Stephen Frost, Jeremy Hardy, John Hegley, Kit Hollerbach, John Lenahan, Sean Hughes (as Sean Murphy), Michael Redmond, Steve Rawlings, Kevin Day, Arthur Smith, Mark Thomas.

The Big 3-0 (1991)

Paddy Ashdown MP, Michael Aspel, Rick Astley, Roseanne Barr, Jeremy Beadle, Brookside cast, Sam Brown, Antoine de Caunes, Julian Clary, John Cleese, Brian Clough, Steve Coogan, Phil Cornwell, Coronation Street cast, Jason Donovan, Drop the Dead Donkey (Susannah Doyle, Jeff Rawle, Haydn Gwynne, Robert Duncan, Victoria Wicks, Neil Pearson, Stephen Tompkinson), EMF, Eastenders cast, French and Saunders (Dawn French, Jennifer Saunders), David Gilmour, Greatest Show on Legs (Martin Soan, Malcom Hardee with Keith Chegwin), Hale and Pace (Gareth Hale, Norman Pace), Daryl Hall, Have I Got News For You (Angus Deayton, Paul Merton, Ian Hislop), John Hegley, Jools Holland, James, Tom Jones, Neil Kinnock MP, Mark Little, London Chamber Orchestra & Choir of St Mary's Church, London Community Gospel Choir, John Major MP, Simon Mayo, Roger McGough, Cathy McGowan, Michael

McShane, Kylie Minogue, Morrissey, Steve Nieve, Emo Philips, Punt & Dennis (Hugh Dennis, Steve Punt), Red Dwarf (Chris Barrie, Craig Charles, Hattie Hayridge, Robert Llewellyn, Danny John-Jules), Reeves & Mortimer (Bob Mortimer, Vic Reeves), Anneka Rice, Rowland Rivron, Jonathan Ross, Alexei Sayle, Seal, Frank Skinner, Smith & Jones (Griff Rhys Jones, Mel Smith), Spinal Tap (Harry Shearer, Christopher Guest, Michael McKean), David A. Stewart, Andrew Strong, Trevor and Simon (Simon Hickson, Trevor Neal), Paul Whitehouse, Kim Wilde, Paula Yates.

We Know Where You Live, Live! (2001)
Eddie Izzard, Badly Drawn Boy, Richard Blackwood, Sam Cadman, Al Campbell, Simon Day, Jack Dee, Harry Enfield, Colin Firth, Dawn French, Goodness Gracious Me (Meera Syal, Nina Wadia, Kulvinder Ghir, Sanjeev Bhaskar with Dave Lamb), Richard E. Grant, Jeremy Hardy, Harry Hill, Dom Joly, Tom Jones, Phill Jupitus, Matthew Kelly, Sean Lock, Kate Moss, Vic Reeves, Alan Rickman, Jonathan Ross, Tim Roth, Stereophonics, Michael Stipe, Emma Thompson, Julie Walters, Paul Whitehouse, U2.

Remember The Secret Policeman's Ball – documentary (2004)
Terry Jones, Stephen Fry, Jonathan Miller, Alan Bennett, Terry Gilliam, Rowan Atkinson, Ruby Wax, Jennifer Saunders, Bob Geldof, Sting, Peter Luff, John Cleese, Michael Palin, Jonathan Lynn, Michael Palin, Jonathan Lynn, Anna Ford, Alexei Sayle, Lenny Henry, Joan Armatrading, Phil Collins, Neil Innes, Dawn French (Narrator).

The Secret Policeman's Ball 2006: The Ball in the Hall
Ronni Ancona, David Armand, Jo Brand, Russell Brand, Dan Clark, James Cook, Jon Culshaw, Julia Davis, Jimmy Fallon, Tara Fitzgerald, Michael Fenton Stevens, Michael Fielding, Nitin Ganatra, Richard E. Grant, Seth Green, Raymond Griffiths, Shobna Gulati, Phil Holden, Natalie Imbruglia, Jeremy Irons, Eddie Izzard, Julian Barrat, Jimmy Carr, Isabella Cascarano, Chevy Chase, Brian Cox, Omid Djalili, Anthony Elvin, Jimmy Fallon, Tara Fitzgerald, Michelle Gomez, The Green Wing (Tamsin Greig, Stephen Mangan, Julian Rhind-Tutt), Darren Horan, Jessica Hynes, Peter Kyriacou, Joanna Lumley, The Magic Numbers, Andrew Maxwell, Stephen Merchant, The Mighty Boosh (Noel Fielding, Julian Barrett), Dylan Moran, Al Murray, Graham Norton, Barunka O'Shaughnessy, Jennifer Saunders, Rebekah Seary, Howard Shannon, Sarah Silverman,

Sam Spedding, Jessica Stevenson, Patrick Stewart, Martha Wainwright, Jack Walters, Shaun Williamson, The Zutons.

The Secret Policeman's Ball (2008)

Lily Allen, Gillian Anderson, David Armand, Matt Berry, Katy Brand, Ed Byrne, Alan Carr, Dan Clark, James Corden, Fearne Cotton, Jon Culshaw, Michael Fenton Stevens, Germaine Greer, Sharon Horgan, Matthew Horne, Russell Howard, Eddie Izzard, Elton John, Shappi Khorsandi, Sean Lock, Jason Manford, Tim Minchin, Sarah Millican, Mitchell & Webb (David Mitchell, Robert Webb), Nick Mohammed, Graham Norton, Katherine Parkinson, Russell Peters (via video-tape), Razorlight, Kristen Schaal, Frank Skinner, Meera Syal, Liza Tarbuck, Johnny Vegas, Gok Wan, Sean Williamson.

The Secret Policeman's Ball (2012)

Fred Armisen, Beavis & Butthead, Matt Berry, Russell Brand, Sir Richard Branson, Hannibal Buress, Jimmy Carr, Coldplay, David Cross, Robert De Niro, Rachel Dratch, Noel Fielding, Micky Flanagan, Marianne Garces, Whoopi Goldberg, Bill Hader, Eric Idle, Eddie Izzard, Rashida Jones, Terry Jones, Taran Killam, Rex Lee, Seth Meyers, Bobby Moynihan, Mumford & Sons, Liam Neeson, Chris O'Dowd, Annette O'Toole Bob Odenkirk, John Oliver, Michael Palin, Piff the Magic Dragon, Jay Pharoah, Tim Roth, Paul Rudd, Kyra Sedgwick, Peter Serafinowicz, Sarah Silverman, Statler & Waldorf (Steve Whitmire, Dave Goelz), Jon Stewart, Ben Stiller, Jason Sudeikis, Catherine Tate, Archbishop Desmond Tutu, David Walliams, Reggie Watts, Jack Whitehall, Kristen Wiig, Zarganar.

AMNESTY THANKS THE WRITERS . . .

(1976) Alan Bennett, Graham Chapman, Peter Cook, Michael Frayn, Barry Humphries, Eric Idle, Neil Innes, Terry Jones, Jonathan Miller, Bill Oddie, Michael Palin. (1977) John Cleese, Peter Cook, Terry Jones. (1979) John Cleese, Peter Cook, Billy Connolly, Michael Palin, Terry Jones, Rowan Atkinson, Eleanor Bron, Clive James, Ken Campbell. (1981) Rowan Atkinson, John Cleese, Ronald Eyre, John Bird & John Fortune, Rory McGrath & Jimmy Mulville, Chris Langham, Tim Brooke-Taylor, Graham Chapman, Marty Feldman, Ronald Eyre, John Wells. (1987) Michael Frayn, Chris Langham, Jonathan Lynn, Johnny Speight.

(**1989**) John Cleese, Michael Palin, Dawn French, Jennifer Saunders, Spitting Image, Graham Chapman, Peter Cook. (**2001**) Ivor Baddiel, Tim Brooke-Taylor, Graham Chapman, John Cleese, Marty Feldman, Robin Ince, George Jeffrie, Richard Parker, Richard Pinto, Sharat Sardana, Bert Tyler-Moore. (**2006**) Jesse Armstrong, James Cary, Kevin Cecil, Andrew Dawson, Steve Dawson, Nick Doody, Roger Drew, John Finnemore, John Holmes, Tim Inman, Matt Kirshen, Steve Punt, James Serafinowicz, Will Smith, Dan Tetsell. (**2008**) Andrew Dawson, Steven Dawson, Sharon Hogan, Tim Inman, Graham Linejham, David Mitchell, James Serafinowicz, Holly Walsh, Robert Webb. (**2012**) DJ Javerbaum, James Serafinowicz, Seth Myers.

AMNESTY THANKS THE PHOTOGRAPHERS ...

(**1976**) David Redfern. (**1979**) Paul Cox & Simon Fowler. (**1981**) Adrian Boot & Michael Putland. (**1987**) Chalkie Davies, Alan Davidson, Alan Grisbrook, Dave Hindley, Dave Hogan, Carol Starr, Dave Wainwright, Stefan Wallgren & Richard Young. (**1991**) Frank Spooner Pictures Ltd. (**2001**) Rankin, PA Photos, Dave Logan. (**2006**) Lindsay Armstrong, Rowan Griffiths, Rich Hardcastle & World News. (**2008**) PA Photos, James McAuley. (**2012**) Chad Batka & Getty Photos.

AMNESTY THANKS THE VISUAL ARTISTS ...

Secret Policeman character: Original 1979–1989, Colin Wheeler. 2006, James Jarvis. 2008, Think Farm. 2012, McBess.

AMNESTY THANKS THE EXECUTIVE PRODUCERS, PRODUCERS AND DIRECTORS ...

Mike Agnew, Katherine Allen, Suzi Aplin, Sarah Ben-Tovim, Neville Bolt, Pete Brown, Paula Burdon, Lisa Chapman, John Cleese, Bob Cousins, Pat Duffy, Beth Earl, Michael Friend, Paul Gambaccini, John Gau, Malcolm Gerrie, Roger Graef, Aaron Grosky, Andy Hackman, Kit Hawkins, Malcolm Hay, David G. Hillier, Judith Holder, Mike Holgate, Tony Hollingsworth, Paul Jackson, Terry Jones, Margy Kinmonth, Julia Knowles,

Martin Lewis, Declan Lowney, Peter Luff, Al MacCuish, Jonathan Miller, Dave Morley, Kerry Moscoguiri, Séamus Murphy-Mitchell, Ken O'Neill, Richard Parker, Geoff Posner, Alison Sanderson, Thomas Schwalm, David Simpson, Graham Smith, Lily Sobhani, Clive Tulloh, John Turner, Lisle Turner, David Tyler, Peter Walker, Bob Weinstein, Harvey Weinstein, Simon Wright.

AND FINALLY . . .

When the first show was planned, it was clear no one imagined we would be writing a history of the Secret Policeman's Balls thirty-five years later. Unfortunately, our archive reflects this and while we have endeavoured to acknowledge all contributors, we have inevitably made mistakes and omissions. Amnesty International and Canongate would like to extend our gratitude to all the writers, publishers and copyright owners listed above who have generously allowed us to reproduce their work in this book free of charge. We have made every effort to trace copyright holders and obtain their permission for the use of copyright material. Amnesty and the publisher apologise for any errors or omissions and would be grateful if notified of any corrections that should be incorporated in future reprints or editions of this book.

These shows have stood the test of time because so many people gave so much to Amnesty International – both on stage and behind the scenes. There are hundreds of you and we thank you all from the bottom of our hearts.

OUR SPECIAL THANKS TO . . .

We would like to give special thanks to the people we have called upon to sit on (unpaid) steering groups and provide advice, support and guidance: Mark Borkowski, Hannah Chambers, Caroline Chignell, John Cleese, Andy Harries, Raffy Manoukian, Paul Roberts, Stewart Till, Ed Smith and Clive Tulloh.

Finally, a huge thank you to our audiences. Thank you for laughing, for joining Amnesty and for helping promote and protect human rights around the world.

INDEX